bake

RACHEL ALLEN

Collins

For my sister and best friend Simone

HarperCollins Publishers Ltd
77–85 Fulham Palace Road
London W6 8JB

www.collins.co.uk

Collins® is a registered trademark of
HarperCollins Publishers Limited

First published 2008 by Collins

Text © Rachel Allen, 2008
Photographs © Mark Read, 2008; except
pages 37, 54 and 106, Noel Murphy, 2008
Illustrations © Gordon Hurden, 2008

12 11 10 09 08
9 8 7 6 5 4 3 2 1

A catalogue record for this book is available from
the British Library

Isbn-13 978-0-00-725970-0

Editorial Director: Jenny Heller
Senior Development Editor: Lizzy Gray
Editors: Emma Callery, Kate Parker and Kathy Steer
Design: Smith & Gilmour
Food Stylist: Annie Rigg
Prop Stylist: Wei Tang

Colour reproduction by Colourscan, Singapore
Printed and bound by Lego, Italy

CONTENTS

INTRODUCTION

Baking has always been one of my greatest joys. I have such happy memories of my sister and I when we were little, standing on kitchen chairs so that we could help Mum make biscuits or buns for the family. Even today, the wonderful, warm aromas of baking bread, cakes or cookies always transport me back to these times.

Baking makes you stop and really enjoy your time in the kitchen. Of course, there is a lot more to baking than just cakes and cookies, it's a versatile and very homely method of cooking, whether you're baking a fresh loaf of bread or just a simple jacket potato. It's warming, comforting and nurturing, and fills the house with such welcoming smells.

Giving something that you have baked to someone you love is real generosity – whether it be a delicious pie for friends on a cold winter's evening or a special cake for a birthday.

There is no mystery to baking; baking is a simple science, which is precisely why it is so satisfying. Your friends may think you're a genius if you present them with a beautiful cake, but it's really just the right ingredients in the right quantities!

I have chosen my favourite baking recipes in this collection to give you a wide range of delicious treats and meals that can be baked in your oven. I hope these become part of your everyday life. There are also many special recipes for those once-in-a-while occasions and celebrations. If you can master a set of weighing scales, then you have all the skills you need to bake ... so what are you waiting for? Get that pinny on and start baking!

Rachel x

PS The oven temperatures in this book are for a conventional oven, but if I am using a fan oven, then I usually reduce the temperature by 10 per cent.

SWEET
MOUTHFULS

OATMEAL AND RAISIN COOKIES

110g (4oz) butter,
  softened
110g (4oz) caster sugar
110g (4oz) soft light
  brown sugar
1 egg
2 tbsp water
1 tsp vanilla extract
250g (9oz) porridge oats
110g (4oz) self-raising
  flour
1 level tsp salt
110g (4oz) raisins

An American favourite, these cookies are moist, sweet and very moreish.

1 Preheat the oven to 180°C (350°F), Gas mark 4.

2 Cream the butter in a large bowl or in an electric food mixer until soft. Add the sugars and beat until the mixture is light and fluffy. Add the egg, water and vanilla extract while still beating. Reduce the speed and gently mix in the oats, flour, salt and raisins to form a dough.

3 Using your hands, roll the dough into walnut-sized balls and place spaced slightly apart on two baking trays (no need to grease or line).

4 Bake in the oven for 15–25 minutes or until light golden brown, but still slightly soft in the centre.

5 Allow to cool on the trays for a minute before transferring to a wire rack to cool.

VARIATION

Oatmeal and chocolate: Chocolate chips can be used instead of raisins, if you prefer.

BASIC COOKIE RECIPE

MAKES ABOUT 35 COOKIES

225g (8oz) butter,
  softened
110g (4oz) caster sugar
275g (10oz) plain flour
Ground spices or finely
  grated zest (optional;
  see Variations below)

This recipe is a basis for many combinations. Experiment with ingredients – flavourings, dried fruits, nuts, spices and even herbs such as lavender – to find your favourite.

1 Preheat the oven to 170°C (325°F), Gas Mark 3.
2 Cream the butter in a large bowl or in a food mixer until soft. Add the sugar and beat until the mixture is light and fluffy.
3 Sift in the flour and spices or grated zest (if using) and bring the mixture together to form a dough.
4 Using your hands, roll the dough into walnut-sized balls and place them slightly apart on a baking tray (no need to grease or line). Flatten them slightly with the back of a damp fork and bake in the oven for 13–15 minutes or until they are light golden brown and slightly firm on top.
5 Carefully transfer the cookies to a wire rack to cool.

VARIATIONS

Poppy seed: Add 2 tablespoons of poppy seeds to the flour.
Lemon: Add the finely grated zest of 1 lemon to the flour.
Orange: Add the finely grated zest of 1 orange to the flour.
White chocolate and orange: Dip the tops of the orange cookies in 50g (2oz) melted white chocolate, then allow to set on greaseproof paper.
Spices (cinnamon, mixed spice, ginger): Add 1 teaspoon of a ground spice to the flour.
Crystallised ginger and dark chocolate: Add 25g (1oz) finely chopped crystallised ginger to the flour. When the cookies are baked and cooled, dip the tops in 50g (2oz) melted dark chocolate, then allow to set on greaseproof paper.
Double chocolate chip: Use 250g (9oz) plain flour and add 50g (2oz) sifted cocoa powder to the flour. Bring the dough together and mix in 125g (4^1/$_2$oz) dark or white chocolate chips.

White chocolate and dried cranberry: Add 50g (2oz) chopped dried cranberries to the flour. When the cookies are baked and cooled, dip the tops in 50g (2oz) melted white chocolate and allow to set on greaseproof paper.

RACHEL'S BAKING TIPS

✳ Roll leftover dough into a log shape, 2–3cm (^{3}/$_4$–1^1/$_4$in) in diameter, then leave in the fridge for up to 2 weeks, or freeze for up to a couple of months. To bake, cut off slices, about 1cm (^{1}/$_2$in) thick, and cook on a baking tray in a preheated oven.
✳ Always remove cookies from their baking trays while still warm otherwise they will stick.

GERMAN SPICE AND HAZELNUT COOKIES

MAKES 25-30 COOKIES

125g (4^1/$_2$oz) butter, softened
80g (3^1/$_2$oz) soft light brown sugar
1 egg, lightly beaten
1 tsp vanilla extract
200g (7oz) plain flour
1/2 tsp bicarbonate of soda
1/4 tsp freshly grated nutmeg
1/4 tsp mixed spice
1 dsp caster sugar
1 dsp ground cinnamon
25g (1oz) hazelnuts, roughly chopped

The fragrant spices in these cookies make them a delicious and aromatic treat.

1 Preheat the oven to 180ºC (350ºF), Gas mark 4.
2 Cream the butter in a large bowl or a food mixer until soft. Add the brown sugar and beat together again until light and fluffy. Beat in the egg and vanilla extract until combined.
3 Sift in the flour, bicarbonate of soda and spices and gently bring the mixture together to form a dough. Wrap the dough in cling film and allow it to chill in the fridge for 30 minutes.
4 Mix the caster sugar and cinnamon in a medium-sized bowl. Roll the dough into walnut-sized balls and toss in the sugar and cinnamon. Place on baking trays (no need to grease or line) about 7cm (2^3/$_4$in) apart and sprinkle with the hazelnuts. Bake for 15 minutes, or until golden and firm at the edges.
5 Leave for 2 minutes, then transfer to a wire rack to cool.

OAT AND VANILLA SHORTBREAD COOKIES

MAKES ABOUT 40 COOKIES

200g (7oz) butter, softened
100g (3¹/₂oz) icing sugar, sifted
1 tsp vanilla extract
200g (7oz) plain flour
¹/₂ tsp baking powder
100g (3¹/₂oz) porridge oats
Caster sugar, for sprinkling

The oats give these cookies a wonderful crumbly texture in this delicious variation on the classic shortbread biscuit.

1 Preheat the oven to 180°C (350°F), Gas mark 4.

2 Cream the butter in a large bowl or in an electric food mixer until soft. Add the icing sugar and vanilla extract and beat until the mixture is light and fluffy.

3 Sift in the flour and baking powder, then stir in the oats and bring the mixture together to form a dough.

4 Using a sheet of cling film to cover the dough, roll it into a log about 30cm (12in) long and 6cm (2¹/₂in) in diameter. Allow to chill in the fridge, covered in the cling film, for about 30 minutes until firm.

5 Remove the cling film, slice the log into rounds about 5mm (¹/₄in) thick and place slightly apart on a baking tray lined with parchment paper. Bake in the oven for 15 minutes or until light golden brown and dry to the touch.

6 Carefully transfer the cookies to a wire rack to cool.

CHOCOLATE AND COCONUT BARS

MAKES 16 BARS

225g (8oz) butter, softened

150g (5oz) golden caster sugar

150g (5oz) desiccated coconut

75g (3oz) crushed cornflakes (I do this in a bag with a rolling pin)

Pinch of salt

150g (5oz) self-raising flour, sifted

25g (1oz) cocoa powder, sifted

175g (6oz) good-quality dark chocolate

18 x 28cm (7 x 11in) Swiss roll tin

These crunchy, chocolatey treats are perfect for picnics and parties.

1 Preheat the oven to 180ºC (350ºF), Gas mark 4. Butter or line the Swiss roll tin with greaseproof paper.

2 Cream the butter in a large bowl or in an electric food mixer until soft. Add the sugar and beat until the mixture is light and fluffy. Add the coconut, cornflakes and salt, then gradually add the sifted flour and cocoa powder and bring the mixture together to form a fairly dry dough.

3 Place the dough in the prepared Swiss roll tin and spread it out evenly (I sometimes place a layer of cling film over it and roll it with a rolling pin or empty jam jar).

4 Remove the cling film and bake in the oven for 20 minutes or until dry to the touch. Allow to cool in the Swiss roll tin.

5 Melt the chocolate in a heatproof bowl set over a saucepan of simmering water, then spread over the cooled biscuit base in the tin. Place somewhere cool (preferably not in the fridge) until the chocolate has hardened, then cut into bars.

GINGER AND HONEY SNAPS

MAKES ABOUT 20 COOKIES

225g (8oz) self-raising
flour
2 tsp bicarbonate
of soda
Pinch of salt
1 tsp ground ginger
1 tsp mixed spice
1/2 tsp ground
cinnamon
100g (3¹/₂oz) caster
sugar, plus 1 tbsp
extra, for sprinkling
125g (4¹/₂oz) butter,
cubed
100g (3¹/₂oz) runny
honey

For a variation on the classic ginger biscuit, these are
the perfect accompaniment to a mid-morning cuppa.

1 Preheat the oven to 180°C (350°F), Gas mark 4. Grease
a large baking tray with vegetable oil.
2 Sift the flour, bicarbonate of soda, salt and spices into
a large bowl, add the 100g (3¹/₂oz) sugar and mix well.
Add the butter and, using your fingertips, rub it into
the flour until the mixture resembles breadcrumbs.
3 Heat the honey gently in a small saucepan, then pour
it into the flour and butter mixture and bring together
to form a dough using a wooden spoon.
4 Sprinkle the 1 tablespoon of caster sugar over a plate.
Using floured hands, roll the dough into small balls, then
roll in the caster sugar and place on the greased baking
tray about 5cm (2in) apart. Flatten down with the back of
a damp fork and bake in the oven for 10–12 minutes or until
they are medium brown. If the cookies are too dark, they
will taste bitter.
5 Leave on the baking tray for 2 minutes before carefully
transferring to a wire rack to cool.

RACHEL'S BAKING TIP

To make fresh cookies a couple of days later, you can roll
some or all of the mixture into a sausage shape, wrap tightly
in cling film and allow to chill in the fridge. Remove from the
fridge 30 minutes before cooking. Cut off pieces of dough,
roll them in your hands, then in the caster sugar and bake
as above. They won't be as big but they are still delicious!

LITTLE PECAN PUFFS

110g (4oz) shelled
   pecans
110g (4oz) butter,
   softened
50g (2oz) caster sugar
1 tsp vanilla extract
110g (4oz) plain flour,
   sifted
25g (1oz) icing sugar,
   sifted, plus extra
   for dusting

These buttery and crumbly little morsels are tossed in icing sugar so they look like small puffy clouds – hence their name!

1 Preheat the oven to 150°C (300°F), Gas mark 2.

2 Place the pecans in a food processor and grind until quite fine.

3 Cream the butter in a large bowl or in an electric food mixer until soft. Add the sugar and vanilla extract and beat until the mixture is light and fluffy. Add the ground pecans and flour and bring together to form a dough.

4 Using your hands, roll the dough into small, marble-sized balls, then flatten slightly using the palm of your hand and place on a baking tray (no need to grease or line).

5 Bake in the oven for 40 minutes or until they are a very pale golden brown and slightly firm around the edges.

6 Sift the icing sugar into a shallow bowl or onto a large plate. Allow the cookies to cool for 2 minutes, then carefully remove them from the tray and, while they are still hot, roll them in the sifted icing sugar.

7 Allow to cool on a wire rack, then dust generously with more icing sugar.

BAKEWELL BARS

MAKES 12 BARS

75g (3oz) butter,
  softened
25g (1oz) caster sugar
1 egg yolk
175g (6oz) plain flour,
  plus extra for dusting
Half a jar
  (approximately
  200g/7oz) raspberry
  jam (or make your
  own – see page 277)

For the topping
100g (3½oz) butter,
  melted and cooled
  slightly
2 eggs, beaten
A few drops of almond
  essence
100g (3½oz) ground
  almonds
100g (3½oz) semolina
100g (3½oz) caster
  sugar
Flaked almonds,
  for sprinkling

20 x 20cm (8 x 8in)
  square cake tin

I love the classic combination of light almond sponge
and buttery shortbread, sandwiched together with a tasty
layer of raspberry jam. You can use any type of jam you
wish, of course – apricot would make a delicious alternative
in this recipe. You can also double the quantity to fit into
a 23 x 30cm (9 x 12in) Swiss roll tin.

1 Preheat the oven to 180°C (350°F), Gas mark 4. Butter the
sides of the cake tin and line the base with greaseproof paper.
2 First, make the biscuit base. Cream the butter in a large
bowl or in an electric food mixer until soft. Add the sugar
and beat until the mixture is light and fluffy. Add the egg
yolk and mix well, then sift in the flour and mix together
to form a dough.
3 Roll the pastry out on a lightly floured work surface to
the right size to fit the base of the tin and then press into
the prepared tin. Spread the raspberry jam over the top,
then allow to chill in the fridge while you make the topping.
4 Place the melted butter in a bowl, add the beaten eggs and
almond essence and mix well. Stir in the ground almonds,
semolina and caster sugar.
5 Take the tin out of the fridge and spread the almond
dough over the jam, being careful not to mess up the jam
too much. (I usually place the almond dough in dots over
the jam, then join it all together using the back of a spoon.)
6 Sprinkle the top with the flaked almonds and bake in the
oven for about 25–30 minutes or until golden and set in the
centre. Allow to cool in the tin, then cut into fingers.

ALMOND AND ORANGE BUTTER FINGERS

MAKES ABOUT 32 FINGERS

225g (8oz) butter, softened
125g (4¹/₂oz) caster sugar
1 tsp finely grated orange zest
110g (4oz) plain flour
175g (6oz) ground almonds
Flaked almonds, for sprinkling

These lovely old-fashioned, shortbread-like biscuits are moist and crumbly, with a citrus zing.

1 Preheat the oven to 170°C (325°F), Gas mark 3.

2 Cream the butter in a large bowl or in an electric food mixer until soft. Add the sugar and orange zest and beat until the mixture is light and fluffy. Sift in the flour then stir in the ground almonds and bring the mixture together to form a dough.

3 Using your hands, roll the dough into walnut-sized balls and form into oval shapes. Sprinkle with the flaked almonds, making sure they are well dispersed and pressed in. Transfer to a plate and allow to chill in the fridge for 20 minutes.

4 Place the fingers slightly spaced apart on a large baking tray (no need to grease or line) and bake in the oven for 15 minutes or until light golden brown.

5 Carefully transfer the fingers to a wire rack to cool.

SNICKERDOODLES

MAKES ABOUT 26 BISCUITS

125g (4¹/₂oz) butter,
   softened
110g (4oz) caster sugar,
   plus 1 dsp extra,
   for rolling
1 egg, lightly beaten
1 tsp vanilla extract
250g (9oz) plain flour
¹/₂ tsp freshly grated
   nutmeg
³/₄ tsp baking powder
Pinch of salt
1 dsp ground cinnamon

A somewhat soft and cakey biscuit with a spicy,
autumnal flavour.

1 Preheat the oven to 180ºC (350ºF), Gas mark 4.
2 Cream the butter in a large bowl or in an electric food
mixer until soft. Add the 110g (4oz) caster sugar and beat
until the mixture is light and fluffy. Beat in the egg and
vanilla extract until combined.
3 Sift in the flour, nutmeg, baking powder and salt and
gently mix together to form a dough.
4 Mix the dessertspoon of sugar and the cinnamon together
in a medium-sized bowl. Using your hands, roll the dough
into walnut-sized balls then roll in the sugar and cinnamon
mixture and place on two baking trays (no need to grease
or line), each ball spaced about 3cm (1¹/₄in) apart. Flatten
them down with the palm of your hands.
5 Bake in the oven for about 15 minutes, or until they feel
firm around the edges.
6 Allow to stand for 2 minutes on the baking trays, then
carefully transfer to a wire rack to cool.

DATE BARS

250ml (9fl oz) water
200g (7oz) dates (stoned weight), chopped
175g (6oz) plain flour
1/2 tsp bicarbonate of soda
175g (6oz) soft light brown sugar
100g (31/2oz) porridge oats
Good pinch of salt
175g (6oz) butter, diced

20 x 20cm (8 x 8in) square cake tin

We used to make these sticky sweet bars when I worked in a food shop in Vancouver. They're great for a little afternoon pick-me-up and much better than any bought variety. They are perfect for lunchboxes, too, and will keep very fresh in an airtight box for up to a week. They can also be frozen.

1 Preheat the oven to 180°C (350°F), Gas mark 4. Butter the sides of the cake tin and line the base with greaseproof paper.
2 Place the water and chopped dates in a medium-sized saucepan and bring up to a simmer. Cook for about 10 minutes, uncovered, on a low–medium heat until the date mixture is very soft and thick, stirring occasionally. Remove from the heat and allow to cool to room temperature.
3 Sift the flour and bicarbonate of soda into a large bowl. Add the sugar, oats and salt and mix well. Add the butter and, using your fingertips, rub it in until moist clumps form.
4 Press half of the oat mixture evenly over the base of the prepared tin. Spread the cooked date mixture over this, then sprinkle with the remaining oat mixture. Press gently with the palm of your hand to flatten it on top.
5 Bake in the oven for approximately 40 minutes or until golden brown at the edges and set in the centre.
6 Allow to cool completely in the tin, then cut into bars and serve.

PEANUT BUTTER AND WHITE CHOCOLATE BLONDIES

125g (4½oz) plain flour
1 tsp baking powder
100g (3½oz) butter, softened
150g (5oz) crunchy peanut butter
175g (6oz) soft light brown sugar
1 egg, beaten
1 tsp vanilla extract
75g (3oz) white chocolate, chopped

20 x 20cm (8 x 8in) square cake tin

Tired of brownies? Try blondies! These little squares are great on their own; eaten with ice cream they are simply sinful.

1 Preheat the oven to 170°C (325°F), Gas mark 3. Butter the sides of the cake tin and line the base with greaseproof paper.

2 Sift the flour and baking powder into a small bowl and set aside.

3 In a large bowl, cream the butter and peanut butter together until very soft. Add the sugar, egg and vanilla extract and beat until combined. Add the flour, baking powder and the chopped chocolate and mix to form a dough.

4 Place the dough in the prepared tin and bake in the oven for 25–30 minutes or until golden brown and almost firm in the centre.

5 Allow to cool in the tin, before removing and cutting into squares.

CARROT AND PECAN SQUARES

MAKES 16 SQUARES

175g (6oz) wholemeal
   self-raising flour
1/2 tsp salt
3 tsp baking powder
1 tsp mixed spice
1 tsp ground ginger
50g (2oz) raisins
   (optional)
150ml (1/4 pint)
   sunflower oil
150g (5oz) soft light
   brown sugar
3 eggs
1 tsp vanilla extract
225g (8oz) carrot,
   finely grated
50g (2oz) shelled
   pecans, chopped,
   plus 25g (1oz) for
   sprinkling
1 x quantity cream
   cheese icing
   (see page 267)

20 x 20cm (8 x 8in)
   square cake tin

These are denser and richer than Carrot Cake (see page 67). The recipe uses a classic cream cheese icing, but the cakes are equally good un-iced.

1 Preheat the oven to 180°C (350°F), Gas mark 4. Butter the sides of the cake tin and line the base with greaseproof paper.

2 Sift the flour, salt, baking powder and spices into a large bowl. Add the raisins (if using) and mix well.

3 Whisk the oil, brown sugar, eggs, vanilla extract, grated carrot and chopped pecans in a separate bowl, then mix in the flour and spice mixture. Spoon into the prepared tin and bake in the oven for 25–30 minutes, or until springy to the touch and a skewer, when inserted in the centre, comes out clean.

4 Allow to cool, then remove from the tin and place on a serving plate.

5 Make the cream cheese icing as described on page 267, then, using a palette knife or back of a spoon, spread the icing onto the cooled cake. Sprinkle with additional chopped pecans and cut into squares to serve.

LIGHT SWEET SCONES

MAKES 10-12 SCONES

500g (1lb 2oz) light
  Italian or plain flour
1 rounded tsp
  bicarbonate of soda
2 rounded tsp cream
  of tartar
1 tsp sea salt
125g (4¹/₂oz) unsalted
  cold butter, cubed (if
  you are using salted
  butter, decrease the
  salt to ¹/₂ tsp)
25g (1oz) caster sugar
1 egg, beaten
275ml (9fl oz)
  buttermilk or milk,
  plus extra for the
  egg wash
50g (2oz) caster or
  granulated sugar
  (optional)

6cm (2¹/₂in) cutter

My friend Oisin makes these divine scones. He uses a very light Italian flour, but you can use plain flour if you wish.

1 Preheat the oven to 220°C (425°F), Gas mark 7.

2 Sift the flour, bicarbonate of soda, cream of tartar and salt into a large bowl. Using your fingertips, rub in the butter until the mixture resembles breadcrumbs. Add the sugar and mix well.

3 Set aside about a third of the beaten egg and combine the rest with the buttermilk, then add to the flour mixture and mix briefly to combine into a moist dough. Place on a lightly floured work surface and knead ever so slightly to bring together, then press or roll out to a thickness of 2cm (³/₄in).

4 Using the cutter, cut out approximately 12 scones and place on a floury baking tray. Add about a teaspoon or so of buttermilk to the remainder of the beaten egg to make an egg wash.

5 Brush the scones with the egg wash (and dip the tops in sugar if you wish) and bake in the oven for 10–12 minutes or until golden brown on top. Eat as soon as possible!

VARIATIONS

Cinnamon: Add 2 teaspoons of ground cinnamon to the flour.
Orange: Add the finely grated zest of 1 orange to the flour.
Chocolate chip: Add 100g (3¹/₂oz) of dark or milk chocolate chips (or chopped chocolate) to the dry ingredients before you add the liquid.
Sultana or raisin: Add 100g (3¹/₂oz) of sultanas or raisins to the dry ingredients before you add the liquid. I also sometimes add 100g (3¹/₂oz) dried cranberries or dried blueberries instead of the sultanas.

CINNAMON PECAN BUNS

MAKES 12 BUNS

For the filling
100g (3¹/₂oz) butter,
    softened
1 tsp ground cinnamon
100g (3¹/₂oz) soft light
    brown sugar
100g (3¹/₂oz) toasted
    pecans, chopped
    (see Rachel's baking
    tips opposite)

For the dough
375g (13oz) plain flour
1 tsp baking powder
1 tsp ground cinnamon
25g (1oz) caster sugar
50g (2oz) butter,
    softened
1 egg, beaten
200ml (7fl oz) milk

For the icing
75g (3oz) icing sugar
1¹/₂–2 tbsp boiling water

25cm (10in) diameter
    cake tin

These sweet, buttery and nutty treats are delicious with a cup of tea or coffee. Normally made with a yeast-risen dough, the buns in this recipe are made using a slightly faster method.

1 Preheat the oven to 230°C (450°F), Gas mark 8, and butter and flour the cake tin.

2 First, make the filling. Cream the butter and cinnamon together in a large bowl or in an electric food mixer until soft. Add the brown sugar and beat until the mixture is light and fluffy and then stir in the chopped toasted pecans. Set aside (not in the fridge).

3 Next, make the dough. Sift the flour, baking powder and cinnamon together into a large bowl. Add the caster sugar, then add the butter and, using your fingertips, rub it in until the mixture resembles breadcrumbs. Whisk the beaten egg and milk together in a separate bowl, then make a well in the centre of the dry ingredients and pour in most of the liquid (all but 60ml/2fl oz). Using one hand with your fingers outstretched like a claw, move your hand around in one direction (clockwise or anti-clockwise) until the dough comes together. You may need to add the rest of the milk as the dough should be soft and a little sticky.

4 To make the buns, tip the dough out onto a floured work surface and dust with flour. Using a rolling pin, roll out the dough until it is a 35 x 25cm (14 x 10in) rectangle and about 2cm (³/₄in) thick.

5 Spread the filling all over the rectangle, then with the widest end facing you, roll up the dough away from you so that it resembles a Swiss roll. Cut the 'log' 11 times to make 12 slices, each 3cm (1¹/₄in) thick. Place the pieces cut side facing up, with a tiny bit of space between each 'swirl', in the prepared cake tin.

6 Bake in the oven for 10 minutes, then reduce the oven temperature to 200°C (400°F), Gas mark 6 and cook for a further 25–35 minutes or until risen, golden brown and cooked in the centre. They should have joined together to make a lovely cluster of buns.

7 Allow to stand in the tin for 2–3 minutes before carefully turning out and cooling on a wire rack. When cool, transfer to a serving plate or cake stand.

8 To make the icing, sift the icing sugar into a bowl, add 1 tablespoon of boiling water and mix well, adding another $1/2$–1 tablespoon of boiling water if necessary, until the icing is soft but not too runny. Drizzle the icing over the buns. To serve, break each bun off with your hand or cut into slices.

VARIATION

Cinnamon scones: Instead of rolling up the dough and cutting it, you could make simple cinnamon scones. Roll the dough out until it is about 3cm ($1^1/4$in) thick, then cut into ten squares or rounds, each about 6cm ($2^1/2$in) in diameter. Brush the tops with beaten egg, then dip the wet top into crunchy granulated sugar so that they are covered in an even layer. Place on a baking tray and bake in a preheated oven at 230°C (450°F), Gas mark 8 for about 10–15 minutes or until golden on top and sounding hollow when tapped on the base. Allow to cool then split in half and serve with the cinnamon pecan filling spread on each half.

RACHEL'S BAKING TIPS

✳ To toast the pecans, roughly chop them and then spread out on a baking tray and cook in a preheated oven at 230°C (450°F), Gas mark 8 for 4 minutes. Allow to cool before using.

✳ To reduce the cooking time, place the buns on a baking tray, spacing them further apart than in step 5. Bake for 12–15 minutes until golden on top and firm at the edges.

ECCLES CAKES

300g (11oz) good-quality bought or homemade puff or flaky pastry (see pages 257–8)
1 egg, beaten

For the filling
40g (1½oz) butter, melted
75g (3oz) currants
75g (3oz) soft light or dark brown sugar
40g (1½oz) mixed peel, chopped
Finely grated zest of 1 orange
½ tsp ground cinnamon
¼ tsp freshly grated nutmeg

For the top
About 2 tbsp milk
About 2 tbsp demerara sugar

An Eccles cake is a small, round cakey biscuit made with puff pastry, filled with currants, sugar and spices and topped with crunchy demerara sugar. They are named after the town of Eccles, near Manchester, where they have been made for the last 250 years!

1 Preheat the oven to 200°C (400°F), Gas mark 6.
2 Mix all the ingredients together for the filling and set aside.
3 On a lightly floured work surface, roll out the pastry to a thickness of 2–3mm (1/16–1/8in) and cut into 8cm (3¼in) discs. Bring the pastry scraps together and roll them out too.
4 Place 1 teaspoon of the filling in the centre of each disc. Lightly brush the edges with beaten egg or water and bring the edges together into the centre, 'wrapping up' the filling. Turn the disc over, seam side down, and flatten it slightly with the rolling pin until it is about 5cm (2in) in diameter.
5 Brush the tops with milk, then sprinkle with demerara sugar (you can dip the tops in the sugar, if you wish). Make three incisions with a knife, about 1cm (½in) long, and place the cakes on a baking tray (no need to grease or line), spaced slightly apart to allow room for spreading.
6 Bake in the oven for 10–12 minutes or until golden brown. The currants and sugar caramelise through the holes in the top of the little cakes. Carefully transfer to a wire rack to cool.

VARIATIONS

Mincemeat: Replace the filling with mincemeat (see page 278). Place 1 teaspoon in each disc and continue as above.
Orange and almond puffs: Replace the filling with 1 small beaten egg, 100g (3½oz) ground almonds, 50g (2oz) caster sugar and the finely grated zest of 1 orange. Mix together and continue as above.

LEMON CUPCAKES

125g (4¹/₂oz) butter,
softened
125g (4¹/₂oz) caster
sugar
Finely grated zest
of ¹/₂ large lemon
(keeping the zest
of the remaining
¹/₂ lemon for the
lemon icing –
see below)
2 eggs, beaten
150g (5oz) plain flour
¹/₄ tsp baking powder

For the lemon
butter icing
75g (3oz) butter,
softened
175g (6oz) icing sugar,
sifted
Finely grated zest
of ¹/₂ large lemon
1–2 tsp freshly
squeezed lemon juice
12 crystallised flowers
(optional; or make
your own – see page
271)

12-hole fairy cake tin

I love these zesty little treats with an afternoon cup of tea.

1 Preheat the oven to 180°C (350°F), Gas mark 4. Line
a 12-hole fairy cake tin with 12 paper cases.

2 Cream the butter in a large bowl or in an electric food
mixer until soft. Add the sugar and grated lemon zest and
beat until the mixture is light and fluffy. Gradually add the
beaten eggs, then sift in the flour and baking powder and
fold into the mixture. Alternatively, whiz all the ingredients
together in an electric food mixer.

3 Divide the mixture between the paper cases and bake in
the preheated oven for 7–10 minutes, until risen and golden.
When cooked, the centre of each cake should be slightly
springy to the touch. Remove the cakes from the tin and
place on a wire rack to cool before you ice them.

4 To make the lemon butter icing, cream the butter in a bowl
with a wooden spoon or hand-held electric beater until very
soft. Gradually add the icing sugar and beat into the butter,
along with the lemon zest and enough lemon juice to soften
the icing to a spreadable consistency.

5 When the cupcakes are cool, spread a generous heaped
teaspoon of lemon butter icing over the top of each one.
Decorate with the crystallised flowers (if using).

FAIRY CAKES

MAKES 24 MINI OR 12 MEDIUM-SIZED FAIRY CAKES

125g (4¹/₂oz) butter,
    softened
125g (4¹/₂oz) caster
    sugar
1 tsp vanilla extract
2 eggs
150g (5oz) plain flour
¹/₄ tsp baking powder

For the filling
100ml (3¹/₂fl oz)
    raspberry or
    strawberry jam
    (or make your own –
    see pages 276–7)
200ml (7fl oz) crème
    chantilly – see page
    270) or vanilla
    buttercream icing
    (see page 268)
Icing sugar, for dusting
Dragées (metallic
    sugared balls), to
    decorate (optional)

12-hole fairy cake tin

These are the prettiest little cakes for a birthday party or just for a special treat; they are also known as butterfly buns.

1 Preheat the oven to 190°C (375°F), Gas mark 5. Line a 12-hole fairy cake tin, or a 24-hole tin for mini cakes, with 12 (or 24) paper cases.

2 Cream the butter in a large bowl or in an electric food mixer until soft. Add the sugar and vanilla extract and beat until the mixture is light and fluffy.

3 Add the eggs, one at time, beating continuously, then sift in the flour and baking powder. (If you are pushed for time, and the butter is sufficiently soft, put the butter, sugar, eggs, vanilla, flour and baking powder into an electric food mixer and briefly whiz just until the mixture comes together.)

4 Divide the mixture evenly between the paper cases using two teaspoons for mini cakes or two dessertspoons for larger ones. Cook in the oven for 8–12 minutes, or until golden and springy to the touch. (The mini cakes may take just 5 minutes.) Transfer the cakes to a wire rack to cool.

5 When cooled, cut the top off each cake, then cut the tops in half to make the butterfly wings. Set aside. Spread half a teaspoon or so of jam on the top of the cut cake, then spoon or pipe the crème chantilly or buttercream on top of the jam. Arrange two butterfly wings at an angle on top of each cake. Dust generously with icing sugar and decorate with dragées, if using.

VIENNESE BISCUITS

110g (4oz) butter,
    softened
50g (2oz) icing sugar,
    sifted
1 egg yolk
1/2–1 tsp vanilla extract
150g (5oz) plain flour
25g (1oz) cornflour
Pinch of salt

Piping bag
1–1.5cm (1/2–5/sin)
    star nozzle

Sometimes called 'whirls', these little rosette-shaped biscuits are made with icing sugar and cornflour to give a wonderful melt-in-the mouth texture. You'll need a piping bag to shape them.

1 Preheat the oven to 180°C (350°F), Gas mark 4.
2 Cream the butter in a large bowl or in an electric food mixer until soft. Add the icing sugar and beat until the mixture is light and fluffy. Beat in the egg yolk and vanilla extract until combined.
3 Sift in the flours and salt and mix well to form a dough.
4 Spoon the dough into a cloth piping bag fitted with the star nozzle and onto a lined baking tray pipe 5cm (2in) 'S' shapes, or circles or rosettes for bite-sized ones, spaced 5cm (2in) apart to allow them to spread. Bake in the oven for 12–15 minutes or until pale golden brown.
5 Leave on the baking tray for 2 minutes, then carefully transfer to a wire rack to cool.

VARIATION

Paired biscuits: Sandwich similar shapes together with butter icing or buttercream (see pages 267–8) or apricot jam; or dip in melted chocolate.

CAKES

BUTTER-FREE SPONGE CAKE

SERVES 6-8

3 eggs, separated
225g (8oz) caster sugar
90ml (3fl oz) water
150g (5oz) plain flour
1 tsp baking powder
**2 tsp icing sugar, for
    dusting**

For the filling
**250ml (9fl oz) whipped
    cream**
**100g (3½oz) fresh fruit,
    such as sliced
    strawberries, whole
    raspberries or
    blackberries**

**Two 20cm (8in)
    diameter sandwich
    tins**

This is a good lesson in cake-making for the novice baker: how to combine eggs, water and sugar into the perfect light fluffy 'mousse' before folding in the flour. Once you have mastered the basic cake recipe, the decorations and the filling are up to you, but I've given a classic combination here.

1 Preheat the oven to 180°C (350°F), Gas mark 4. Butter and flour the sides of the sandwich tins and line the bases with greaseproof paper.

2 Place the egg yolks and sugar in an electric food mixer and beat for 2 minutes. Pour in the water and whisk for approximately 10 minutes or until the mixture is firm and creamy.

3 Sift in the flour and baking powder and fold in gently with a metal spoon or spatula.

4 In a separate, spotlessly clean bowl, beat the egg whites until they just hold stiff peaks, then fold them into the flour mixture very gently, again using a metal spoon or spatula.

5 Divide the mixture between the two prepared tins, smooth the surface and bake in the oven for approximately 20 minutes or until just set in the centre.

6 Remove the cakes from the tins by loosening the edges and allow to cool on a wire rack, then sandwich with the whipped cream and fruit. Dust with icing sugar before serving.

RACHEL'S BAKING TIP

You can also make this cake with just one 20cm (8in) spring-form/loose-bottomed tin. Before baking, put a sheet of foil on the top of the cake and reduce the oven temperature to 170°C (325°F), Gas mark 3 after 20 minutes. It takes approximately 35 minutes to cook in total.

ICED ORANGE CAKE

SERVES 6

100g (3½oz) butter
2 eggs
Finely grated zest
  of 1 orange
100g (3½oz) caster
  sugar
100g (3½oz) icing
  sugar, sifted
125g (4½oz) plain flour
1 tsp baking powder

For the topping
100g (3½oz) icing sugar
1–2 tbsp freshly
  squeezed orange juice

20cm (8in) diameter
  spring-form/loose-
  bottomed tin

This is a deliciously moist and tangy cake, perfect for summer dinner parties.

1 Preheat the oven to 180°C (350°F), Gas mark 4. Butter and flour the sides of the cake tin and line the base with greaseproof paper.

2 Melt the butter gently in a saucepan and set aside.

3 Using a hand-held electric beater, whisk together the eggs, grated orange zest and caster and icing sugar for a few minutes until light and slightly fluffy. Stir in the melted butter and sift in the flour and baking powder. Fold it all together gently.

4 Pour the cake mixture into the prepared tin, smooth the surface and bake in the oven for 35–40 minutes or until golden and set in the centre and a skewer inserted into the middle comes out clean.

5 Place the tin on a wire rack and allow to stand for about 10 minutes before removing the cake carefully from the tin. Allow to cool on the wire rack.

6 To make the topping, sift the icing sugar into a bowl and stir in just enough orange juice until it is soft but not runny.

7 When the cake is cool, place it on a serving plate or cake stand and spread the icing over the top. Dipping a spoon or table knife in boiling water makes it easier to spread the icing.

UPSIDE-DOWN CRANBERRY CAKE

SERVES 8

50g (2oz) butter
300g (11oz) caster sugar
225g (8oz) fresh or
　frozen cranberries
200g (7oz) plain flour
1 tsp baking powder
1/2 tsp salt
1/4 tsp bicarbonate
　of soda
2 eggs
200ml (7fl oz)
　buttermilk
75ml (2 1/2fl oz)
　vegetable or
　sunflower oil

To serve
Softly whipped cream
Brown sugar

25cm (10in) diameter
　ovenproof pan

You can use many different kinds of fruit for an upside-down cake, such as gooseberries, blueberries, blackberries or slices of apple or pear. The buttery, sugary juices of the cooked fruit soak into the cake once you flip it over, making it incredibly moist. If you are using a red fruit such as cranberries – as in this recipe – the juices stain the cake a beautiful pink.

1 Preheat the oven to 180°C (350°F), Gas mark 4.
2 Melt the butter in the ovenproof pan. Stir in half the sugar and cook over a gentle heat for approximately 2 minutes. Add the cranberries and set aside.
3 Sift the flour, baking powder, salt and bicarbonate of soda into a large bowl. Whisk the eggs in a measuring jug or small bowl and add the remaining sugar, the buttermilk and oil and mix together. Pour this mixture into the dry ingredients and whisk to form a liquid batter. Pour the batter over the cranberries in the pan.
4 Place the pan in the oven and bake for 30–35 minutes or until the cake feels firm in the centre.
5 Allow to cool for 5 minutes before turning out by placing an inverted plate over the top of the pan and turning the pan and plate over together in one quick movement. Serve warm or at room temperature with softly whipped cream and sprinkled with brown sugar.

ITALIAN HAZELNUT CAKE

SERVES 6-8

200g (7oz) hazelnuts
(with skins on)
1 tsp baking powder
or gluten-free
baking powder
1 tsp ground cinnamon
100g (3½oz) butter,
softened
5 eggs, separated
175g (6oz) caster sugar
1 tsp vanilla extract
Pinch of salt

20cm (8in) diameter
spring-form/loose-
bottomed tin

This elegantly simple cake doesn't need to try too hard to be absolutely delicious. It's light, heavenly with ice cream, and the hazelnuts give it an incredible texture – delicate and nutty at the same time.

1 Preheat the oven to 170°C (325°F), Gas mark 3. Butter and line the sides and base of the cake tin with greaseproof paper.
2 Grind the hazelnuts with the baking powder and ground cinnamon in a food processor until fine. Add the butter and combine.
3 Place the egg yolks in the bowl of an electric food mixer or use a hand-held electric beater. Add the sugar and whisk until the mixture become slightly 'moussey' and the mix holds a trail when you lift the beater. Add the hazelnut mixture and the vanilla extract and whisk until combined.
4 Whisk the egg whites and salt together in a large, spotlessly clean bowl until stiff peaks form, then gently fold into the nut mixture in three stages so as not to deflate the whites.
5 Pour the mixture into the prepared tin, smooth the surface and bake in the oven for 55–70 minutes or until the cake feels firm and a skewer inserted into the middle comes out clean. The mixture is quite delicate so don't be tempted to open the oven until close to the end of the cooking time.
6 Allow to cool in the tin for 15 minutes, then very gently ease the sides of the cake out of the tin using a palette knife. Remove the base after another 15 minutes and leave to cool before cutting into slices.

VARIATION
Chocolate: Substitute the ground cinnamon with 50g (2oz) dark chocolate (whizzed up in the food processor with the hazelnuts).

CHOCOLATE AND VANILLA MARBLE CAKE

SERVES 6-8

225g (8oz) butter,
  softened
225g (8oz) caster sugar
4 eggs
2 tsp vanilla extract
225g (8oz) plain flour
2 tsp baking powder
50ml (1³/4fl oz) milk
Scant 50g (2oz) cocoa
  powder, sifted

20cm (8in) diameter
  spring-form/loose-
  bottomed tin

I just love this simple, old-fashioned cake as it always reminds me of when I was little. Made using a basic Madeira cake recipe, the mixture is separated into two bowls, cocoa powder is folded into one and then the two mixtures are swirled gently together. This cake will keep for a couple of days in an airtight box, or it can be frozen. Serve it plain or dusted with icing sugar, or drizzle some hot chocolate sauce (see page 274) over the top.

1 Preheat the oven to 180°C (350°F), Gas mark 4. Butter and flour the sides of the cake tin and line the base with greaseproof paper.

2 Cream the butter in a large bowl or in an electric food mixer until soft. Add the sugar and beat until the mixture is light and fluffy.

3 Whisk the eggs and vanilla extract together in a small bowl. Gradually add the eggs to the butter mixture, beating all the time. Sift in the flour and baking powder and fold in gently to mix, then add the milk and mix gently to combine.

4 Tip half of the cake mixture into another large bowl and, into this bowl, fold in the sifted cocoa powder.

5 Place the cake mixtures into the prepared tin by alternating spoonfuls of the vanilla batter with the chocolate batter, then with a skewer or similar implement, gently draw swirls through the cake mixture to 'marblise' it. Don't overmix or you won't have that wonderful marble effect. Bake in the oven for 45 minutes or until a skewer inserted into the middle comes out clean.

6 Turn the cake out onto a wire rack and allow to cool.

DUTCH APPLE CAKE
MAKES 12–16 SQUARES

2 eggs
175g (6oz) caster sugar,
  plus 15g (¹/₂oz) extra
  sugar, for sprinkling
¹/₂ tsp vanilla extract
 (3oz) butter
75ml (2¹/₂fl oz) milk
125g (4¹/₂oz) plain flour
¹/₂ tsp ground
  cinnamon
2¹/₄ tsp baking powder
2 small (or 1 large)
  cooking apples
75ml (2¹/₂fl oz) double
  cream, to serve

20 x 20cm (8 x 8in)
  square cake tin

This cake has been made at Ballymaloe for years. We even have guests who ask for it specifically every time they visit. The fruit sinks to the bottom as it cooks, leaving a light sponge on top with a lovely sugary crust.

1 Preheat the oven to 200°C (400°F), Gas mark 6. Line the sides and base of the cake tin with parchment paper.
2 Using an electric whisk, whisk the eggs, 175g (6oz) caster sugar and vanilla extract in a large bowl until the mixture is thick and mousse-like and the whisk leaves a figure of eight pattern (this will take about 5 minutes).
3 Melt the butter in a saucepan with the milk, then pour onto the eggs, whisking all the time. Sift in the flour, cinnamon and baking powder and fold carefully into the batter so that there are no lumps of flour. Pour the mixture into the prepared tin and smooth the surface.
4 Peel and core the apples and cut into thin slices, then arrange them over the batter. They will sink to the bottom (this is meant to happen!). Sprinkle with the remaining sugar and bake in the oven for 10 minutes. Reduce the oven temperature to 180°C (350°F), Gas mark 4 and bake for a further 20–25 minutes or until well risen and golden brown.
5 Allow to cool in the tin, cut into squares and serve warm. It is delicious with cream!

VARIATION

Raspberry and pear: Instead of the cinnamon, mix the finely grated zest of 1 orange into the batter. Instead of the apples, sink 100g (3¹/₂oz) fresh or frozen raspberries and thin slices of 2 pears into the batter and cook in the same way.

CHERRY CRUMBLE CAKE

SERVES 6

350g (12oz) juicy,
ripe fresh cherries
(weight after stones
have been removed)
150g (5oz) self-raising
flour
Pinch of ground
cinnamon
50g (2oz) caster sugar
1 egg
30ml (1fl oz) milk
100g (3½oz) butter,
melted
Icing sugar, for dusting
(optional)

For the crumble
topping
25g (1oz) plain flour
¼ tsp ground
cinnamon
25g (1oz) caster sugar
25g (1oz) butter, cubed

20cm (8in) diameter
spring-form/loose-
bottomed tin

Everyone loves a crumble topping, so why not put it on
a cake? Use fresh cherries, if possible, or canned or frozen
ones (but not glacé).

1 Preheat the oven to 180°C (350°F), Gas mark 4. Butter the
sides of the cake tin and line the base with greaseproof paper.
2 Remove the stalks and stones from the cherries using
a cherry pitter if you have one, to keep the fruit whole,
otherwise cut them in half and discard the stones. Set the
cherries aside.
3 Sift the flour and cinnamon into a large bowl, add the
sugar, mix together and make a well in the centre.
4 Whisk the egg, milk and melted butter together in another
bowl, then pour into the dry ingredients and combine with
a wooden spoon or whisk. Beat well to make a thick, smooth
mixture, then spoon into the prepared tin and spread evenly.
Scatter the cherries over the mixture and gently press them
in with the back of a fork.
5 To make the topping, tip all the ingredients into a bowl.
Rub in the butter with your fingertips to make a crumb-like
mixture and scatter the topping over the cherries.
6 Bake in the oven for 30–35 minutes or until the top is lightly
golden and a skewer inserted into the middle comes out clean.
7 Leave in the tin for about 10 minutes until cool enough
to handle, then run a knife around the edge and remove
the cake from the tin. Allow to cool on a wire rack.
8 Dust with icing sugar, if you wish, and serve.

RACHEL'S BAKING TIP

If using butter straight from the fridge, you can grate
it into the flour and mix it without having to rub it in.

POPPY SEED CAKE WITH VANILLA BUTTERCREAM ICING

SERVES 8–10

150g (5oz) butter, softened
100g (3½oz) caster sugar
3 eggs, beaten
100g (3½oz) plain flour
1 tsp baking powder
75g (3oz) poppy seeds
1 x quantity vanilla buttercream icing (see page 268)

20cm (8in) diameter spring-form/loose-bottomed tin

This cake came about when our German au pair told me how much she missed her mum's poppy seed cake – so we decided to make it in Ireland. After a little bit of experimenting, we came up with this recipe. It is incredibly rich – one small slice generally suffices – and it is absolutely divine! This cake will keep for a few days but it can also be frozen un-iced.

1 Preheat the oven to 170°C (325°F), Gas mark 3. Butter the sides of the cake tin and line the base with greaseproof paper.
2 Cream the butter in a large bowl or in an electric food mixer until soft. Add the sugar and beat until the mixture is light and fluffy. Gradually add the beaten eggs, beating well between each addition.
3 Sift in the flour and baking powder, add the poppy seeds and stir until combined.
4 Spoon the mixture into the prepared cake tin, making a slight hollow in the centre with the back of a spoon. Bake in the oven for 25–28 minutes or until it is cooked in the centre and a skewer inserted into the middle comes out clean.
5 Allow the cake to stand for 5 minutes before carefully removing it from the tin and transferring it to a wire rack to cool.
6 Make the vanilla buttercream icing as described on page 268. If you wish, when the cake is cool, split it in half using a long-bladed serrated knife. Place one layer of the cake on a serving plate and spread over 2 generous tablespoons of the vanilla buttercream, then place the other half of the cake on top. Spread the remaining icing over the top and sides with a palette knife or table knife. The cake can also be kept whole, with the icing spread over the top and sides.

MOCHA CAKE

175g (6oz) self-raising
  flour
50g (2oz) cocoa powder
225g (8oz) soft light
  brown sugar
175g (6oz) butter,
  melted
4 medium eggs,
  separated
60ml (2fl oz) very
  strong coffee, cooled
3 tbsp water
1 x quantity coffee
  butter icing (see
  page 267)
Easy chocolate curls
  (see page 271) or
  chocolate coffee
  beans, to decorate

13 x 23cm (5 x 9in)
  loaf tin

This sumptuous coffee cake is great for sharing with friends
over a large cappuccino and a gossip.

1 Preheat the oven to 190°C (375°F), Gas mark 5. Oil and
line the loaf tin with parchment paper so that it comes
over the sides of the tin. Sift the flour and cocoa powder
into a large bowl, add the sugar and stir to combine.
2 Using a wooden spoon or a hand-held whisk, beat in the
melted butter, egg yolks, coffee and water until smooth.
3 Whisk the egg whites in a large clean bowl until fairly stiff
peaks form, then gently fold into the cake mixture in three
batches making sure there are no lumps of egg white left.
4 Turn the mixture into the prepared loaf tin and smooth the
surface. Give the tin a tap to remove any air bubbles. Bake in
the oven for 35 minutes, then reduce the oven temperature
to 160°C (325°F), Gas mark 3 for the last 20 minutes or until
a skewer inserted into the middle comes out clean.
5 Allow the cake to cool in the tin for 10 minutes then lift out
by the parchment paper onto a wire rack to cool completely.
6 Make the icing as described on page 267. When the cake is
cold, remove the parchment paper. Using a bread knife, split
the cake horizontally and spread about a third of the icing
on the lower half with a palette knife. Place the other half of
the cake back on top and spread the rest of the icing over it.
7 Decorate as desired. It's best to leave the cake for 30 minutes
to settle before cutting.

VARIATION
Cupcakes: This mixture also makes lovely cupcakes.
Divide into 12 cupcake cases and bake for 15 minutes in
an oven preheated to 190°C (375°F), Gas mark 5, then cool
and simply dust with icing sugar.

RED VELVET CAKE

SERVES 10-12

150g (5oz) butter,
    softened
300g (11oz) caster sugar
1 tsp vanilla extract
3 eggs, separated
250g (9oz) plain flour
25g (1oz) cornflour
1 tsp baking powder
2 level tbsp good-
    quality cocoa powder
250ml (9fl oz)
    buttermilk
Red food colouring
    (use 2 tbsp liquid
    colour or 1/2 tsp thick
    red food paste)
Pinch of salt
1 tsp white wine vinegar
1 tsp bicarbonate of
    soda

For the white frosting
2 large egg whites
250g (9oz) caster sugar
50g (2oz) golden syrup
Pinch of salt
1/4 tsp cream of tartar
2 tbsp water
1 tsp vanilla extract

Two 23cm (9in)
    diameter sandwich
    tins, each about 5cm
    (2in) deep

This delicious treat has layers of vampy red cake contrasting with snowy white frosting. The result is quite spectacular, both to look at and to eat. A journalist once wrote in *The New York Times* that this is the Dolly Parton of cakes – rich and tacky, but much loved all the same!

1 Preheat the oven to 180°C (350°F), Gas mark 4. Butter and flour the sides of the cake tins and line the bases with parchment paper.

2 Cream the butter in a large bowl or in an electric food mixer until soft. Add the sugar and beat until the mixture is pale and fluffy. Add the vanilla extract and the egg yolks, one by one, beating well after each addition.

3 Place the flour, cornflour, baking powder and cocoa powder in a sieve resting on a plate. Measure the buttermilk with the food colouring and mix together. It should be very red, so add more if you need to.

4 Sift one-third of the dry ingredients into the butter and eggs mixture until just combined, then pour in one-third of the buttermilk mixture and mix until just combined. Continue, combining a third at a time, until both are incorporated.

5 Whisk the egg whites and salt in a large, spotlessly clean bowl until stiffish peaks form. Add one-quarter to the batter and mix. Add the remaining egg whites in three stages, folding them in gently with a large metal spoon until just incorporated, leaving as much air in the egg whites as possible.

6 In a small bowl, mix the vinegar and bicarbonate of soda until it bubbles up, then gently fold this into the batter. Quickly pour the batter into the two prepared tins and smooth the tops. Bake in the oven for 25–30 minutes or until a skewer inserted into the middle comes out clean

and the cakes feel slightly springy on top.

7 Leave in the tins for 15 minutes, then carefully remove
the cakes from the tins, running a table knife or a palette
knife slowly around them to loosen them, and invert them
onto a wire rack to cool.

8 To make the white frosting, place the egg whites, sugar,
golden syrup, salt, cream of tartar and water in a stainless
steel or heatproof bowl set over a saucepan of simmering
water. (The base of the bowl should not touch the water.)
Bring the water to a steady simmer. With a hand-held electric
beater or a balloon whisk (to build up your muscles!), whisk
the mixture until you have shiny, satiny soft peaks. Remove
the bowl from the simmering water and continue to whisk
for a further 2 minutes – it will get a bit stiffer. Whisk in
the vanilla extract.

9 Immediately ice the middle, top and sides of the cake with
a palette knife, fluffing the frosting up to form little peaks
all over the cake. You need to work fast to ice the cake, as
the icing sets very quickly. Leave for at least 30 minutes
to allow a thin crust to form outside a creamy interior.

RACHEL'S BAKING TIP

After the cakes have cooled completely and before frosting,
cover them loosely with cling film and place them in the
freezer for 30 minutes–1 hour. This really helps when it
comes to icing delicate crumbly cakes.

CHOCOLATE, MARMALADE AND HAZELNUT CAKE
SERVES 12

175g (6oz) butter
175g (6oz) good-quality dark chocolate (at least 70% cocoa solids)
5 eggs, separated
175g (6oz) caster sugar
150g (5oz) hazelnuts (with skins on), ground in a food processor
200g (7oz) fine-cut marmalade
Zest of 1 orange, finely grated

For the topping
75g (3oz) good-quality dark chocolate (at least 70% cocoa solids)
75ml (2½fl oz) double cream
Zest of 1 orange, finely grated

22cm (8½in) diameter spring-form/loose-bottomed tin

If you love the combination of chocolate with orange, this is the cake for you! It's incredibly rich and intense in flavour.

1 Preheat the oven to 190°C (375°F), Gas mark 5. Butter the sides of the cake tin and line the base with greaseproof paper.

2 Melt the butter and chocolate together in a heatproof bowl set over a saucepan of simmering water. Do not let the base of the bowl touch the water.

3 In a separate bowl, whisk the egg yolks and sugar together with a hand-held electric beater until the mixture is light and mousse-like.

4 Add the ground hazelnuts, marmalade and orange zest to the melted chocolate mixture.

5 Meanwhile, whisk the egg whites in a large, spotlessly clean bowl until stiff peaks form.

6 Fold the egg yolk and sugar mixture into the chocolate mixture until combined, then gently fold in the egg whites in three stages so as not to deflate them. Pour the mixture into the prepared tin and bake in the oven for 20 minutes. Reduce the oven temperature to 170°C (325°F), Gas mark 3 and continue to cook for a further 35–40 minutes or until a skewer inserted into the middle of the cake comes out clean.

7 Allow to cool for 20 minutes, then carefully remove from the tin to a wire rack to cool completely.

8 When the cake is cool, melt the chocolate, cream and orange zest in a heatproof bowl set over a saucepan of simmering water. Make sure the base of the bowl does not touch the water. Place the cake on a serving plate and pour over the topping. Using a palette knife, smooth the icing, allowing it to fall down the sides of the cake. Allow to set for 30 minutes–1 hour.

KUGELHOPF

1 tbsp flaked almonds
   or whole almonds
75g (3oz) raisins
3 tbsp brandy
160g (5³/₄oz) strong
   white flour
¹/₄ tsp salt
Pinch of freshly grated
   nutmeg
3 tbsp caster sugar
75ml (2¹/₂fl oz) barely
   warmed-up full fat
   milk
1¹/₂ tsp dried yeast
   or 15g (¹/₂oz) fresh
   yeast or 1 x 7g sachet
   fast-acting yeast
2 eggs
1 egg yolk
150g (5oz) butter,
   softened
Icing sugar, sifted,
   for dusting (optional)

For the glaze
50g (2oz) butter
1–2 tbsp caster sugar

23cm (9in) diameter
   Kugelhopf or
   bundt tin or 23cm
   (9in) diameter
   spring-form/loose-
   bottomed tin

This buttery, light, bread-like cake comes from the Alsace region in France and is quite like Italian panettone. Indeed, the word 'Kugelhopf' is related to the German *kugel*, meaning 'ball' or 'globe', evoking the round shape of the cake. It is simple to make using an electric food mixer, but of course can also be made by hand. The cake does, however, require a fair amount of time overall, so start the day before if possible.

1 Generously butter and flour the Kugelhopf tin or cake tin. Sprinkle with the almonds.

2 In a small saucepan, gently simmer the raisins in the brandy for 2 minutes. Remove from the heat, cover and set aside for at least 30 minutes to plump up.

3 Sift the flour, salt and nutmeg into the bowl of an electric food mixer.

4 In a measuring jug, mix the caster sugar with the warm milk and yeast and let stand in a warm place for 5 minutes until frothy. Add to the flour, nutmeg and salt, or, if using fast-acting yeast, the sugar, milk and yeast can go straight into the ingredients.

5 With the dough hook attached to the electric food mixer, mix together on a low speed.

6 Whisk the eggs and single yolk in another bowl. With the food mixer on a low speed, slowly pour in the egg, increasing the speed slightly for about 5 minutes or until the dough looks smooth and satiny. Slow it down again and add the butter, mixing until fully incorporated. Increase the speed to medium and beat quite vigorously for about 8 minutes, scraping down the bowl now and then, until the dough is still very soft but elastic. Add the raisins and mix through the dough. Remove the hook and scrape off the dough.

7 Lightly oil a large clean bowl and scrape the dough into it,

covering with a butter wrapper or greaseproof paper and a loose plastic bag (it needs to be airtight). Place in a draught-free warm place for about $1^1/_2$ hours or until doubled in size.

8 Knock back the dough. Cover and chill in the fridge for a minimum of 2 hours – it can be left overnight.

9 Remove and shape the dough into a round disc (no kneading required). Make a hole in the centre, place in the prepared tin and cover with a butter wrapper or greaseproof paper.

10 Place the tin back into the plastic bag again and leave in a warm place for about 2–3 hours or until it has risen two-thirds of the way up the tin. You can leave it in a cool place for up to 8 hours (for example, leave it overnight to bake in the oven the next morning).

11 Preheat the oven to 190°C (375°F), Gas mark 5. Remove the tin from the bag and bake on the middle shelf of the oven, covered lightly with the butter wrapper, for 10 minutes. Reduce the oven temperature to 170°C (325°F), Gas mark 3 and bake for a further 25 minutes.

12 Remove the cake from the oven, carefully unmould it onto a baking tray and return to the oven for 5–10 minutes to crisp the outside.

13 Turn the cake right side up on the baking tray, place the tray and cake on a wire rack and allow to cool for 10 minutes.

14 Melt the butter for the glaze and spoon over the cake, sprinkling over the caster sugar, which will form a lovely crust. Allow to cool. When ready to serve, lightly dust with icing sugar, if you wish.

RACHEL'S BAKING TIPS

* This cake is best eaten on the day it is cooked, but it is still great toasted and buttered after a day or so. Keep in an airtight container for up to a week.
* For safety reasons, I put my mixer on the floor when it has to work hard, as it has to in this recipe!

SWISS ROLL

SERVES 8

4 eggs
125g (4½oz) caster
   sugar, plus 3 tbsp
   for sprinkling (or
   use icing sugar
   for dusting)
2 tbsp warm water
1 tsp vanilla extract
125g (4½oz) plain flour

For the filling
6 tbsp (approximately)
   raspberry or
   strawberry jam
   (or make your own –
   see pages 276–7)
225ml (8fl oz) double
   cream, whipped

25 x 38cm (10 x 15in)
   Swiss roll tin

Despite appearances, Swiss rolls are in fact very simple to make. The cake itself has no butter in it, so you can feel justified in spreading it with lashings of jam and whipped cream. Use any kind of jam you like; apricot or blackberry, for instance, would do just as well as raspberry or strawberry.

1 Preheat the oven to 190°C (375°F), Gas mark 5. Line the base of the Swiss roll tin with greaseproof paper, brush the base and sides of the tin with melted butter and dust with flour.

2 Whisk the eggs and caster sugar together in a large bowl or in an electric food mixer until light and fluffy, then add the water and vanilla extract.

3 Sift in the flour, about one-third at a time, and fold it into the mixture using a large metal spoon.

4 Pour the mixture gently into the prepared Swiss roll tin and bake in the oven for 12–15 minutes, or until the centre of the cake is slightly springy and the edges have shrunk a little from the sides of the tin.

5 Spread out a piece of greaseproof paper (slightly larger than the tin in size) on a work surface and sprinkle evenly with caster sugar (this stops the roll from sticking to the paper). Turn the Swiss roll tin onto the sugared greaseproof paper, then carefully remove the tin and greaseproof paper from the bottom of the cake.

6 Place a slightly damp, clean tea towel over the cake while it cools – this will prevent it drying out and cracking when you roll it.

7 When the cake is cool, spread it sparingly with raspberry jam, followed by the whipped cream. With the longest side facing you, roll up the Swiss roll away from you, then transfer to a plate to serve. Sprinkle with caster sugar or dust with icing sugar to finish.

ALMOND PRALINE CAKE

SERVES 8–10

225g (8oz) butter,
    softened
225g (8oz) caster sugar
4 eggs
225g (8oz) plain flour
1 tsp baking powder
3 tbsp almond praline
    (see below)
1 tbsp milk

For the praline
250g (9oz) caster sugar
250g (9oz) unskinned
    (unblanched)
    almonds

For the praline
buttercream icing
125ml (4fl oz) water
350g (12oz) caster sugar
7 egg yolks
350g (12oz) butter
    (preferably
    unsalted), softened
1 tsp vanilla extract
6 tbsp almond praline

Two 20cm (8in)
    diameter sandwich
    tins

This delicious cake has been made at Ballymaloe for many years. It keeps very well, due to the large amount of nuts it contains and because the icing keeps the moisture in the cake. It is ideal for a special tea party.

1 Preheat the oven to 180°C (350°F), Gas mark 4. Butter and flour the sides of the tins and line each base with parchment paper.

2 To make the praline, place the sugar in a non-stick pan or a medium saucepan with low sides and scatter the nuts over the top. Set over a low heat until the sugar turns a caramel colour. Do not stir, but you may carefully 'swirl' the pan to allow the sugar to caramelise evenly.

3 When the caramel has turned a deep whiskey colour, pour the mixture onto a baking tray lined with parchment paper and allow to cool. When the praline is cool and hard, place in a food processor and whiz to a gritty powder. Alternatively, place the praline in a plastic bag and crush with a rolling pin.

4 To make the cake, cream the butter in a large bowl or electric food mixer until soft. Add the sugar and beat until light and fluffy. Add the eggs one by one, beating well between each addition. Sift in the flour and baking powder and stir in gradually. Add 3 tablespoons of the crushed praline and mix lightly, adding the milk to moisten.

5 Divide equally between the two prepared tins and bake in the oven for 25–30 minutes, or until a skewer inserted into the centre of each cake comes out clean. Allow to cool in the tin for a few minutes before turning out onto a wire rack.

6 Meanwhile, make the buttercream icing. In a low-sided medium saucepan, bring the water and sugar to the boil, stirring until the sugar dissolves. Turn the heat up high and let the syrup boil for 4–5 minutes to the 'thread' stage,

when the last few drops that fall from a metal spoon dipped into the syrup come off in one long, quite thick and syrupy thread.

7 While the syrup is boiling, beat the egg yolks for 1 minute with an electric hand-held beater or an electric food mixer, then very gradually add the hot syrup. Continue beating until all the syrup is added and the mixture has cooled. The consistency should be stiff, mousse-like and able to hold a figure of eight pattern made by the beater.

8 Place the softened butter in another bowl and beat well with a hand-held electric beater until very soft. Continuing to beat, gradually add the mousse, a spoonful at a time. Then stir in the vanilla extract and 6 tablespoons of the crushed praline.

9 To assemble, slice each cake in half horizontally. Spread the inside of each sparingly with butter icing and sandwich together, stacking each layer above the other as evenly as possible. Brush all over the cake to remove any crumbs.

10 Ice the top and sides with the remaining icing. Sprinkle the remaining crushed praline all over, including the sides.

VARIATION

Hazelnut praline: Replace the almonds with 250g (9oz) skinned hazelnuts (see Rachel's baking tip, below), still using 3 tablespoons of hazelnut praline for the cake and 6 tablespoons of hazelnut praline for the buttercream icing.

RACHEL'S BAKING TIP

For some reason, it is necessary to skin hazelnuts, though not almonds, for praline. To skin hazelnuts, place them on a baking tray and bake at 180°C (350°F), Gas mark 4 for a few minutes until the skins come off when rubbed with a finger. Wrap the hazelnuts in a clean tea towel (not a pale-coloured one, as this tends to stain the cloth) and rub them for a few seconds to remove the skins. Pour them back onto the baking tray, place outside and let the skins just blow away (you can speed up the process by blowing gently on the hazelnuts).

CARROT CAKE
SERVES 12

2 eggs
140ml (5fl oz)
   vegetable oil
200g (7oz) soft light
   brown sugar
300g (11oz) grated
   carrot (weight
   when grated)
100g (3¹/₂oz) raisins
75g (3oz) pecans or
   walnuts, chopped
   (optional)
180g (6¹/₂oz) self-
   raising flour
Pinch of salt
¹/₂ tsp bicarbonate
   of soda
1 tsp ground cinnamon
¹/₂ tsp freshly grated
   nutmeg
¹/₂ tsp mixed spice

For the orange cream
cheese icing
250g (9oz) cream
   cheese (straight
   from the fridge)
50g (2oz) butter,
   softened
1 tsp vanilla extract
275g (10oz) icing sugar,
   sifted
Finely grated zest
   of 1 orange

13 x 23cm (5 x 9in)
   loaf tin

Who doesn't love this classic cake? It's perfect just as it is with a cup of tea or coffee, but you could also try decorating it with candied violets to add a little visual 'oomph'.

1 Preheat the oven to 150°C (300°F), Gas mark 2. Oil and line the loaf tin with greaseproof paper.
2 Beat the eggs in a large bowl, then add the oil, brown sugar, grated carrot, raisins and chopped nuts.
3 Sift in the dry ingredients and bring the mixture together using a wooden or large metal spoon.
4 Pour the mixture into the prepared loaf tin, smooth the surface and bake in the oven for 1–1¹/₄ hours or until a skewer inserted into the middle comes out clean.
5 Allow to cool in the tin for about 5 minutes before removing. Cool completely on a wire rack before serving.
6 To make the icing, beat the cream cheese and butter together in a bowl until combined. Add the vanilla extract, icing sugar and finely grated orange zest and mix to combine. The icing should be smooth and quite thick. Using a palette knife, spread the icing evenly over the cooled cake, dipping the knife into a bowl of hot water if the icing is hard to spread out. Cut into slices to serve.

VARIATIONS
Instead of using jam for the filling, why not try lemon curd (see page 278) or melted chocolate. Alternatively, spread the sponge with raspberry or blueberry cream (see pages 270–1).

RACHEL'S BAKING TIP
Un-iced, this cake is also delicious sliced and buttered.

CHOCOLATE CAKE

SERVES 6-8

For the cake
125g (4¹/₂oz) dark
   chocolate
3 tbsp milk
150g (5oz) butter,
   softened
150g (5oz) caster sugar
3 eggs
200g (7oz) plain flour
1 tbsp good-quality
   cocoa powder
1 tsp baking powder
¹/₄ tsp bicarbonate
   of soda
Cocoa powder or icing
   sugar, for dusting
   (optional)

**For the chocolate
butter icing**
75g (3oz) butter,
   softened
1 tbsp cream
1 tsp vanilla extract
175g (6oz) icing sugar
1 tbsp good quality
   cocoa powder

Two 20cm (8in)
   diameter sandwich
   tins

This is such a great, simple, yet versatile, chocolate cake. Add the finely grated rind of 1 orange to give the cake a chocolate orange flavour or replace the vanilla extract with 1 tbsp of instant coffee powder for a mocha flavour. This can also be turned into chocolate cupcakes if you wish – the recipe will fill 12 paper cases in a cupcake or muffin tray, and will take about 18–20 minutes to cook. Ice them generously with the chocolate buttercream and decorate to your heart's content.

1 Preheat the oven to 180°C (350°F), Gas mark 4. Butter and flour the sides of the sandwich tins and line the bases with greaseproof paper.

2 Place the chocolate and the milk in a bowl sitting over a saucepan of gently simmering water and heat until the chocolate has melted.

3 Beat the butter until very soft then add the caster sugar and continue to beat until the mixture is light and fluffy. Beat in the eggs, one at a time, then fold in the melted chocolate.

4 Sift in the flour, cocoa powder, baking powder and the bicarbonate of soda, and fold in gently to mix. Divide the mixture between the two tins and bake in the oven for about 25 minutes, or until a skewer inserted into the middle of each cake comes out clean.

5 Remove the cakes from the oven and allow to sit for a few minutes before turning them out of their tins and placing them on a wire rack to cool.

6 While the cakes are cooling, make the chocolate butter icing. Beat the butter, cream and the vanilla extract until very soft. Then gradually sift in the icing sugar and the cocoa powder, beating all the time, until it is all added. Continue to beat until very soft, then whisk the mixture until it is light

and fluffy. (I normally make the chocolate butter icing in an electric food mixer, using the whisk all the way through.)

7 Once the cakes are cool, sandwich them together (I normally sandwich them together bottom to bottom – if you know what I mean!) with the chocolate butter icing. Place the cake on a plate or a cake stand and dust with cocoa powder or icing sugar if you wish.

HONEY LOAF
SERVES 12

300g (11oz) plain flour
2 tsp baking powder
1/2 tsp salt
100g (3 1/2 oz) butter, softened
175g (6oz) runny honey
2 eggs, beaten
75ml (3fl oz) milk
1 tbsp warm honey, for brushing

13 x 23cm (5 x 9in) loaf tin

The honey flavour really comes through in this wonderful loaf cake, especially when toasted and buttered.

1 Preheat the oven to 170°C (325°F), Gas mark 3. Oil and line the loaf tin with greaseproof paper.

2 Sift the flour, baking powder and salt into a bowl, add the salt and set aside.

3 Cream the butter in a large bowl or in an electric food mixer until soft. Add the honey and beat until the mixture is light and fluffy. Continuing to beat, gradually adding the eggs.

4 Fold in the flour with a spatula or metal spoon, then fold in the milk to form a soft dough. Place in the prepared loaf tin and bake in the oven for 45–55 minutes, or until golden and when a skewer inserted in the centre comes out clean.

5 Allow to stand for 3 minutes, then remove from the tin and place on a wire rack. Brush the loaf generously with warm honey and allow to cool.

BANANA BREAD
SERVES 10-12

100g (3¹/₂oz) raisins (small ones are best)
75ml (2¹/₂fl oz) Irish whiskey or black rum
250g (9oz) self-raising flour
Pinch of salt
1 level tsp baking powder
150g (5oz) caster sugar
100g (3¹/₂oz) butter, softened, plus extra to serve
50g (2oz) walnuts or pecans, chopped (optional)
2 eggs
1 tsp vanilla extract
Finely grated zest of 1 orange (optional)
475g (17oz) whole bananas (about 4 small ones), peeled
50g (2oz) glacé cherries (preferably organic), halved

13 x 23cm (5 x 9in) loaf tin

This is called 'bread' simply because it's cooked in a loaf tin. It's actually wonderfully sweet and a perfect afternoon indulgence. It's also delicious toasted and buttered for a breakfast treat.

1 Preheat the oven to 170°C (325°F), Gas mark 3. Lightly oil and line the loaf tin with parchment paper.

2 In a small saucepan, gently simmer the raisins in the whiskey or rum for 2–3 minutes, then remove from the heat, cover and leave for 1 hour to plump up.

3 Sift the flour, salt and baking powder into a large bowl. Add the sugar, butter and chopped nuts (if using) and, using your fingertips, rub it in until the mixture resembles coarse breadcrumbs.

4 Whisk the eggs, vanilla extract and orange zest in another bowl. Add the bananas and mash very well with a potato masher. Add the cherries.

5 Make a well in the centre of the dry ingredients and pour in the banana mixture. Gently but thoroughly bring all the ingredients together with a wooden spoon, then pour into the prepared loaf tin. Smooth the top and bake in the oven for 1–1¹/₄ hours or until a skewer inserted into the middle comes out clean.

6 Allow to cool for 5 minutes before removing the cake from the tin. Serve sliced and buttered.

VARIATION

Banana and chocolate bread: As an alternative, leave out the raisins and cherries and add 75g (3oz) dark chocolate chips when adding the bananas in step 4, or you can melt the chocolate and fold it in to the banana mixture. Continue as above.

MEREDITH'S ZUCCHINI BREAD

MAKES 2 LOAVES

400g (14oz) plain flour
1/2 tsp salt
1 tsp bicarbonate
  of soda
1/2 tsp baking powder
1 tsp ground cinnamon
1/4 tsp freshly grated
  nutmeg
1/4 tsp ground cloves
300g (11oz) caster sugar
100g (3 1/2 oz)
  demerara sugar
3 eggs, beaten
200ml (7fl oz)
  sunflower oil
2 tsp vanilla extract
380g (13oz) courgettes,
  grated (with the skin
  left on)
75g (3oz) walnuts,
  chopped

Two 13 x 23cm (5 x 9in)
  loaf tins

This delicious loaf cake became a staple at Ballymaloe after an American girl named Meredith came to work in the kitchen – hence 'zucchini' rather than 'courgette'. It is still very popular in the café. Don't be put off by the idea of courgettes baked in a cake: the result is rather like Banana Bread (see page 71) and it is perfect toasted and buttered.

1 Preheat the oven to 150°C (300°F), Gas mark 2. Butter or oil and flour the loaf tins.

2 In a large bowl, sift in the flour, salt, bicarbonate of soda, baking powder and spices. Add both sugars and stir well to mix.

3 Add the beaten eggs, oil, vanilla extract and grated courgettes to the dry ingredients and mix well until combined. Add the walnuts, mix in and divide the mixture between the two prepared loaf tins.

4 Bake in the oven for 1–1 1/4 hours or until a skewer inserted into the middle comes out clean. Allow to cool in the tin for about 20 minutes before turning out onto a wire rack. Serve on its own or toasted and buttered.

RACHEL'S BAKING TIP

Tightly wrapped in cling film, these loaves keep well for up to 10 days.

SWEET POTATO AND PECAN BREAD
SERVES 12

3 eggs
150ml (1/4 pint)
    vegetable oil
200g (7oz) soft light
    brown sugar
300g (11oz) sweet
    potato, peeled and
    grated
100g (3 1/2 oz) pecans,
    chopped
180g (6 1/2 oz) self-
    raising flour
Pinch of salt
1 tsp ground cinnamon
1/2 tsp freshly grated
    nutmeg
1/2 tsp mixed spice

13 x 23cm (5 x 9in)
    loaf tin

Like Banana Bread (see page 71), this is, in fact, a loaf-shaped cake. The sweet potato adds moistness and sweetness, as well as a mellow flavour and lovely orangey colour. You can use walnuts instead of pecans, if you like, or add raisins or other dried fruit.

1 Preheat the oven to 150°C (300°F), Gas mark 2. Line the loaf tin with parchment paper.

2 Beat the eggs in a large bowl, then add the oil, sugar, grated sweet potato and chopped pecans.

3 Sift in the dry ingredients and bring the mixture together using a wooden or metal spoon.

4 Pour the mixture into the prepared loaf tin, smooth the surface and bake in the oven for 1–1 1/4 hours or until a skewer inserted into the middle comes out clean.

5 Allow to cool in the tin for about 5 minutes before removing. Cool completely on a wire rack before serving.

PUDDINGS

BAKED CHEESECAKE WITH BLUEBERRIES

SERVES 10-12

175g (6oz) digestive
  biscuits
75g (3oz) butter, melted
175g (6oz) blueberries,
  plus extra for
  decorating
450g (1lb) cream cheese
150g (5oz) caster sugar
1 tsp vanilla extract
4 eggs, lightly beaten
Icing sugar, to dust

24cm (9¹/₂in) diameter
  spring-form/loose-
  bottomed tin

This wonderfully rich cheesecake is equally good made with other fruit. Use whatever is in season, or whatever you happen to have in the freezer. Raspberries and blackberries are particularly delicious.

1 Preheat the oven to 180°C (350°F), Gas mark 4. Butter the sides and base of the cake tin.

2 Place the biscuits in a food processor and whiz until quite fine. Alternatively, place them in a plastic bag and bash with a rolling pin. Mix the crushed biscuits with the melted butter and press down into the base of the tin so that it is nice and even. Spread the blueberries over the base and allow to chill in the fridge while you make the topping.

3 Beat the cream cheese, sugar, vanilla extract and the eggs together in a large bowl until smooth and creamy. Pour over the top of the blueberries and then bake in the oven for 40 minutes or until it is pale golden and should only wobble very slightly when you gently shake the tin.

4 Allow to cool in the tin for about 10 minutes, then run a knife around the edge to loosen it and carefully remove the cheesecake from the tin. Transfer to a serving plate. Sprinkle over a few blueberries, if you wish, then dust with icing sugar. Cut into slices to serve. This cheesecake is best eaten when it is at room temperature.

RACHEL'S BAKING TIP

You can experiment with all kinds of (dry) sweet biscuits or cookies for the base; just crush them the way you would the digestives above. Try using a chocolate biscuit base and omitting the blueberries.

DATE BREAD AND BUTTER PUDDING WITH BOOZY TOFFEE SAUCE

SERVES 4-6

50g (2oz) butter, softened, plus extra for greasing
10 slices of good-quality white bread, crusts removed
200g (7oz) dates (stoned weight), chopped
350ml (12fl oz) double cream
150ml (1/4 pint) milk
3 eggs
75g (3oz) caster sugar
1/2 tsp vanilla extract
1 tbsp soft light brown sugar, for sprinkling

To serve
Boozy toffee sauce or toffee sauce (see page 274)
Softly whipped cream

20cm (8in) square, round or oval ovenproof dish

This oh-so-comforting pudding is a great way to use up stale bread. Slightly sweet or aromatic breads such as Cardamom Bread (see page 104) or Cornish Saffron Bread (see page 122) are particularly good, but plain white bread will work perfectly well.

1 Preheat the oven to 180°C (350°F), Gas mark 4.
2 Butter the bread, leaving 4 slices whole and cutting the remaining 6 slices in half to make triangles. Grease the sides and base of the dish. Place the 4 whole slices of bread buttered side up on the base of the ovenproof dish, then sprinkle the chopped dates over the top. Arrange the triangles of bread buttered side up on top to cover the dates.
3 Heat the cream and milk in a saucepan almost to the boil. While it heats up, whisk the eggs and sugar in a heatproof bowl, then pour the very hot milk and cream on top, whisking as you pour. Pour this custard over the bread, and allow to soak for 20 minutes.
4 Place the pudding in a large roasting tin and carefully pour in enough hot water to come halfway up the sides of the dish (known as a bain-marie). Bake in the oven for 50 minutes–1 hour or until the top is golden and the centre just set.
5 Serve with warm toffee sauce or boozy toffee sauce and some softly whipped cream.

RACHEL'S BAKING TIPS
* Try and find large, plump Medjool dates for this recipe.
* This recipe can be made a day ahead and then re-heated in the oven at 180°C (350°F), Gas mark 4 for 8–10 minutes or until hot in the centre.

SCHEITERHAUFEN

SERVES 4-6

75–110g (3–4oz)
   butter, softened
1/2 tsp mixed spice
2 cooking apples,
   peeled, cored and
   sliced
12 slices of Cardamom
   Bread or White Yeast
   Bread (see pages
   104 and 119), crusts
   removed
75g (3oz) white
   chocolate buttons
   or chopped white
   chocolate
350ml (12fl oz) double
   cream
350ml (12fl oz) milk
4 eggs, lightly beaten
1 tsp vanilla extract
150g (5oz) caster sugar,
   plus 2 tbsp extra
   for sprinkling
50g (2oz) flaked
   almonds (optional)
1 x quantity crème
   Anglaise (see page
   273), to serve

19 x 23cm (7 1/2 x 9in)
   roasting tin

If you want a more wicked version of bread and butter pudding, try this spectacular Austrian alternative, made with apples and white chocolate. 'Scheiterhaufen' means 'pyre' in German, but this dessert is far from funerary!

1 Butter the roasting tin. Melt 25g (1oz) of the butter in a medium saucepan, add the mixed spiced and then the cooking apples. Stir with a wooden spoon until the apples are coated in the butter.

2 Butter the bread with the remaining butter and arrange 4 slices, buttered side up, in a single layer in the roasting tin. Sprinkle the bread with half of the apples and half the chocolate. Arrange another layer of bread over the top, buttered side up, add the remaining apples and chocolate and finish off with another layer of the bread.

3 Heat the cream and milk in a saucepan to just under the boil. While it is heating up, whisk the eggs, vanilla extract and sugar together in a heatproof bowl, then pour the very hot milk and cream on top, whisking as you pour. Pour this custard over the bread pudding, making sure all the bread gets soaked, and then sprinkle the remaining sugar and almonds (if using) on top. Cover and chill for 1 hour or overnight.

4 Preheat the oven to 180°C (350°F), Gas mark 4. Place the pudding in a large roasting tin and carefully pour in enough hot or boiling water to come halfway up the sides of the pan (also called a bain-marie). Bake in the oven for 1 hour or until golden on top. Cover with foil if the pudding is getting too dark towards the end of cooking. Make the crème Anglaise as described on page 273 and serve with the warm pudding.

APPLE AND OAT CRUMBLE

SERVES 6

3–4 large cooking
  apples, peeled,
  cored and cut into
  big chunks
1 tbsp water
2–3 tbsp caster sugar
Whipped cream or
  vanilla ice cream,
  to serve

For the crumble
150g (5oz) plain flour
1 tsp ground cinnamon
  (optional)
75g (3oz) butter, chilled
  and cubed
25g (1oz) porridge oats
75g (3oz) soft light
  brown sugar

1 litre (1³/4 pint) pie
  dish or six ramekins

Adding oats to a good old-fashioned crumble gives a lovely nutty flavour and crunchy texture.

1 Preheat the oven to 180°C (350°F), Gas mark 4.

2 Place the apples, water and sugar into a saucepan set over a gentle heat and cook, stirring every minute or so to prevent it sticking, for approximately 10 minutes or until the apples become a soft pulp. Taste and add more sugar if necessary. Transfer into the pie dish or six ramekins and allow to cool slightly.

3 Next, make the crumble. Place the flour and cinnamon (if using) in a large bowl, add the butter and, using your fingertips, rub it in until the mixture resembles very coarse breadcrumbs. (Don't rub in too much or the crumble will not be crunchy.) Add the oats and sugar and mix to combine.

4 Sprinkle this crumble mixture over the slightly cooled apple and bake for 15 minutes for small crumbles or 30–45 minutes for a large one until cooked and golden. Serve warm with whipped cream or vanilla ice cream.

VARIATIONS

Peach and raspberry crumble: Put 375g (13oz) peaches (about 5), peeled, stoned and cut into chunks, and 200g (7oz) raspberries into the pie dish or ramekins and sprinkle over 25g (1oz) caster sugar. Make the crumble as above, replacing brown sugar with demerara or granulated and omitting the oats. Scatter the crumble over the fruit and bake as above until golden and bubbly.

Rhubarb and strawberry crumble: Add about 225g (8oz) sliced strawberries to 450g (1lb) chopped rhubarb, scatter with the sugar and cover with the crumble. Bake as above.

BAKED BROWN SUGAR CUSTARDS

MAKES 4

2 eggs
50g (2oz) soft dark
  brown sugar
200ml (7fl oz) milk
100ml (3¹/₂fl oz)
  double cream
Finely grated zest
  of 1 small orange
  (optional)
A little soft dark brown
  sugar, for sprinkling

Four 100ml (3¹/₂fl oz)
cups or ramekins

These gorgeous and very simple little desserts are somewhat like crème caramel or French 'flan'. The brown sugar adds a delicious, rich, toffee-ish flavour. You can even bake them in little espresso cups.

1 Preheat the oven to 170°C (325°F), Gas mark 3.
2 Whisk the eggs in a bowl. Add the brown sugar and mix well.
3 Place the milk, cream and orange zest (if using) into a saucepan and bring up to simmering point. Remove from the heat and gradually pour onto the egg and sugar mixture, whisking all the time. Pour the mixture through a sieve into a large jug and skim off any froth from the surface.
4 Place the cups or ramekins in a baking dish or wide shallow pan and fill them up with the custard. Pour enough hot water into the baking dish to come halfway up the sides of the cups or ramekins (known as a bain-marie) and cover with foil. Bake in the oven for about 40 minutes or until the custards are just set in the centre.
5 Remove the custards from the baking dish and serve warm or allow to cool. Either way, sprinkle a little bit of extra brown sugar on top just before serving.

RACHEL'S BAKING TIPS
❋ If you wish, use a kitchen blow torch to caramelise, or 'brûlée', the brown sugar on top for a lovely crunchy surface.

STICKY TOFFEE PUDDING
SERVES 6

225g (8oz) dates (stoned weight), chopped
250ml (9 fl oz) black tea (not too strong)
100g (3½oz) unsalted butter, softened
175g (6oz) golden caster sugar
3 eggs
1 tsp mixed spice
1 tsp vanilla extract
225g (8oz) self-raising flour
¾ tsp bicarbonate of soda
Vanilla ice cream or whipped cream, to serve
1 x quantity toffee sauce (see page 274)

20cm (8in) diameter spring-form/loose-bottomed tin, or a 20 x 20cm (8 x 8in) square cake tin

Moist, sweet, moreish and very straightforward to make, this is a guaranteed crowd pleaser. It can be prepared entirely in advance and will keep very well once cooked, lasting five or six days in an airtight box in the fridge or up to three months in the freezer. Before serving, just warm it up in a low oven for about 15 minutes covered (defrost first if it has been frozen).

1 Preheat the oven to 180°C (350°F), Gas mark 4. Butter and flour the sides of the tin and line the base with greaseproof paper.

2 Place the chopped dates and tea in a saucepan and bring to the boil. Cook for a few minutes to soften the dates, then remove from the heat and set aside.

3 Beat the butter in a large bowl or an electric food mixer until soft. Add the sugar and beat until the mixture is pale and fluffy. Beat in the eggs, one at a time, then beat in the mixed spice and vanilla extract. Fold in the date mixture. Sift in the flour and bicarbonate of soda and fold in gently until mixed.

4 Pour the mixture into the prepared tin and bake for about 45 minutes or until the top is just firm to the touch and a skewer inserted into the middle comes out clean.

5 Allow to stand in the tin for about 5 minutes before removing and transferring to a serving plate. While the cake is cooking, make the toffee sauce as described on page 274.

6 To serve, cut into slices (or squares if it is in a square tin) and serve with a scoop of vanilla ice cream or whipped cream and a very generous drizzle of warm toffee sauce over the top!

RACHEL'S BAKING TIP
This can also be served with boozy toffee sauce (see page 274) instead of the regular toffee sauce above.

COCONUT MERINGUE ROULADE WITH LEMON CURD CREAM AND RASPBERRIES

SERVES 6–8

4 egg whites
225g (8oz) caster sugar
50g (2oz) desiccated
   coconut

For the filling
100–150ml (3¹/₂–5fl oz)
   double cream,
   lightly whipped
150ml (¹/₄ pint) lemon
   or lime curd (or
   make your own –
   see page 278)
250–300g (9–11oz) fresh
   or frozen raspberries

To decorate
Icing sugar, for dusting
Fresh raspberries
Fresh mint leaves
   (optional)

23 x 33cm (9 x 13in)
   Swiss roll tin

The word 'roulade' comes from the French word for 'to roll' (*rouler*). Roulades can be savoury – made with meat or vegetables and filled with various ingredients – or sweet: made as a cake or meringue and filled with fruit and cream, as I've done here. Meringue roulades make wonderful summer desserts. I love the combination of crunchy, chewy and creamy textures. The meringue can be made a day in advance and stored unfilled and covered with foil. Just fill and roll the roulade on the day you intend to serve it.

1 Preheat the oven to 180°C (350°F), Gas mark 4. Line the Swiss roll tin with foil, folding the sides up to make a frame 4cm (1¹/₂in) high and squeezing the corners together. Brush lightly with vegetable oil.

2 Place the egg whites in the spotlessly clean bowl (stainless steel is best) of an electric food mixer (or use a hand-held electric beater) and whisk until soft peaks form.

3 Add the sugar all in one go (but if using a hand-held beater, add the sugar in stages) and whisk at full speed for about 4–5 minutes until stiff peaks form. Using a large metal spoon, fold in the coconut firmly and quickly.

4 Smooth the meringue into the prepared tin with a palette knife and bake in the oven for 15–20 minutes, until faintly browned and firm to the touch.

5 Allow the meringue to cool for a few minutes, then turn out onto a sheet of foil (slightly bigger than the roulade) – deftly turning it upside down onto the sheet and gently removing the foil on the base. Allow to cool completely.

6 For the filling, stir the cream and curd together. Adjust

to taste – it should have a good 'lemony'/'limey' tang to contrast with the sweet meringue.

7 Spread the curd cream mixture evenly over the meringue, leaving the long edge nearest to you free of cream for about 4cm (1½in). Cover the cream with the fruit.

8 Holding the foil closest to you, roll up the roulade away from you and leave it in the foil until you are ready to serve (it will hold neatly here for a couple of hours in the fridge).

9 When ready to serve, unwrap the roulade and gently push it onto a serving dish using a palette knife or cake slice.

10 Dust with icing sugar and decorate with a few more raspberries and mint leaves, if you wish.

VARIATIONS

Irish coffee meringue roulade: Make as above, but at the end of step 2, fold in 1 tablespoon of instant coffee powder. For the filling, whip 425ml (15fl oz) whipping cream in a bowl, fold in 1 teaspoon of instant coffee powder, 1 tablespoon of sifted icing sugar and 2 tablespoons of Irish whiskey, and then follow steps 7–9.

Pavlova meringue roulade with cherries and rosewater mascarpone: Make as above, but at the end of step 2, fold in 2 teaspoons of rosewater, 1 teaspoon of red or white wine vinegar and 1 teaspoon of sifted cornflour (no desiccated coconut) and bake for 20–30 minutes. For the filling, soften 250g (9oz) mascarpone with a spoon, then add 1 tablespoon of caster sugar and 1–2 tablespoons of rosewater to taste (you may need to add 1–2 tablespoons of cream to loosen the mascarpone and make it more spreadable.) Spread over the meringue as above. Scatter 300g (11oz) halved and stoned fresh cherries over the mascarpone. Follow steps 7–9 and decorate with extra cherries.

RACHEL'S BAKING TIP

Edible rosewater is available from specialist shops and most chemists.

BAKED ALASKA

**1 litre (1³/₄ pints)
homemade or bought
good-quality ice
cream (flavour of
your choice)
Sauce of your choice,
to serve (see pages
274–5) (optional)**

For the biscuit base
**25g (1oz) butter, at
room temperature
25g (1oz) caster sugar
1 medium egg yolk
¹/₈ tsp vanilla extract
60g (2¹/₂oz) plain flour
Pinch of baking powder**

For the meringue
**3 egg whites
Pinch of cream
of tartar
200g (7oz) caster sugar**

**1 litre (1³/₄ pint) round
heatproof pudding
basin**

This seriously impressive dessert comes from my friend Dervilla. Wonderfully redolent of the 1960s and 70s, it is making a long overdue comeback. This is a simple recipe but may take a little practice – it'll be the only time you ever bake ice cream in the oven! Get it right and your guests will be talking about it for weeks. Depending on your choice of ice cream for the dish, serve it with a raspberry, strawberry or coffee sauce (see pages 274–5).

1 If using homemade ice cream, set it in the pudding basin. If using bought ice cream, leave it out of the freezer until it is easily 'mashable' to mould into the pudding basin (don't let it melt!). Spoon the ice cream into the mould and mash it up and press it down to get a smooth surface (give it a few gentle bangs to help). Cover with cling film and return to the freezer to keep it fresh and to stop it melting.

2 Next, make the biscuit base. Cream the butter in a large bowl or in an electric food mixer until soft. Add the sugar and beat until the mixture is light and fluffy. Add the egg yolk and vanilla extract and beat until combined. Sift in the flour and baking powder and mix until all the flour is incorporated. Bring the dough together into a ball, slightly flatten it with the palm of your hand and then place in a plastic bag or wrap in cling film. Allow the dough to chill in the fridge for at least 30 minutes.

3 When the dough is ready to roll, preheat the oven to 180°C (350°F), Gas mark 4. Place the dough on a lightly floured work surface, sprinkle on a bit more flour and roll out keeping it round and giving the dough a quarter turn with each roll to prevent it from sticking to the surface. If you need to flour the work surface again, do so sparingly. Roll the dough out to a thickness of 1cm (¹/₂in). ***Continued overleaf***

4 Measure the diameter of the pudding basin containing the ice cream and cut out your dough 3cm (1¹/₄in) wider than the basin. (Use any leftover dough to make cookies and bake in the same at the same temperature for 5–8 minutes.) Carefully lift the dough onto a large baking tray lined with parchment paper and bake in the oven for about 8–10 minutes or until pale golden. Allow to cool, then transfer to a wire rack to cool. When cold, return the biscuit base to the baking tray.

5 Before you prepare the meringue, preheat the oven to 220°C (425°F), Gas mark 7. In a large, spotlessly clean bowl, whisk the egg whites until soft peaks form. Add half the caster sugar and the cream of tartar and whisk until stiff peaks form and the meringue is satiny and glossy. Fold in the remaining sugar with a metal spoon.

6 Remove the ice cream from the freezer. Allow it to sit for about 10 minutes and then, carefully holding the container upside down, pour some hot water over the base of the bowl. Ease out the ice cream with the aid of a flexible metal spatula, place on a large plate and then slide onto the centre of the cold biscuit base. Quickly spoon the meringue thickly and in peaks over the ice cream, spreading it down to the base and covering it to the edge. Return to the freezer for 30 minutes or place immediately in the centre of the hot oven for 3–4 minutes or until the meringue is set and pale gold in colour. Serve straight away on its own or with the sauce of your choice.

MOCHA-PECAN MERINGUE ICE CREAM SANDWICHES

MAKES 9–10 MERINGUE SANDWICHES

125g (4¹/₂oz) shelled pecans, lightly toasted
50g (2oz) good-quality dark chocolate (at least 55% cocoa solids), finely chopped
2 egg whites
Pinch of salt
¹/₄ tsp cream of tartar
150g (5oz) soft light brown sugar or 50g (2oz) caster sugar and 110g (4oz) soft light brown sugar
1 tsp good-quality instant coffee granules or powder
18–20 pecan halves
Homemade or bought good-quality vanilla or coffee ice cream, slightly softened, to serve
1 x quantity hot chocolate sauce (see page 274)

These are a fun and frivolous summery treat. Make them in advance and keep in the freezer so they are ready to take out when the sun puts in an appearance. They get lovely and chewy in the freezer, but be sure to keep them well covered because the meringue may absorb other flavours.

1 Preheat the oven to 110°C (225°F), Gas mark ¹/₄. Line two large baking trays with lightly oiled foil or parchment paper.
2 Place half the toasted pecans in a food processor and whiz until quite fine, then add the rest of the toasted nuts and the chocolate and whiz briefly so they are still coarse.
3 Whisk the egg whites, salt and cream of tartar together in the spotlessly clean bowl of an electric food mixer until soft peaks form. Gradually add the sugar, beating at full speed, until the mixture is very stiff, about 4–5 minutes. Fold in the nut mixture and the coffee (the granules will not dissolve) with a large metal spoon.
4 Using a dessertspoon, heap little mounds of the batter onto the prepared trays leaving 4–5cm (1¹/₂–2in) between each one to allow room for spreading. Lightly press a pecan half into each.
5 Bake in the oven for 1–1¹/₄ hours or until they are dry underneath. Turn off the oven and allow to cool in the oven leaving the oven door ajar if you can.
6 When ready to serve, place 1 tablespoon of the ice cream on the base of a meringue, then gently press the base of another meringue onto the ice cream. Place on flat trays lined with cling film, and freeze for approximately 1 hour or until firm.
7 Make the hot chocolate sauce as described on page 274. Serve warm drizzled over the meringues sandwiches.

CHOCOLATE LAVA CAKES

MAKES 4 LAVA CAKES

**150g (5oz) good-quality
    dark chocolate**
125g (4¹/₂oz) butter
3 eggs and 3 egg yolks
75g (3oz) caster sugar
50g (2oz) plain flour
**25g (1oz) good-quality
    cocoa powder, plus
    extra for dusting**

**Four 8cm (3¹/₄in)
    diameter ramekins**

These gorgeous little puddings should be deliciously spongy on the outside and molten in the centre. Do not overcook them or they will be set all the way through. They are delicious served with vanilla ice cream.

1 Preheat the oven to 180°C (350°F), Gas mark 4. Butter the ramekins and place on a baking tray.
2 Break or chop the chocolate and melt with the butter in a heatproof bowl set over a saucepan of simmering water.
3 Whisk the eggs and egg yolks with the sugar in a large bowl until the mixture is pale and fluffy. Add the egg mixture to the chocolate mixture and fold in to mix. Sift in the flour and cocoa powder and fold in gently with a metal spoon or spatula until just mixed.
4 Transfer the mixture to the prepared ramekins and bake in the oven for 8–10 minutes or until risen and just firm to the touch. The outer part should be cooked and the inner part liquid. Very carefully, run a knife around the inside of each mould to loosen the puddings, then gently turn them out onto individual warmed serving plates. Dust with cocoa powder and serve immediately.

RHUBARB CREMA CATALANA

SERVES 6

200ml (7fl oz) water
225g (8oz) caster sugar
150g (5oz) rhubarb,
   sliced into 2cm
   (³/₄in) pieces
250ml (9fl oz) full
   fat milk
200ml (7fl oz) double
   cream
Strips of orange peel
   from 1 orange (use
   a vegetable peeler)
1 cinnamon stick,
   snapped in half
4 egg yolks
2 level tsp cornflour
4 tbsp demerara sugar,
   for sprinkling

Six 8cm (3¹/₄in)
   diameter ramekins
   or other individual
   ovenproof dishes

Here I have added rhubarb and a hint of orange to this classic dessert from northern Spain – not dissimilar to crème brûlée.

1 Preheat the oven to 150°C (300°F), Gas mark 2.
2 Place the water in a saucepan with 150g (5oz) of the caster sugar and stir over a medium heat until the sugar dissolves. Add the rhubarb and bring to the boil, then immediately take off the heat and cover. Leave to cook in the residual heat for 10–20 minutes or until the rhubarb is soft.
3 To make the custard, heat the milk, cream, orange peel and cinnamon stick in a medium-sized saucepan until they just begin to simmer. Remove from the heat and set aside for 15 minutes to allow the cream to soak up the flavours.
4 Meanwhile, whisk together the egg yolks, cornflour and remaining caster sugar in a large bowl until just combined.
5 When you think the cream has absorbed the flavours, remove the cinnamon and orange peel (the cinnamon stick can be washed off and dried and used again) and pour onto the egg mixture, whisking all the time until just combined. Transfer to a large jug.
6 Drain the rhubarb from the syrup with a slotted spoon and divide among the ramekins. Gently pour over the custard.
7 Place the ramekins in a large roasting tin. Pour in enough hot water to reach halfway up the ramekins (known as a bain-marie). Bake for 45 minutes, covering with foil or parchment paper for the last 20 minutes. Remove from the oven and allow to cool. They may seem a bit wobbly but will gradually set.
8 When ready to serve, preheat the grill to maximum. Sprinkle the tops with demerara sugar and grill until the sugar melts but does not burn! Remove and the tops will harden in seconds. They will hold like this for only 15–20 minutes, so serve immediately.

CREAMY VANILLA RICE PUDDING

SERVES 4-6

75g (3oz) short-grain
   rice, such as pearl
   rice
2 tbsp caster sugar
700ml (23fl oz) milk
150ml (1/4 pint) double
   cream
1 tsp vanilla extract
Soft dark brown sugar,
   for sprinkling
   (optional)

1 litre (1³/4 pint)
   pie dish

This is an old favourite of mine. Serve it on its own or with fruit poached in a saucepan with a little sugar syrup – rhubarb, plums or peaches work especially well. Or sprinkle the pudding with soft dark sugar and extra cream.

1 Preheat the oven to 170°C (325°F), Gas mark 3.
2 Place the rice and sugar in the pie dish, mixing together and spreading evenly over the base.
3 In a large saucepan, bring the milk and cream to the boil. Add the vanilla extract and carefully pour over the rice and sugar (I usually do this while the dish is sitting on the rack in the oven).
4 Bake in the oven for 1¹/4–1¹/2 hours or until the rice is soft. Serve on its own or with a sprinkling of brown sugar, if you wish.

VARIATIONS

Creamy chocolate rice pudding: Reduce the quantity of sugar to 1 tablespoon and melt 150g (5oz) chopped dark or milk chocolate with the milk and cream. Bake as above, then dust with cocoa powder after it's cooked and serve with softly whipped cream.

Individual creamy rice puddings: For each 8cm (3¹/4in) diameter ramekin, place 1 generous dessertspoon of short-grain rice, 2 teaspoons of caster sugar (or to make a chocolate alternative, use 1 teaspoon of sugar and 25g/1oz chocolate), 75ml (2¹/2fl oz) milk and 25ml (1fl oz) cream into five 8cm (3¹/4in) ramekins. Bake as above for 1 hour.

RASPBERRY JAM STEAMED PUDDING

SERVES 8-10

200g (7oz) butter, at
    room temperature
200g (7oz) caster sugar
3 eggs, lightly beaten
1/2 tsp vanilla extract
250g (9oz) plain flour
1 level tsp baking
    powder
1/2 level tsp bicarbonate
    of soda
3 tbsp buttermilk
125ml (4fl oz) raspberry
    jam (or make your
    own – see page 277)
Lightly whipped cream,
    to serve

1 litre (1³/4 pint)
    heatproof pudding
    basin

Steamed puddings are wonderfully comforting and moist.
In this recipe the jam is cooked on the bottom and, when
the pudding is turned out, oozes down the sides of the cake.
Simply irresistible!

1 Lightly butter the pudding basin.

2 Cream the butter in a large bowl or an electric food mixer
until soft. Add the sugar and beat until the mixture is light
and fluffy. Gradually add the beaten eggs and vanilla extract,
beating well between each addition. (Beating the butter and
sugar really well in the beginning gives the best results.)

3 Sift in the flour, baking powder and bicarbonate of soda and
mix into the batter until just incorporated. Next, add the
buttermilk and mix together to make a dropping consistency.

4 Pour the jam into the base of the prepared pudding basin
and spoon in the sponge batter.

5 Cut out a sheet of parchment paper at least 4cm (1¹/2in)
larger than the top of the basin, crease it in the middle and
tie the sheet over the lip of the bowl with heatproof string.

6 Place the pudding in a saucepan not much larger than the
basin (place an inverted saucer beneath the pudding bowl just
in case the pan should boil dry; this will then prevent the base
of the pudding burning) and carefully pour in enough hot
water to come up no higher than three-quarters of the way up
the basin. Cover and simmer for approximately 1 hour until a
skewer inserted in the centre of the pudding comes out clean
and it feels spongy to the touch. Keep the water topped up in
the saucepan during cooking, otherwise it may boil dry.

7 Carefully remove the basin from the pan and turn out onto
a warmed serving plate, allowing the jam to fall down the
sides. Serve with lightly whipped cream.

BAKED BANANAS WITH MAPLE SYRUP, TOASTED PECANS AND CHOCOLATE SAUCE

SERVES 4

4 tbsp maple syrup
4 tbsp freshly squeezed orange juice
4 bananas, peeled
16 toasted pecans or walnuts, halved
1 x quantity hot chocolate sauce (see page 274) or whipped cream, to serve

When bananas are baked, they turn beautifully sweet – perfect for a last-minute dessert.

1 Preheat the oven to 200°C (400°F), Gas mark 6.
2 In a small bowl, mix the maple syrup with the orange juice.
3 Cut out four sections of foil, each long and wide enough to wrap up a banana. Place a banana in the centre of each, scrunching up the sides. Pour in the maple syrup mix and seal the parcels.
4 Place on a baking tray and bake in the preheated oven for 20 minutes. Carefully place the parcels on a serving plate, opening the foil wide enough to scatter over the pecans. Leave the bananas in the parcels for serving or turn out into bowls. Serve with hot chocolate sauce or whipped cream.

VARIATIONS

Baked bananas with rum: Mix together 4 tablespoons each of rum and water, pour over the bananas in their foil parcels, sprinkle over 2–3 teaspoons soft dark brown sugar and seal. Cook as above and serve with either toffee sauce (see page 274) or whipped cream.

Baked bananas with orange and honey mascarpone: Cut the bananas crossways and squeeze into large ramekins. Whisk together 6 teaspoons of honey, 4 rounded tablespoons of mascarpone, freshly squeezed juice from 2 oranges and 2 tablespoons of lemon juice until smooth. Pour over the bananas, cover with foil and bake in the preheated oven for 10 minutes. Remove the foil, turn the bananas over and bake for a further 10 minutes. Serve hot and bubbling.

BAKED FIGS

8 ripe figs
8 tsp runny honey
2 tbsp chopped
    pistachios, to serve

Choose from one of
the following for the
topping:
Vanilla ice cream
Greek yoghurt and
    honey
Soft goat's cheese,
    such as Ardsallagh,
    and balsamic vinegar

Small gratin dish
    or four ramekins

This is a terrific two-way Mediterranean dish, served either
as a sweet dessert with vanilla ice cream or Greek yoghurt
and honey, or as a more savoury version with goat's cheese
and balsamic vinegar. You can sprinkle chopped pistachios
over the dish, either way you serve it. It's perfect with a
sticky dessert wine like Sauternes.

1 Cut each fig into four but only halfway down, not all the
way through to the base. Pack them fairly tight into the
gratin dish or ramekins – this will help them soak up the
juices when cooking. (Don't roast the figs on a baking tray
or the juices will run out and evaporate.)
2 Drizzle each fig with a teaspoon of honey and bake for
10 minutes or until soft, juicy and bubbling (no more than
15 minutes in total).
3 Once cooked, choose your topping. If using ice cream,
place one small scoop on top of each serving. If using Greek
yoghurt and honey, spoon the yoghurt liberally over the top
and then drizzle with honey. If you opt for the more savoury
version, place a tablespoon of goat's cheese on the top of
each serving, followed by a small drizzle of balsamic vinegar.

BAKED PEACHES WITH AMARETTI

SERVES 4

4 ripe peaches, cut
in half and stones
removed
8 small dark amaretti
biscuits, crushed
75g (3oz) soft light or
dark brown sugar
25g (1oz) nibbed
(chopped) almonds
1 egg yolk
Vanilla ice cream
or whipped cream,
to serve

These quick-and-easy baked peaches make a simple dinner party dessert, delicious served with a small glass of amaretto. The peaches can be prepared and stuffed, ready to bake, then stored in the fridge for a few hours.

1 Preheat the oven to 180°C (350°F), Gas mark 4.
2 Butter the sides and base of a medium-sized ovenproof dish and place the peach halves, cut side up. They should preferably be quite snug in the dish so as not to lose any of the juices.
3 In a small bowl, beat together with a wooden spoon the crushed amaretti biscuits, brown sugar, nibbed almonds and the egg yolk. Spoon the mixture into each peach half.
4 Bake in the preheated oven for 15–20 minutes, or until peaches are soft but still hold their shape. Serve warm with vanilla ice cream or softly whipped cream.

BREADS
AND
SAVOURY
BITES

CARDAMOM BREAD
MAKES 1 LOAF

125ml (4fl oz) water
75g (3oz) butter
50g (2oz) caster sugar,
plus 1 tsp caster
sugar
175ml (6fl oz) warm
water
1½ tsp dried yeast
or 15g (½oz) fresh
yeast or 1 x 7g sachet
fast-acting yeast
1 egg
½ tsp salt
1 tbsp freshly ground
cardamom using
the seeds from
approximately
28 pods
600g (1lb 6oz) plain
flour, sifted

To serve
1 tsp butter, softened
Plain flour, for dusting

This recipe is adapted from one given to me by a cookery school student, Wendy. It's perfect for breakfast: a rich, eggy white bread that is delicious fresh or toasted, with jam. You can make it plaited, as here, or as a simple unplaited loaf.

1 Butter or oil a baking tray. Place the 125ml (4fl oz) water and butter in a saucepan and bring to the boil. Once the butter is melted, pour the mixture into a large bowl and allow to cool.

2 In a measuring jug, mix the teaspoon of caster sugar with 60ml (2fl oz) of the warm water and yeast and allow to stand in a warm place for 5 minutes until frothy. Or, if using fast-acting yeast, they can go straight into the ingredients.

3 In another bowl, whisk together the eggs, the 50g (2oz) caster sugar and the salt, then add the remaining warm water and whisk until blended.

4 When the butter and water mixture has cooled but is still warm, add the yeast mixture, the egg mixture and the ground cardamom and stir until blended. Add the flour and mix.

5 Turn onto a floured surface and knead for about 10 minutes until smooth and soft. Add more flour if the dough is sticky.

6 Place the dough in a large oiled bowl, cover with cling film or a clean tea towel and allow to rise in a warm, draught-free place for about 2 hours or until doubled in size.

7 Preheat the oven to 180°C (350°F), Gas mark 4. Knock back the dough in the bowl and then turn it onto a lightly floured work surface and knead for a few seconds.

8 Shape the dough into a plaited or plain loaf and place on the prepared baking tray. Cover with a clean tea towel and allow to rise for 20–30 minutes or until doubled in size. Bake in the oven for 30–35 minutes or until it sounds hollow when tapped on the base. Remove the loaf from the oven and transfer to a wire rack. Rub with the butter and dust with sugar.

EASY SODA FOCACCIA

MAKES 1 LOAF

450g (1lb) plain flour
1 tsp salt
1 level tsp bicarbonate
of soda
350–400ml (12–14fl oz)
buttermilk or sour
milk (see Rachel's
baking tip, overleaf)
A good drizzle of olive
oil, about 60–75ml
(2–2¹/₂fl oz)
Sea salt, such as
Maldon, for
sprinkling

23 x 33cm (9 x 13in)
Swiss roll tin or
roasting tin

As this recipe uses no yeast, it is not, strictly speaking, a proper Italian focaccia, but a quirky Irish/Italian mix, using a soda bread recipe. It's very quick to make, either with olive oil and sea salt, or covered with a host of additional ingredients, as in the variations below.

1 Preheat the oven to 220°C (425°F), Gas mark 7. Brush the inside of the tin generously with olive oil.
2 Sift the dry ingredients into a large bowl and make a well in the centre. Pour most of the buttermilk in at once and, using one hand with your fingers outstretched like a claw, mix in the flour from the sides of the bowl, adding more buttermilk if necessary. The dough should be softish, but not too wet and sticky. When it all comes together, turn it out onto a floured board and roll it out so that it will fit into the Swiss roll tin. Make dimples all over with your fingertips, on the top of the dough, then drizzle generously with olive oil. Sprinkle with sea salt.
3 Bake in the oven for about 30 minutes or until the bread is nice and golden on the top and bottom. If the bread is a good golden colour and you don't want it to darken any more during cooking, reduce the oven temperature to 200°C (400°F), Gas mark 6 and continue to bake for the specified time.
4 When the focaccia is cooked but still hot, drizzle just a little more olive oil over the top and allow to cool slightly before serving.

VARIATIONS

Red onion, olive and rosemary: Place the chunks of a peeled red onion cut first into 6 wedges lengthways, then half crossways on the raw dough (3 across and 4 down, so that there are 12 altogether), so that each 'square' will have some of everything. Next to the red onion place a pitted olive (press it down slightly) and a little sprig of rosemary. Finish with the drizzle of olive oil and a sprinkling of sea salt. Bake as above.

Gruyère and thyme leaf: Sprinkle 150g (5oz) grated Gruyère cheese and 2 teaspoons of thyme leaves over the raw dough, then drizzle with just a little olive oil and sprinkle with sea salt. Bake as above.

Sun-dried tomato and basil: Add a small handful of sun-dried tomatoes, about 50g (2oz), roughly chopped, and 1 tablespoon of chopped or torn basil to the dry ingredients at the start. Continue as above.

Brown soda focaccia: Replace 150g (5oz) of the flour with wholemeal flour and continue as above.

RACHEL'S BAKING TIP

To make your own sour milk, heat the milk gently until warm, then remove from the heat, add the juice of $1/2$ lemon and leave at room temperature overnight. If you are allergic to dairy products, this recipe works well with soy or rice milk soured in this way.

QUICK BROWN BREAD WITH TREACLE AND SESAME SEEDS

MAKES 1 LOAF

400g (14oz) coarse
  wholemeal flour
100g (3¹/₂oz) plain
  flour, sifted
50g (2oz) sesame seeds
  (or a mixture of
  sesame, sunflower
  and pumpkin)
1 scant rounded tsp
  bicarbonate of
  soda, finely sifted
1 tsp salt
1 tsp treacle or
  molasses
400ml (14fl oz)
  buttermilk
1 egg, beaten
2 tbsp oil, such as
  sunflower oil
1 tbsp sesame seeds,
  for sprinkling

13 x 23cm (5 x 9in)
  loaf tin

This 'no-rise' bread is quick and easy to make if you're in a hurry.

1 Preheat the oven to 200°C (400°F), Gas mark 6. Oil the loaf tin.

2 Place the dry ingredients in a large bowl and mix thoroughly. Make a well in the centre.

3 Place the treacle or molasses in a measuring jug, add the buttermilk and stir to mix. Add the beaten egg and oil, then pour the wet ingredients into the dry ingredients and mix with a wooden spoon or your hands to form a soft and sloppy dough.

4 Pour the dough into the prepared tin and sprinkle with the sesame seeds. Bake in the oven for 55–65 minutes. (I usually take it out of the tin after 50 minutes and continue cooking the loaf on a rack in the oven without the tin until it sounds hollow when tapped on the base.)

RACHEL'S BAKING TIPS

✴ If you cut a line down lengthways through the top of the raw loaf before sprinkling with sesame seeds, it will rise evenly.

✴ It is important that the loaf tin is completely dry before using it otherwise the bread will stick to it. After washing up the tin, I always put it back in the oven for a few minutes to dry.

RUSTIC BACON AND CHEDDAR BREAD

MAKES 1 LOAF

320g (11¹/₂oz) plain
    flour
1 tbsp baking powder
¹/₂ tsp salt
¹/₄ tsp freshly ground
    black pepper
100g (3¹/₂oz) Cheddar
    cheese, grated
100g (3¹/₂oz) bacon
    lardons, cooked until
    just crisp in a little
    sunflower oil and
    cooled
200ml (7fl oz) milk
2 eggs
1 tbsp wholegrain
    mustard
60ml (2fl oz) olive oil

13 x 23cm (5 x 9in)
    loaf tin

This is a seriously easy and no-nonsense recipe for savoury bread. Serve with soup or just on its own, spread with butter.

1 Preheat the oven to 180°C (350°F), Gas mark 4. Lightly oil and line the loaf tin with parchment paper.
2 Sift all the dry ingredients into a large bowl. Add the grated cheese and the cooled bacon lardons and mix well.
3 Pour the milk into a large measuring jug, add the eggs, mustard and olive oil and whisk to combine.
4 Make a well in the centre of the dry ingredients and slowly pour in the liquid, stirring all the time until it is fully incorporated, to form a fairly liquid dough.
5 Pour the mixture into the prepared tin and bake in the oven for 50 minutes. Remove from the tin and allow to cook for a further 10 minutes on the oven shelf to crisp up the bottom. When cooked, it will sound hollow when tapped on the base. Allow to cool on a wire rack before eating.

VARIATIONS

Pumpkin seed, Gruyère and thyme leaf bread:
In a frying pan, toss 2 tablespoons of pumpkin seeds and 1 tablespoon of sesame seeds in 1 tablespoon of olive oil over a medium heat until they start to pop. Add these with 1 teaspoon of chopped thyme leaves and grated Gruyère cheese instead of the Cheddar. Omit the bacon and the mustard. Sprinkle the bread with sea salt before baking as above.

Sun-dried tomato, rosemary and olive bread: Add 1 teaspoon of chopped rosemary, 2 tablespoons of chopped sun-dried tomatoes and 2 tablespoons of chopped black or green olives instead of the Cheddar, bacon and mustard. Continue as above.

NAAN BREAD

1 tbsp caster sugar
200ml (7fl oz) warm
  water (not hot)
1½ tsp dried yeast
  or 15g (½oz) fresh
  yeast or 1 x 7g sachet
  fast-acting yeast
300g (11oz) strong
  white flour, sifted
200g (7oz) plain flour
  or Maida (available
  in Indian speciality
  shops), sifted
1½ tsp salt
125ml (4fl oz) natural
  yoghurt
40g (1½oz) melted ghee
  or butter (optional)
Seeds such as sesame,
  mustard, poppy,
  cumin, onion, fennel,
  or salt crystals, such
  as Maldon, for
  sprinkling (optional)
Chopped coriander or
  garlic, for topping
  (optional)

If you're going to the trouble of cooking your own Indian curry, why not make your own naan bread to accompany it? Naan is a traditional, tear-shaped, flat but leavened bread that is typically made in a tandoor (a clay oven with a charcoal fire). If you have a pizza brick or quarry tiles to cook it on, you'll get great results but a heavy baking tray will do equally well.

1 In a jug, mix the sugar with the warm water and yeast and let stand in a warm place for 5 minutes until frothy. If using fast-acting yeast, there is no need to let the mixture stand.

2 In a large bowl or an electric food mixer fitted with a dough hook, mix together the two flours, salt and yeast mixture until combined. In a separate bowl, whisk the yoghurt and melted ghee or butter together.

3 If making by hand, make a well in the centre of the flour mixture and slowly add the wet ingredients, bringing all the ingredients together to form a soft and satiny dough, adjusting with more flour or water as necessary.

4 If making with a food mixer, use the lowest setting and add the liquid slowly to form the dough.

5 Knead for 10 minutes by hand or in a food mixer with a dough hook for 5 minutes to form a soft elastic dough. Place in an oiled bowl, turning to coat with oil. Cover with cling film or put into a large plastic bag. Leave in a warm (not hot), draught-free place for 1–3 hours until doubled in size.

6 Preheat the oven to 230°C (430°F), Gas mark 8. Place your pizza brick, baking tiles or heavy baking tray in the centre of the oven and preheat for at least 15 minutes before baking or the naans will be heavy and hard. Punch the dough down and knead for 2 minutes, then allow to rest for 15 minutes.

7 Divide into 8 portions and roll into balls. While you shape

one, keep the rest covered. You can probably work with two at a time if they will both fit in the oven. On a dry, lightly floured work surface, roll or stretch the dough into a teardrop shape, about 20–22cm (8–8^1/$_2$in) long and 12cm (4^1/$_2$in) wide – with one end narrower than the other. (Don't worry if it seems too thin, it will puff up.) You can dampen your fingers and dimple the surface all over with your fingertips, but don't let the underside get wet or it will stick in the oven. Sprinkle with seeds or salt crystals, if you wish, or leave plain.

8 Lift the naans onto the hot baking surface and bake for approximately 4–5 minutes, turning after 3 minutes. They should puff up, probably unevenly.

9 When cooked, remove from the oven and, if you wish, brush with melted ghee and sprinkle with chopped coriander or garlic. Eat immediately or keep warm in a tea towel.

VARIATIONS

Kheema naan: Sauté a chopped clove of garlic with 200g (7oz) minced beef or lamb for 10 minutes. Add ^{1}/$_2$ teaspoon of ground coriander, ^{1}/$_2$ teaspoon of ground cumin and salt and pepper and cook for a further 5 minutes over a medium heat, stirring occasionally. Allow to cool. When cold, roll a dough ball into a flat circle, putting 1 tablespoon of the mix in the middle. Fold the dough over the mix, sealing the edges with a drop of water. Roll into the teardrop shape, trying to prevent the filling squeezing out. Bake as above.

Pashwari naan: Mix 25g (1oz) desiccated coconut, 25g (1oz) finely nibbed (chopped) almonds, 25g (1oz) chopped raisins with 25g (1oz) caster sugar. Roll out a dough ball into a flat circle, putting 1 tablespoon of the mix into the middle, fold the dough over the mix, sealing the edges with a drop of water. Roll this gently into the teardrop shape, trying to prevent the filling squeezing out. Bake as above.

Garlic or coriander naan: Place ^{1}/$_2$ teaspoon of chopped coriander or garlic in the flat circle and continue as above.

EASY GLUTEN-FREE WHITE BREAD

MAKES 1 LOAF

225g (8oz) white or brown rice flour (brown rice flour can be used instead of white; the end product is still a pale-coloured bread)

25g (1oz) potato flour

50g (2oz) fine cornmeal

25g (1oz) soya flour

25g (1oz) dried milk powder

1 rounded tsp xanthum gum (available from health food shops)

1/2 tsp salt

25g (1oz) caster sugar

1 x 7g sachet fast-acting yeast

25g (1oz) sesame or linseed seeds

2 medium eggs

300–320ml (10–11fl oz) tepid water

13 x 23cm (5 x 9in) loaf tin

You'll need a food processor for this one. The rice flour gives the bread a different consistency to that which you would expect from a traditional loaf, but this is an essential recipe to have to hand if you are feeding friends or family members with gluten intolerance.

1 Oil and line the loaf tin with parchment paper.

2 Sift all the dry ingredients together and place in the bowl of a food processor. Add the yeast and seeds and whiz for approximately 20 seconds to combine.

3 Whisk the eggs and tepid water together in a medium-sized bowl. With the motor running, pour in the liquid quite steadily and quickly, adding more water if you need to in order to have a wettish mix (it will be too wet to knead).

4 Spoon the mixture into the prepared loaf tin, smooth the top and give the tin a tap to even out. Place the tin in a very loose plastic bag or cover loosely with cling film and a clean tea towel and leave in a warm place for 25–40 minutes until risen to the top of the tin.

5 Preheat the oven to 190°C (375°F), Gas mark 5. Uncover the loaf and bake in the oven for 55–60 minutes, gently removing the loaf from the tin about 10 minutes before the end of the cooking to crisp up the bottom. When cooked, it will sound hollow when tapped on the base. Allow to cool on a wire rack.

BALLYMALOE WHITE SODA BREAD

MAKES 1 LOAF

450g (1lb) plain flour
1 level tsp caster sugar
1 level tsp bicarbonate
of soda
1 tsp salt
350–425ml (12–15fl oz)
buttermilk or sour
milk (see Rachel's
baking tip on
page 108)

We bake this bread every day at the cookery school, and it is very quick and simple to make at home too. This is the basic recipe but there are so many sweet and savoury variations that you can try – chocolate, raisins, cinnamon, cubes of crispy bacon, cheese, herbs . . . the possibilities are endless. The deep cross in the loaf (see step 3) is supposed to let out the fairies – so that the bread won't be jinxed by evil spirits! In reality, of course, it's just to allow the heat to penetrate the loaf as it's cooking.

1 Preheat the oven to 230°C (425°F), Gas mark 8.
2 Sift the dry ingredients into a large bowl and make a well in the centre. Pour in most of the buttermilk (leaving about 60ml/2fl oz in the measuring jug). Using one hand with your fingers outstretched like a claw, bring the flour and liquid together, adding more buttermilk if necessary. Do not knead the mixture or it will become heavy. The dough should be softish, but not too wet and sticky.
3 When it comes together, turn onto a floured work surface and bring together a little more. Pat the dough into a round about 4cm (1½in) deep and cut a deep cross in it.
4 Place on a baking tray and bake in the preheated oven for 15 minutes, then turn down the heat to 200°C (400°F), Gas mark 6 and cook for 30 minutes more. When cooked, the loaf will sound slightly hollow when tapped on the base and be golden in colour. I often turn it upside down for the last 5 minutes of cooking. Allow to cool on a wire rack.

VARIATIONS

White soda scones: Make the dough as above but flattened into a round approximately 2.5cm (1in) deep. Cut into scones and cook for 15–20 minutes at 230°C (450°F), Gas mark 8.

White soda bread or scones with herbs: Add 2–3 tablespoons freshly chopped herbs – such as rosemary, sage, thyme, chives, parsley or lemon balm – to the dry ingredients, and make as above.

Spotted dog: Add 100g (3½oz) sultanas, raisins or currants, or a mixture of all three, to the dry ingredients, and make as above.

BROWN SODA BREAD
MAKES 1 LOAF

225g (8oz) wholemeal
  flour
225g (8oz) plain flour
1 tsp salt
1 tsp bicarbonate
  of soda
50g (2oz) mixed seeds,
  such as sesame,
  pumpkin or
  sunflower, or golden
  linseeds (optional)
25g (1oz) butter
  (optional)
1 egg
375–400ml (13–14fl oz)
  buttermilk

For this wholemeal version of soda bread (see page 117), the method differs, so don't just swap half of the plain flour for wholemeal.

1 Preheat the oven to 220°C (425°F), Gas mark 7.

2 Sift together the flours, salt and bicarbonate of soda in a large bowl and mix with the seeds (if using). Add the butter (if using), and rub into the flour mixture with your fingertips until it resembles breadcrumbs. Make a well in the centre.

3 In another bowl, whisk the egg with the buttermilk and pour most of the liquid into the flour mixture. Using one hand with your fingers outstretched like a claw, bring the flour and liquid together, adding more buttermilk if necessary. The dough should be quite soft, but not too sticky.

4 Turn onto a floured work surface, and gently bring it together into a round about 4cm (1½in) deep. Cut a deep cross on top.

5 Place on a baking tray and bake in the preheated oven for 15 minutes, then turn down the heat to 200°C (400°F), Gas mark 6 and cook for 30 minutes more. When cooked, the loaf will sound slightly hollow when tapped on the base. Allow to cool on a wire rack.

WHITE YEAST BREAD
MAKES 2 LOAVES

2 tsp caster sugar
425ml (15fl oz)
 warm water
2¹/₂ tsp dried yeast or
 20g (³/₂oz) fresh yeast
 or 1¹/₂ x 7g sachets
 fast-acting yeast
750g (1lb 10oz) strong
 white flour, plus
 extra for dusting
 (optional)
2 tsp salt
40g (1¹/₂oz) butter
 or 4 tbsp olive oil
1 egg, beaten, and
 poppy or sesame
 seeds, for the top of
 the loaf (optional)

With this recipe you can be as creative as you wish, from simple oval loaves to plaited masterpieces. Or make a whole variety of rolls, from basic round ones to more complex shapes: pretzel-type knots or, if you're feeling particularly inventive, small animals – snakes, mice, even hedgehogs!

1 In a measuring jug, mix the sugar with 150ml (¹/₄ pint) of the warm water and yeast and let stand in a warm place for 5 minutes until frothy. If using fast-acting yeast, there is no need to let the mixture stand.

2 Sift the flour and salt into a large bowl. Rub in the butter and make a well in the centre. (If using olive oil instead of butter, pour the olive oil into the remaining water.) Pour in the yeast mixture and most of the remaining water (and the olive oil, if using). Mix to a loose dough, adding the remaining water if needed, plus extra if necessary.

3 Knead for about 10 minutes or until the dough is smooth and springy to the touch. (If kneading in an electric food mixer with a dough hook, 5 minutes is usually long enough.) Put the dough in a large oiled bowl. Cover the top tightly with cling film and place somewhere warm to rise until doubled in size. This may take up to 2 or even (on a cold day) 3 hours.

4 Preheat the oven to 220°C (425°F), Gas mark 7.

5 When the dough has more than doubled in size, knock back and knead again for 2–3 minutes. Leave to relax for 10 minutes before you begin to shape the bread.

6 Shape the bread into loaves (for a plaited loaf, see the instructions on page 262) or rolls, transfer to a baking tray and cover with a clean tea towel. Allow to rise again in a warm place for 20–30 minutes, until the shaped dough has again doubled in size. When fully risen, it should leave a dent when you gently press the dough with your finger. ***Continued overleaf***

7 Gently (as the bread is full of air at this point and therefore very fragile) brush with egg wash and sprinkle with poppy or sesame seeds (if using), or dust lightly with flour for a rustic-looking loaf.

8 Bake in the oven for 10–15 minutes for rolls or 30–45 minutes for a loaf, depending on its size. Turn the heat down to 200°C (400°F), Gas mark 6 after 15 minutes for the remaining cooking time. When cooked, the bread should sound hollow when tapped on the base. Transfer to a wire rack to cool.

RACHEL'S BAKING TIPS

✳ Slow rising gives bread an amazing texture and flavour, if you have the time I would recommend trying it. Use cold water instead of warm water and at step 3, leave the dough to rise in a cool place (or fridge) overnight. Then, when the dough is shaped (step 6), leave to rise again for 8 hours in a cool place.

SOURDOUGH

MAKES 2 LARGE LOAVES

For the sourdough starter
1½ tsp dried yeast or 15g (½oz) fresh yeast or 1 x 7g sachet fast-acting yeast
500ml (18fl oz) warm water
300g (11oz) plain flour

This is a simplified version of a sourdough, which, while delicious to eat, can be quite fiddly to make at home. Classic sourdough starter has no added yeast, however I do use a little bit in this faster version. I leave the starter for three days to 'sour' (ferment), but if you prefer a stronger flavour, you can leave it for four days. Sometimes I add a little wheatgerm or bran (about 1 or 2 tablepoons) to the starter (after three days). I often divide it and make some white sourdough, and some rye or wholemeal sourdough.

1 Three or four days before you intend to bake the bread, place the yeast for the sourdough starter in a medium-sized bowl,

For white sourdough
900g (2lb) strong white flour, plus extra for dusting
2 tsp salt
1 x sourdough starter
400ml (14fl oz) warm water

add the water and mix together. Sift in the plain flour and hand whisk to mix, then cover with cling film and leave to stand at room temperature for three or four days.

2 When you are ready to make the bread, sift the strong white flour and the salt into a large bowl (or the bowl of an electric food mixer). Mix together the sourdough starter and the warm water, then pour into the flour.

3 Mix all the ingredients together, and knead for 10 minutes, or 5 minutes if using an electric food mixer (with the dough hook attached). Stop kneading when the dough feels springy to the touch.

4 Place in a large, oiled bowl, cover with cling film or a clean tea towel and leave in a warm place for about about 1^1/$_2$ hours, until doubled in size. (To test whether the dough has fully risen, push your finger into the dough – it should leave a dent that does not spring back.)

5 Knock the dough back and knead on a floured work surface for 2 minutes before shaping it into loaves, round or oval.

6 Place the loaves spaced apart on a floured baking tray, dust with flour, then score the top of each loaf a few times with a sharp knife. Cover with a clean tea towel, and place somewhere warm to rise again – about 30–45 minutes.

7 Preheat the oven to 220°C (425°F), Gas mark 7 and bake the loaves for 30–45 minutes. After 15 minutes, you may need to turn the oven down to 200°C (400°F), Gas mark 6 if the bread has already risen and is golden in colour.

8 The bread is cooked when it is a deep golden brown all over and sounds hollow when tapped on the base. Remove from the oven and place on a wire rack to cool.

VARIATIONS

Rye sourdough: Replace half the strong white flour with 450g (1lb) rye flour.

Wholemeal sourdough: Replace half the strong white flour with 450g (1lb) wholemeal flour.

CORNISH SAFFRON BREAD

MAKES 1 LOAF

350g (12oz) strong
  white flour, sifted
50g (2oz) caster sugar
100g (3¹/₂oz) butter,
  softened
75g (3oz) raisins
¹/₂ tsp saffron threads
200ml (7fl oz) cold milk
1¹/₂ tsp dried yeast or
  15g (¹/₂oz) fresh yeast
  or 1 x 7g sachet fast-
  acting yeast

13 x 23cm (5 x 9in)
  loaf tin

This is a traditional, sweet, yeast-risen loaf. The saffron gives it a warm yellow glow, while the saffron threads look beautiful baked throughout. Serve the bread either fresh or toasted, sliced and spread with butter.

1 Oil and line the loaf tin with parchment paper.
2 Place the flour and sugar in a large bowl, add the butter and, using your fingertips, rub it in until the mixture resembles breadcrumbs. Add the raisins.
3 In a small saucepan, bring the saffron and milk to the boil over a low heat. Remove from the heat and set aside to cool. When at body temperature, add the yeast and leave to sit for 4–5 minutes. If using fast-acting yeast, simply add to the saffron and milk, but don't leave to sit.
4 Pour the saffron and yeast milk into the dry ingredients, mix well and knead for 10 minutes (I normally do this in an electric food mixer with the dough hook).
5 Place the dough in a large bowl, cover with a tea towel and leave in a warm place to rise (or in the fridge overnight) until doubled in size.
6 Punch the dough to knock it back and knead for a minute, then place in the prepared loaf tin and cover with a clean tea towel or napkin. Place in a warm place for a further 1–2 hours or until the dough has doubled in size.
7 Preheat the oven to 180°C (350°F), Gas mark 4. Place the risen dough in the oven to cook for 50 minutes–1 hour. When cooked, the loaf should be a deep golden colour and sound hollow when tapped on the base.

CORN BREAD

MAKES 11–12 ROLLS

150g (5oz) plain flour
³/₄ tsp salt
1¹/₄ rounded tsp
   baking powder
¹/₂ tsp bicarbonate
   of soda
150g (5oz) coarse maize
   meal or cornmeal
   (available from
   health food shops)
50–75g (2–3oz) caster
   sugar
175ml (6fl oz)
   buttermilk
50ml (1³/₄fl oz) milk
1 egg, beaten
50g (2oz) butter, melted

12-hole muffin tin and
   paper cases

Often served with Mexican soups and dishes such as chilli con carne, the slight sweetness of this bread helps take away the sting of hot spices.

1 Preheat the oven to 190°C (375°F), Gas mark 5. Line the muffin tin with 11–12 muffin cases.

2 Sift the flour, salt, baking powder and bicarbonate of soda into a medium-sized bowl. Add the maize meal and sugar and mix together. Add in different ingredients for variations at this stage (see below). In a measuring jug, pour in both milks, then add the beaten egg and lightly whisk together.

3 Make a well in the middle of the dry ingredients. Pour in the milk mixture and the melted butter and mix together. Scoop tablespoons of the batter into the muffin cases, filling them three-quarters of the way up.

4 Bake for 10 minutes, then reduce the oven temperature to 180°C (350°F), Gas mark 4 and bake for a further 10 minutes or until the rolls spring back when gently pushed.

5 Allow the rolls to cool on a wire rack.

VARIATIONS

Cheese and onion: Sweat 125g (4¹/₂oz) finely chopped onions in 1 teaspoon of melted butter in a saucepan, covered with a butter wrapper. Allow to cool. Add to the dry ingredients with 100g (3¹/₂oz) grated strong Cheddar cheese and mix well. Add the wet ingredients and continue as above.

Red pepper and chorizo: Add 100g (3¹/₂oz) diced peeled roasted red pepper and 75g (3oz) diced chorizo to the dry ingredients, then add the wet ingredients. Continue as above.

Bacon and blue cheese: Add 100g (3¹/₂oz) fried diced bacon, and 40–50g (1³/₄–2oz) chopped blue cheese to the dry ingredients, then add the wet ingredients. Continue as above.

BROWN SCONES WITH SEEDS

MAKES ABOUT 12 SCONES

225g (8oz) wholemeal
flour

225g (8oz) plain flour,
sifted

75g (3oz) seeds, such
as sesame, pumpkin,
sunflower, or golden
linseeds, plus extra
for sprinkling
(optional)

1 tsp salt

1 tsp bicarbonate of
soda, finely sifted

25g (1oz) cold butter,
cubed (optional)

1 egg

375–400ml (13–14fl oz)
buttermilk or milk

Suspiciously healthy though these may sound, these scones
are definitely delicious!

1 Preheat the oven to 220°C (425°F), Gas mark 7.

2 In a large bowl, mix together the wholemeal and white
flours, the seeds, salt and bicarbonate of soda. Add the
butter (if using) and rub it in until the mixture resembles
breadcrumbs.

3 Whisk the egg in another bowl, stir in the buttermilk and
pour most of the liquid into the dry ingredients. Using one
hand with your fingers outstretched like a claw, mix in a full
circle, bringing the flour and liquid together, and adding more
liquid if necessary. The dough should be quite soft, but not
too sticky.

4 Turn the dough out onto a floured work surface. Do not
knead it but gently bring it together into one piece. With the
lightly floured palm of one hand, flatten the dough slightly
to about 4cm (1 1/2 in) high.

5 Cut the dough into square scones (if you wish you could
brush any leftover liquid over the top and sprinkle with some
extra seeds) and place on a lightly floured baking tray. Cook
in the oven for 15–20 minutes (depending on the size). Have
a look at them after 10 minutes; if they are already a deep
golden brown, reduce the oven temperature to 200°C (400°F),
Gas mark 6 for the remainder of the time. When cooked they
should sound hollow when tapped on the base. Allow to cool
on a wire rack.

PAPER-THIN CRISPBREAD

MAKES ABOUT 15 LARGE CRISPBREADS

375g (13oz) plain flour,
  sifted or 225g (8oz)
  plain flour and 150g
  (5oz) wholemeal flour
1 tsp salt
1 tbsp sesame or
  poppy seeds
2 tsp chopped herbs,
  such as rosemary
  or thyme, or crushed
  cumin, fennel,
  black pepper or
  coriander seeds
1 egg
1 tbsp olive oil, plus
  extra for brushing
  (optional)
125ml (4 fl oz) water
Sea salt, for sprinkling
  (optional)

This recipe is amazingly versatile: it can be made with plain flour, or a mixture of plain and wholemeal, and a great variety of different seeds can be put into or sprinkled on top of it. Fresh herbs, such as chopped rosemary or thyme, added to the dough before baking, make another delicious alternative.

1 Place the dry ingredients in a large bowl and mix together.

2 Whisk the egg in another bowl, add the olive oil and water. Mix well. Pour the wet ingredients into the dry ingredients and, using your hands or in the bowl of a food processor, mix to a dough. Knead for 2 minutes until the dough is smooth, then wrap in cling film and set aside to rest for 20 minutes.

3 Preheat the oven to 200°C (400°F), Gas mark 6 and lightly oil several baking trays.

4 Divide the dough into two pieces and roll out each piece until it is about 20cm (8in) wide, fold the dough in half then in half again and continue to roll until the dough is paper thin, like pasta, approximately 1–2mm (^{1}/$_{16}$in) thick. Each piece should be about 45cm (18in) square. You will probably need to use some flour while rolling out.

5 Cut the dough into rectangles about 8 x 14cm (3^1/$_4$ x 5^1/$_2$in) in size and place in a single layer on the prepared baking trays. If you want to sprinkle sea salt or seeds on top of the crispbreads, then first brush the top of the raw crispbreads with olive oil so that they stick to the surface.

6 Bake in the oven for 10–14 minutes or until pale golden brown and slightly curled up at the edges. They will feel dry when cooked, but will only really crisp up when they have cooled. Check after 8–10 minutes of cooking and if they are golden brown underneath, but still quite pale on top, then turn them over. Allow to cool on wire racks.

SPICY BACON AND GRUYERE SCONES

MAKES 15-20 SCONES

450g (1lb) plain flour
1 level tsp bicarbonate
    of soda
1 level tsp cayenne
    pepper
1 tsp salt
30g (1oz) cold butter,
    cubed
110g (4oz) bacon,
    grilled and finely
    chopped
110g (4oz) Gruyère
    or Cheddar cheese,
    finely grated
1 egg
375ml (13fl oz)
    buttermilk or milk

5cm (2in) plain cutter
    (optional)

These savoury scones are a scrumptious, rather sophisticated variation on a traditional theme.

1 Preheat the oven to 220°C (425°F), Gas mark 7.
2 Sift the flour, bicarbonate of soda, cayenne pepper and salt into a large bowl. Add the butter and rub it in until the mixture resembles breadcrumbs, then mix in the bacon and grated cheese.
3 Whisk the egg in another bowl and stir in the buttermilk. Pour this into the dry ingredients and mix to a soft dough using one hand going around the inside of the bowl in one direction – do not knead!
4 Roll the dough out on a lightly floured work surface until it is 2cm (3/4in) thick, then cut into squares with a knife or into rounds with the plain cutter.
5 Place on a floured baking tray and bake in the oven for 10–14 minutes until well risen and golden brown. Allow to cool on a wire rack.

ALICIA'S EASY CHEESE STRAWS

MAKES ABOUT 12 CHEESE STRAWS

250g (9oz) good-quality bought or homemade puff pastry (see page 257), chilled
1 egg white, lightly beaten, for brushing
100g (3¹/₂oz) Parmesan cheese, finely grated
100g (3¹/₂oz) Cheddar cheese, finely grated
Good pinch of cayenne pepper

Alicia Wilkinson, a cookery school regular, made this recipe at the school during a visit from South Africa. Her cheese straws are so delicious that I had to include them here.

1 Preheat the oven to 190°C (375°F), Gas mark 5.

2 Roll the chilled puff pastry out on a lightly floured work surface or a marble slab into a large rectangle, 3mm (¹/₈in) thick, and brush the lower half of the pastry with the egg white.

3 Mix the cheeses with a good pinch of cayenne pepper, then sprinkle half of the mixture liberally over the egg white and press down gently.

4 Fold the upper half of the pastry down over the lower half and press with a rolling pin to seal. Roll out the pastry to the original size, again about 3mm (¹/₈in) thick, and brush the entire sheet with egg white. Sprinkle over the remaining cheese and spice mixture and allow to chill in the fridge for approximately 10 minutes.

5 Cut the pastry into thin 1cm (¹/₂in) strips and twist into straws. Place on baking trays and bake in the oven for 10–15 minutes or until golden brown, puffed up and cooked through. Allow to cool on a wire rack.

RACHEL'S BAKING TIPS

⁎ Serve the straws in interesting containers, such as a tall glass or beaker. We sometimes use a scalloped zinc pot or children's tin sand buckets, depending on the occasion.

⁎ The raw prepared cheese straws may be laid on parchment paper and frozen for up to 3 months. To cook, lift the paper onto a baking tray and bake as in step 5, but allow a minute or so extra cooking time.

OATCAKES

MAKES ABOUT 30 OATCAKES

200g (7oz) oatmeal
  flakes
1/4 tsp salt
1/4 tsp baking powder
25g (1oz) butter,
  softened
1 tbsp olive oil
100ml (3¹/₂fl oz) boiling
  water
A handful of fine
  oatmeal, for rolling
Mixed seeds, such as
  sesame, millet,
  poppy, or golden
  linseeds, freshly
  ground black pepper
  or salt crystals, such
  as Maldon, for
  sprinkling (optional)

5–8mm (2–3¹/₄in) plain
  cutter (optional)

Why buy oatcakes when they're so easy to make? They're also perfect for anyone with wheat intolerance. Few things rival them for serving with cheese.

1 Preheat the oven 170°C (325°F), Gas mark 3.

2 Place the oatmeal, salt and baking powder in the bowl of a food processor and whiz for 2 minutes until it is finer in texture and looks similar to ground almonds. Add the butter and whiz until combined.

3 With the motor running, pour in the olive oil and boiling water, stopping frequently to check if it's coming together. Don't let it get too wet.

4 Turn the dough out onto a work surface dusted with fine oatmeal and knead just to bring it together. Roll the dough out as thinly as possible, about 2–3mm (¹/₁₆–¹/₈in) thick, then sprinkle the dough with seeds or grind some pepper or sprinkle some salt on top, if you wish. Give the dough another light roll to make sure they stay on.

5 Using the plain cutter or a knife, cut the dough into triangles, rounds or squares. You can re-roll and use the scraps as well.

6 Place on baking trays (don't oil or butter) and bake for about 15–20 minutes until lightly browned on the edges and crisp. Transfer to a wire rack to cool.

SOFT PRETZELS

MAKES 10-14 PRETZELS

450g (1lb) strong
    white flour, sifted
150g (5oz) strong
    brown flour, sifted
1 level tsp fast-acting
    yeast
2 tbsp soft light
    brown sugar
1 tsp salt
1 tbsp vegetable oil
375ml (13fl oz) warm
    water
Salt crystals, such as
    Maldon, and seeds,
    such as sesame or
    poppy, for sprinkling
    (optional)

For the bicarbonate
of soda solution
75g (3oz) bicarbonate
    of soda
1 litre (1¾ pints) water

Soft pretzels warm from the oven are so evocative of German bakeries or those wonderful New York street vendors. Pretzels are essentially a type of bread, and like most yeast-based dough you can get the kids punching and rolling it if they want to join in. The unique pretzel taste comes about after dipping the risen pretzels into a solution of water and bicarbonate of soda and then baking them, so don't skip this step!

1 Mix the two flours, yeast, sugar and salt together in a large bowl or the bowl of an electric food mixer fitted with a dough hook.

2 In measuring jug or bowl, mix the vegetable oil into the warm water. If making by hand, make a well in the centre of the flour mixture and slowly add the water, bringing all the ingredients together to form a soft dough that's not too dry and not too sticky. Adjust by adding a bit more flour or water where necessary. If making in an electric food mixer, run the machine on the lowest setting and add the liquid slowly to form the dough.

3 Knead the mixture for 10 minutes. If kneading by hand, stretch it away with one hand and fold it back on itself with the other, giving it a quarter turn each time, until you have a smooth firm dough that springs back when you gently press your finger into it. Place the dough in an oiled bowl and turn the dough in it to coat it in oil. Cover with cling film or a plastic bag and leave in a warm, draught-free place for approximately 1–3 hours or until it is doubled in size.

4 Preheat the oven to 230°C (450°F), Gas mark 8 and line several baking trays with parchment paper.

5 Place the dough on a dry, lightly floured work surface. Punch down and lightly knead it, then divide into 10–14

balls (I made 10 and they weighed 100g each), keeping them covered with a clean tea towel while you are shaping one at a time. Roll each one into a thin rope, not much thicker than a pencil (if you want crisp ones, roll them thinner) and shape into a pretzel shape (as shown in the photographs), sealing the edges with a dab of water on your finger. Place on the prepared baking trays, cover and allow to rise again for 10–20 minutes.

6 Bring the water to the boil in a large saucepan and dissolve the bicarbonate of soda in it. Leave it on a bare simmer. Gently place each pretzel in the water and bicarbonate of soda mixture, not putting more than three in at a time. Allow 30 seconds on one side then flip them over using a slotted spoon and poach for a further 30 seconds. Drain and return to the lined trays. If you wish, you could sprinkle salt crystals, sesame seeds or poppy seeds on them at this stage. Alternatively, add them after baking (see Variations below).

7 Bake in the oven for 8–10 minutes, turning the pretzels over halfway through cooking. Allow to cool on a wire rack.

VARIATIONS

Savoury additions: While the pretzels are still hot from the oven, you can brush them with melted butter and sprinkle on sesame seeds, poppy seeds or salt crystals if you haven't already, or even garlic butter (see page 202).

Mustard dip: Serve them plain with mustard to dip into.

Honey and cinnamon: For a sweet treat and while the pretzels are still hot from the oven, mix 15g (1/2oz) melted butter with 1 tablespoon of honey, 1 tablespoon of caster sugar and 1/2 teaspoon of ground cinnamon and brush over the pretzels. Allow to cool.

TARTS
AND
PIES

PISSALADIERE
SERVES 6

1 x quantity shortcrust
pastry (see page 254)
together with 1 tsp
water or oil from
a tin of anchovies
(see below), to bind

For the topping
4 tbsp olive oil
900g (2lb) onions,
peeled and thinly
sliced lengthways
2 cloves of garlic,
peeled and crushed
1 tsp chopped
thyme leaves
1 tbsp chopped parsley
salt, freshly ground
black pepper and a
pinch of caster sugar
1–2 x 30g tins
anchovies, drained
and halved
lengthways
Approximately 16
black olives, pitted

23 x 33cm (9 x 13in)
Swiss roll tin

This French dish is like an oniony pizza. The word *'pissaladière'* derives from the Provençal French *pissalo* or 'salt fish', presumably because of the anchovies that are included in the recipe. The base can also be made with puff pastry (see page 257), which does not need pre-baking. French Niçoise olives are best on top, but Greek or Italian will do just as well. Pissaladière is perfect for a summer lunch, served with a crisp green salad. You can also make mini tarts – cook at 220°C (400°F), Gas mark 6, for 15 minutes.

1 To make the pastry, follow the description on page 254.
2 Meanwhile, heat the olive oil in a wide, heavy-bottomed frying pan, then add the onions. (The pan will seem quite full at first, but the onions will melt down considerably after about 10 minutes.) Stir the onions and cook over a low heat, covered, for at least 20 minutes, stirring continuously and scraping the base of the pan every few minutes.
3 Now add the garlic, herbs and salt, pepper and sugar, and continue cooking for 10 minutes until the onions begin to melt and turn golden. Taste for seasoning, adjusting if necessary, and remove from the heat.
4 Preheat the oven to 180°C (350°F), Gas mark 4.
5 Remove the pastry from the fridge, uncover and, with a floured rolling pin, roll out on a floured work surface into a rectangle to fit the Swiss roll tin. Lift it onto the tin and prick the whole base with a fork. Bake in the oven for 10 minutes, then remove.
6 Cover the pre-baked base with an even layer of onions. Arrange the anchovy fillets in a lattice pattern over the onions, placing a whole or halved olive within each diamond.
7 Return to the oven and bake for a further 25 minutes to allow the flavours to blend. Serve hot or cold.

SPINACH, POTATO AND GOAT'S CHEESE TART

SERVES 6 · VEGETARIAN

1 x quantity shortcrust
    pastry (see page 254)
250g (9oz) baby or
    destalked large
    spinach leaves
7 baby new potatoes,
    unpeeled
4 eggs
250ml (9fl oz) double
    cream
Salt and freshly ground
    black pepper
Zest of 1/2 lemon
Pinch of freshly grated
    nutmeg
Pinch of cayenne
    pepper
25g (1oz) Parmesan
    cheese, finely grated
150g (5oz) goat's cheese,
    6–7mm (1/4–1/2in)
    slices

25cm (10in) diameter
    tart tin

This is a delicious tart, full of healthy spinach perfectly complemented by the flavour of the goat's cheese.

1 Make the pastry as described on page 254, leaving to chill for 30 minutes before using.

2 Preheat the oven to 180°C (350°F), Gas mark 4. Line the tart tin and bake 'blind' (see page 255).

3 Wash and spin the spinach, removing any tough stalks and stems if using large spinach leaves. In a medium-sized saucepan, cook the spinach in just the water that's clinging to it over a low heat until it wilts. Drain in a colander or sieve and allow to cool a little, then squeeze most of the moisture out with your hands and chop roughly.

4 Meanwhile, steam or boil the potatoes until just cooked, and cool on a tray or board. When cool enough to handle, cut into 5mm (1/4in) slices.

5 In a medium-sized bowl, whisk the eggs and add the cream, salt and pepper, lemon zest, nutmeg, cayenne pepper and Parmesan. Whisk these ingredients together then add the spinach and mix through. Season well as the potatoes are very mild and need a good contrast.

6 Spread the potato slices over the base of the prepared tart and dot with the goat's cheese (retain a few slices of each to place on the top, if you wish). Gently spoon over the spinach cream mixture as high as you can go. If you are concerned about spillage, carry the tart minus the last few spoons of filling over to the oven. Place in the oven, spoon over the remaining filling and any remaining potato and cheese slices.

7 Bake for 35–40 minutes until the tart is golden brown and just set in the centre. Remove from the oven and allow to cool for about 10 minutes before serving.

CHICKEN AND LEEK PIE

SERVES 6

1 chicken (about 2kg/4lb 8oz), cut into portions on the bone
600ml (1 pint) chicken stock
200ml (7fl oz) white wine
2 large sprigs of thyme or tarragon
Salt and freshly ground black pepper
25g (1oz) butter
4 leeks (about 350g/12oz when sliced), cut into 1cm (1/2in) thick slices
1 tbsp water
1 generous tbsp plain flour
350ml (12fl oz) double cream
2 tsp chopped thyme or 1 tbsp chopped tarragon
1 tsp Dijon mustard
450g (1lb) good-quality bought or homemade puff pastry or flaky pastry (see pages 257–8)
1 egg, beaten

30cm (12in) oval pie dish or 6–8 single pie dishes

This delicious pie is true comfort food and also freezes very well. I save the chicken carcass, the bones and the green tops of the leeks to make a really good chicken stock for later use.

1 Preheat the oven to 230°C (450°F), Gas mark 8.

2 Place the chicken portions in a large ovenproof casserole or saucepan with the stock, white wine, sprigs of herbs and a pinch of salt and pepper. Bring to the boil, then reduce the heat and simmer for approximately 25–30 minutes or until the chicken is completely cooked.

3 While the chicken is cooking, melt the butter in another saucepan. Add the sliced leeks and water. Season with salt and pepper, cover and cook gently until the leeks have softened. Once cooked, remove them from the pan with a slotted spoon and set aside.

4 Add the flour to the buttery juices and stir over a medium heat for 1 minute to make a roux.

5 When the chicken is cooked, remove the portions from the casserole and set aside. Bring the chicken poaching liquid back up to the boil and add the cream. Boil, uncovered, for about 5 minutes or until the mixture has intensified in flavour, then whisk in the roux. Add the herbs and mustard. Once the chicken has cooled enough to handle, pull the meat off the bones and cut into pieces about 2cm (3/4in) square. Add to the sauce with the leeks and salt and pepper to taste.

6 Place the chicken and leek pie filling into the large or four single pie dishes, so they are full, and cover with the pastry (see page 259), rolled out to a thickness of 5mm (1/4in). Brush with the beaten egg and cook in the oven for 10 minutes. Reduce the temperature to 200°C (400°F), Gas mark 6 and cook for a further 20–25 minutes or until the pastry is golden brown and the mixture is bubbling.

ROAST MUSHROOM AND GOAT'S CHEESE TARTLET WITH SWEET ONION JAM

MAKES 1 TARTLET ✳ VEGETARIAN

2 flat mushrooms
1 large clove of garlic,
    peeled and crushed
Olive oil, for drizzling
Salt and freshly
    ground black pepper
A knob of butter
100g (3½oz) spinach
    leaves
125g (4½oz) good-
    quality bought or
    homemade puff
    pastry (see page 257)
50g (2oz) soft goat's
    cheese
5 olives, pitted and
    chopped, for
    sprinkling
1 dsp chopped tarragon
    or marjoram, for
    sprinkling
1 dsp sweet onion jam
    (see page 277),
    to serve

This is a wonderfully flavoursome wintry tart, perfect accompanied by a glass of red wine. Whenever wild mushrooms such as porcini or chanterelles are in season, you should seize the opportunity to make this recipe with them.

1 Preheat the oven to 240°C (475°F), Gas mark 9.

2 Remove the stalks from the mushrooms and place on a baking tray dark side up. Place a little of the garlic on each and drizzle with olive oil. Season with salt and pepper and roast in the oven for 10 minutes.

3 While the mushrooms are cooking, melt the butter in a saucepan, add the spinach and cook for 5 minutes or until it has wilted. Season with salt and pepper.

4 Roll out the pastry on a lightly floured work surface into a rectangle about 5mm (¼in) thick. Trim the edges (use the scraps for Cheese Straws on page 130), giving you a rectangle about 12 x 14cm (4½ x 5½in). Turn the pastry upside down so that the cut edges will rise up nicely. Using the tip of a sharp knife, cut a border 1cm (½in) in from the edges, but just halfway down through the pastry, all the way round.

5 Spread the spinach evenly over the centre of the pastry, keeping it within the borders. Arrange the mushrooms over the spinach then crumble the cheese over the top. Place on a baking tray and bake in the oven and cook for 8–12 minutes.

6 Remove the tart from the oven and sprinkle with the chopped olives and herbs. Serve with onion jam on the side.

CALZONE PUTTANESCA

MAKES 6 CALZONE

**For the roasted
tomato sauce**
**450g (1lb) tomatoes,
    halved**
**3 cloves of garlic,
    peeled and kept whole**
5 tbsp olive oil
3 tbsp balsamic vinegar
**Salt, freshly ground
    black pepper and
    1 tsp caster sugar**

For the pizza dough
**350g (12oz) strong
    white flour, sifted**
1 level tsp salt
2 tsp caster sugar
**25g (1oz) butter,
    softened**
**1 x 7g sachet fast-
    acting yeast**
**2 tbsp olive oil, plus
    extra for brushing**
**175–200ml (6–7fl oz)
    warm water**

**For the puttanesca
filling (per calzone)**
**2 tbsp roasted
    tomato sauce**
**4 olives, pitted and
    roughly chopped**
3 anchovies, chopped
**2 tbsp baby capers or
    chopped large ones**
**50g (2oz) grated
    mozzarella**
**2 tbsp drained tinned
    tuna**

***Ingredients continued
    overleaf***

Calzone (from the Italian word for 'stocking' or 'trouser-leg')
are delicious crescent-shaped parcels with a variety of
different fillings. Made with pizza dough, they are probably
best thought of as inside-out pizzas although, unlike pizzas,
they can take completely different fillings – more like a pie.
This will make around six adult portions or 10–12 children's
portions. The filling given in the main recipe is based on a
classic Italian sauce for pasta, but see the next page for two
other equally delicious variations. There is plenty of tomato
sauce for this recipe – freeze what you don't use.

1 Preheat the oven to 230°C (425°F), Gas mark 7.
2 To make the roasted tomato sauce, lay the halved tomatoes
on a baking tray in a single layer, cut side up. Add the whole
cloves of garlic randomly on the tray, drizzle with the oil and
vinegar and season with salt, pepper and sugar to taste. Cook
in the oven for about 20 minutes until very soft and blistered
in appearance.
3 Liquidise in a liquidiser or food processor and push through
a sieve. Season again to taste. The sauce needs to be thick
enough to coat the back of a spoon: if it needs thickening,
place in a saucepan, bring to the boil and reduce to thicken,
which could take up to 10 minutes.
4 To make the pizza dough, place the flour, salt and sugar
in a large bowl and mix. Rub in the butter, add the yeast
and mix together. Make a well in the centre of the mixture,
add the oil and most, but not all, of the warm water and
mix to a loose dough. Add more water or flour, if needed.
5 Take the dough out of the bowl and place on a lightly floured
work surface, covered with a clean tea towel, for 5 minutes.
Then knead the dough for 10 minutes or until smooth and
slightly springy to the touch. Alternatively, knead the dough

8 basil leaves,
roughly torn
Salt and freshly ground
black pepper
2 tbsp finely grated
Parmesan cheese
Tiny sprinkle of chilli
flakes (optional)

for 5 minutes in an electric food mixer using the dough hook. Let the dough relax for another 5 minutes.

6 Turn the oven up to 240°C (475°F), Gas mark 9. Place an upside-down baking tray or a pizza baking tile in the centre of the oven, allowing at least 15 minutes to heat up fully.

7 To make the puttanesca filling, simply mix all the ingredients together in a medium-sized bowl and season.

8 Lightly dust the work surface and dough ball with flour, rolling it into a disc roughly 23cm (9in) in diameter. (Try to keep the disc as thin as possible as it has to be doubled over.)

9 Spoon the filling onto one half of the disc, keeping it at least 1–2cm (^{1}/2–^{3}/4in) from the edge. Lift the other half over and seal the edges by squeezing them together and pressing with the prongs of a fork, making sure the dough doesn't stick to the work surface. Using either a floured pizza paddle or the floured base of a loose-bottomed tin, slide the calzone onto it and then quickly onto the upside-down tray or baking tile in the oven.

10 Bake for 15–20 minutes, covering with foil towards the end of the cooking time, if necessary, to prevent it burning. Remove from the oven, lightly brush with olive oil and serve with a green salad.

VARIATIONS FOR FILLINGS

Calzone with Italian sausage: Squeeze the sausage meat out of the casing of 100g (3^1/2oz) soft spicy Italian sausages and break up with a fork. Sauté it in 1–2 tablespooons of olive oil over a medium heat for about 10 minutes until fully cooked. Cut ^{1}/4 red onion into large slices lengthways and sauté with ^{1}/2 teaspoon of roughly chopped rosemary in 1 tablespoon of olive oil until the onions are translucent but not browned. Following the instructions above, spread half the base with 2 tablespoons of roasted tomato sauce, then spread over the cooked sausages, 50g (2oz) grated mozzarella and the cooked onions. Fold over the other half of the dough and cook as above, brushing with chilli oil instead of olive oil if you prefer.

Calzone di magro ('without meat'): Poach 75g (6oz) leeks, cut into 1cm (1/2in) rounds, for 5–10 minutes in 75ml (21/2fl oz) water with 15g (1/2oz) butter and seasoned with salt and pepper. Mix together 50g (2oz) grated mozzarella, 2 tablespoons chopped parsley, 1/2 tsp chopped thyme and 1 clove of finely grated or crushed garlic, and taste for seasoning. Spread the cheese mixture over half the base and scatter over the leeks. Fold over the other half of the dough and cook as above, brushing with olive oil.

QUICHE LORRAINE
SERVES 6

1 x quantity shortcrust pastry (see page 254)
1 tbsp olive oil
175g 6oz) streaky bacon, cut into 1cm (1/2in) lardons
100g (4oz) onions, peeled and chopped
2 eggs and 2 egg yokes
250ml (9fl oz) double cream
1 scant tbsp chopped parsley
1 scant tbsp chopped chives
50g (2oz) Cheddar cheese, grated
50g (2oz) Gruyère cheese, grated
Salt and freshly ground black pepper

19cm (71/2in) high-sided tart tin or 23cm (9in) shallow tin

Named after the Lorraine region of north-east France, this classic quiche is delicious served with a green salad and tangy relish. It tastes great cold, too.

1 Make the pastry as described on page 254, leaving to chill for 30 minutes before using.

2 Preheat the oven to 180°C (350°F), Gas mark 4. Line the tart tin and bake 'blind' (see page 255).

3 Heat the oil in a frying pan and cook the bacon until crisp. Remove and dry on kitchen paper. Then sweat the onions gently in the same oil for a further 10 minutes.

4 Meanwhile, whisk the eggs in a medium-sized bowl, add the cream, herbs, cheeses and cool bacon and onions. Mix well and add seasoning.

5 Pour the filling into the pastry base and return to the oven for 30–40 minutes or until the centre has set. Serve warm with a green salad and relish.

PORK, CHORIZO AND SPINACH PIE

SERVES 8-10

1 x quantity hot water
    crust pastry (see
    page 257)
50g (2oz) butter
400g (14oz) spinach
    leaves
Salt and freshly ground
    black pepper
750g (1lb 10oz) minced
    pork
50g (2oz) chorizo, sliced
    and roughly chopped
Pinch of freshly grated
    nutmeg
4 cloves of garlic,
    peeled and crushed
1 tbsp chopped sage
3 eggs, beaten

25cm (10in) diameter
    tart tin, 3cm (1¼in)
    deep

This versatile pie is great eaten either hot or cold and is
perfect for picnics. You can serve it cold with relish and
gherkins for a ploughman's lunch, or piping hot for dinner
after a long winter's walk. It's truly a pie for all seasons.

1 First make the pastry as described on page 257.

2 While the pastry is chilling, cook the spinach. Melt the
butter in a wide saucepan, add the spinach and cook until
wilted. No additional water is necessary; the moisture left
on the spinach is sufficient. Season with salt and pepper.
When cooked, drain and allow to cool.

3 In a large bowl, mix all the other ingredients, including
two-thirds of the beaten eggs, and season with salt and
pepper. Make sure the spinach is cooled, then chop it
roughly and add to the mixture. Mix well.

4 When the pastry is chilled and firm, divide it in half, then
roll out one half on a lightly floured work surface until it is
about 8mm (³⁄₈in) thick and use to line the tart tin. Trim the
edges and then brush with some of the beaten egg. Place the
pork mixture in the pastry case. Roll out the second half of
the pastry until it is also about 8mm (³⁄₈in) thick and place
it on top of the pie (see page 259). Trim the edges and brush
the top with more beaten egg. Roll out the scraps until they
are approximately 5mm (¼in) thick and cut into leaves or
whatever shapes take your fancy, if you wish. Place these
on top of the pie and brush the shapes with a little more
beaten egg to glaze.

5 Make a small hole (5mm/¼in wide) in the centre top of
the pastry and bake in the oven for 15–20 minutes or until
a skewer inserted into the middle comes out hot.

6 Allow to cool for at least 30 minutes before removing from
the tin. When cooled, cut into slices to serve.

BEEF PASTIES WITH MINT, GINGER AND PEAS

MAKES 12 PASTIES

1 x quantity hot water
crust pastry (see page
257) with 1/2 tsp
turmeric and a pinch
of cayenne added
with the flour
2 tbsp olive oil
150g (5oz) onions,
peeled and chopped
2 cloves of garlic,
peeled and chopped
1 tsp finely grated root
ginger
Salt and freshly ground
black pepper
1 tsp coriander seeds
1 tsp cumin seeds
1 tsp black mustard
seeds (optional)
200g (7oz) minced beef
1 tbsp tomato purée
1 tsp English mustard
1 tsp Worcestershire
sauce
100g (3¹/₂oz) fresh or
frozen peas
1 tbsp chopped mint
1 egg, beaten

This great-tasting dish has elements of Mexican empanadas, Indian samosas and classic Cornish pasties all rolled into one.

1 Preheat the oven to 220°C (425°F), Gas mark 7. Make the pastry as described on page 257.

2 While the pastry is chilling, make the filling. Heat the olive oil in a saucepan set over a medium heat, add the onions, garlic and ginger, season with salt and pepper and cook until the onions are soft and slightly golden.

3 Grind the seeds in a mortar with a pestle, then add to the pan with the beef, tomato purée, mustard and Worcestershire sauce. Cook over a medium heat for 15 minutes or until the beef is cooked. Add the peas for the last 1–2 minutes of cooking. Add the chopped mint, then season to taste and allow to cool.

4 Roll the dough out on a lightly floured work surface until it is approximately 2mm (¹/₁₆in) thick. Using a small saucer or something similar, cut the dough into 12cm (4¹/₂in) diameter circles.

5 Lay 1 generous tablespoon of the mixture on one half of the circle and brush the edge of the other half with beaten egg, then fold it over to form a semi-circle. Pinch the edges together to seal, making sure there is no air trapped inside, and mark the edges with a fork. Repeat until all the circles and filling are used up.

6 Brush the tops with beaten egg and bake in the oven for 15–20 minutes or until golden and a skewer inserted in the middle of each comes out hot. Serve hot or at room temperature.

BEEF, STOUT AND ANCHOVY PIE

SERVES 4-6

4 tbsp olive oil

600g (1lb 6oz) stewing beef, trimmed and cut into 2cm (³/₄in) chunks

Salt and freshly ground black pepper

400g (14oz) button mushrooms, cut into quarters

2 large onions (about 500g/1lb 2oz total weight), peeled and sliced

4 large cloves of garlic, peeled and chopped

500ml (18fl oz) beef or chicken stock

250ml bottle of stout

1 tbsp chopped tarragon

30g tin anchovies, drained

1 x quantity hot water crust pastry (see page 257)

1 medium pie dish or 4–6 individual dishes

The sea-salty flavour of anchovies works well here, combining 'turf and surf' as in a steak and oyster pie, but you can leave them out if you prefer.

1 Place a large ovenproof casserole over a medium heat. Add 2 tablespoons of olive oil and the beef and cook until brown (do this in batches if necessary). Season with salt and pepper, then remove with a slotted spoon and set aside.

2 Add 1 more tablespoon of oil and the mushrooms, season, and cook until browned. Remove and set aside.

3 Pour the last tablespoon of olive oil into the casserole and add the onions and garlic. Toss these for 1 minute, then add the beef, mushrooms, stock and stout. Bring to the boil, cover, reduce the heat and simmer gently on the hob or in an oven preheated to 150°C (300°F), Gas mark 2 for 1–1¹/₂ hours or until the meat is lovely and tender. Depending on the meat, it may even take a bit longer.

4 Add the chopped tarragon and season to taste, but go slightly easy on the salt as some anchovies will be going into the pie too. Allow to cool, while you make or prepare the pastry.

5 Preheat the oven to 230°C (450°F), Gas mark 8. Place the pie filling in the pie dish or dishes. Place 1–2 anchovies (I like to roll them up to get a good burst of anchovy flavour) in each individual dish, or all the anchovies in the large dish, spaced apart from each other. Top with the pastry (see page 259) and cook in the oven for 10 minutes before reducing the oven temperature to 200°C (400°F), Gas mark 6 and cooking for a further 20–30 minutes.

VARIATIONS

Puff or flaky pastry: In place of the hot water crust pastry, use 250g of puff pastry or flaky pastry (see page 257–8).

COCONUT MACAROON TART

SERVES 6-8

1 x quantity sweet shortcrust pastry (see page 254)
3 eggs
225g (8oz) caster sugar
1 tsp ground cinnamon
150g (5oz) desiccated coconut
125g (4½oz) butter, melted
Icing sugar, for dusting

23cm (9in) diameter tart tin

This decorative tart goes well with ice cream and makes a good dinner party dessert. The coconut is naturally oily, which helps to preserve the tart for a few days.

1 Make the pastry as described on page 254, leaving to chill for 30 minutes before using.

2 Preheat the oven to 180°C (350°F), Gas mark 4. Line the tart tin and bake 'blind' (see page 255).

3 For the filling, whisk the eggs, sugar and cinnamon together in a bowl. Add the desiccated coconut and the melted butter and mix well. Pour the filling into the cooked pastry case and bake in the oven for 40–45 minutes or until it is golden brown and just set in the centre. (Sometimes I turn the oven down to 170°C (325°F), Gas mark 3 after about 30 minutes if it has already turned golden brown and I don't want it any darker.)

4 Remove from the oven and allow to stand in the tin for about 10 minutes before carefully removing and allowing to cool on a wire rack. Dust the tart with icing sugar to serve.

VARIATION

Coconut and raspberry tart: As an alternative to the ground cinnamon in this recipe, I sometimes spread 1 generous tablespoon of raspberry jam onto the baked pastry base (as in the photograph) before pouring in the coconut filling.

TARTE TATIN

SERVES 4-6

1 x quantity soured
cream shortcrust
pastry (see page 254)
4 eating apples (Granny
Smith is very good or
Golden Delicious; if
using a small variety,
such as Cox's Orange
Pippin, you will need
about 6 apples)
125g (4¹/₂oz) caster
sugar (see Rachel's
baking tips overleaf)
100ml (3¹/₂fl oz) water
25g (1oz) butter
1 egg, beaten
Whipped cream, ice
cream or whipped
cream with a little
icing sugar and
cinnamon or
Calvados, to serve

20–22cm (8–8¹/₂in)
diameter ovenproof
saucepan

Tarte tatin is an absolute classic, created in 1889 at a
French hotel run by the sisters Stéphanie and Caroline Tatin.
This spectacular upside-down tart is rumoured to have been
created accidentally by Caroline when she was making an
apple pie. Finding that the pan of apples cooking in butter
and sugar were beginning to burn, she quickly covered them
with pastry and placed the whole thing in the oven. Turning
it out once the pasty was cooked, she found to her surprise
that the tart was a huge success with the guests. It then
became the signature dish of the hotel. Tarte tatin can be
made with other fruits such as pears (as in the variation
below), pineapple and stone fruit such as peaches (still firm),
or even as a savoury dish with onions, shallots or tomatoes.

1 Make the pastry as described on page 254 and allow to chill.
2 Preheat the oven to 200°C (400°F), Gas mark 6.
3 To prepare the apples, peel them with a peeler to keep them
in a nice rounded shape, then cut into quarters. Remove
the core from each quarter and set aside. Don't worry if they
go brown, and don't cover in water or they will be too wet.
4 Place the sugar and water in an ovenproof saucepan set
over a low–medium heat and stir until the sugar dissolves.
Increase the heat and boil the syrup until it starts to
caramelise around the edges – about 5 minutes. Do not
stir once it has come to the boil otherwise the syrup will
crystallise. Once the syrup starts to turn golden, you may
need to swirl the pan slightly to even out the caramelisation.
5 Once the syrup is a golden caramel in colour, add the butter
and swirl the pan again to distribute it through the caramel.
6 Remove the pan from the heat, and place the apple quarters
in a concentric circle around the outside and any remaining
pieces in the centre, keeping in mind that the tart will be

flipped over when serving. The apples must completely cover the base of the pan; you may need an extra apple!

7 Place the pan back over a medium heat and cook for 10 minutes to slightly caramelise the apples, while you roll out the pastry.

8 Roll the pastry out on a lightly floured work surface to a disc about 2cm (³/₄in) wider in diameter than the pan. Remove the pan from the heat and place the pastry on top of the almost cooked apples. Using the base of a spoon or a fork, tuck the pastry in around the edges of the apples. Brush the pastry with beaten egg then, using a skewer or fork, prick a few holes in the pastry.

9 Bake in the oven for 25 minutes or until the pastry is golden and the apples feel cooked when you insert a skewer through the centre.

10 Remove from the oven and allow to stand for just a few minutes before placing a plate on top of the pan and carefully (it is hot!) but quickly flipping it out. Use a plate with a slight lip to catch the delicious juices. Cut into slices to serve. Serve with whipped cream, ice cream or whipped cream with a little icing sugar and cinnamon or Calvados mixed in.

VARIATION

Pear and ginger tarte tatin: Use 4–5 pears of medium ripeness instead of the apples and add 1 teaspoon of grated root ginger in with the butter.

RACHEL'S BAKING TIPS

* Try adding 1 teaspoon of ground cinnamon to the pastry.
* You can also make this with puff or sweet shortcrust pastry.
* If you wish, use golden caster or granulated sugar, but it is a little trickier to see when it is caramelised, so keep watching the pan. The mixture will go a shade darker than the original golden colour and should take about 5 minutes in total over a medium–high heat. If it burns, I would suggest cutting your losses and starting again!

DATE, ORANGE AND CARDAMOM TART

SERVES 6-8

110g (4oz) caster sugar
Finely grated zest and
  juice of 2 oranges
5 eggs
250ml (9fl oz) double
  cream
Ground seeds of 15
  (as fresh as you can)
  cardamom pods
200g (7oz) dates (weight
  once the stones are
  removed), halved
1 x quantity sweet
  shortcrust pastry
  (see page 254)
25g (1oz) butter
4 tbsp good-quality
  apricot jam, sieved,
  to glaze

23cm (9in) diameter
  tart tin

This is a rich and intensely fragrant tart. The orange
and cardamom go beautifully together, evoking the most
wonderful North African flavours.

1 In a large bowl, mix together the caster sugar, finely
grated orange zest, 4 of the eggs, cream and ground seeds
from the cardamoms and leave in the fridge for at least
8 hours (24 hours is best).
2 In a separate bowl, leave the dates to marinate in the
orange juice for at least 8 hours (24 hours is best).
3 After 8 hours or the next day, make the pastry as described
on page 254, leaving to chill for 30 minutes before using.
4 Preheat the oven to 180°C (350°F), Gas mark 4. Line the
tart tin and bake 'blind' (see page 255). Beat the remaining
egg. Remove the paper and beans from the pastry case, brush
with some of the beaten egg and cook for a further 2 minutes.
5 Reduce the oven temperature to 170°C (325°F), Gas mark 3.
Line the base of the tart evenly with the drained dates.
6 Melt the butter gently in a saucepan and add to the cream
mixture. Pour this gently over the dates to come as far up
to the top of the pastry as possible. Carefully transfer to
the oven and cook for 25–30 minutes or until it is just set.
Allow to cool.
7 Heat the apricot jam gently in a small saucepan until
warm, then brush it over the top and eat immediately.

RACHEL'S BAKING TIP
This tart is best eaten on the day it is made.

SEVILLE ORANGE MERINGUE PIE
SERVES 8

1 x quantity sweet shortcrust pastry (see page 254)
1 x quantity Seville orange curd (see page 278)
4 egg whites
225g (8oz) caster sugar

25cm (10in) diameter spring-form/loose-bottomed tin

This recipe is a perfect balance of citrussy sweet and tangy tartness. The crisp pastry works beautifully with the smooth orange curd topped with the fluffy meringue. If you cannot find Seville oranges (which are only in season in January and February) then use ordinary oranges, but reduce the sugar to 200g (7oz) for the orange curd.

1 Make the pastry as described on page 254, leaving to chill for 30 minutes before using.

2 Preheat the oven to 180°C (350°F), Gas mark 4. Line the tart tin and bake 'blind' (see page 255). Reduce the oven temperature to 150°C (300°F), Gas mark 2.

3 Make the Seville orange curd as described on page 278. Once the curd is cooked, remove from the heat, allow to cool slightly then pour into the cooked pastry case. Spread the mixture out evenly.

4 For the meringue, whisk the egg whites in the spotlessly clean bowl of an electric food mixer until stiff peaks form. Gradually add the caster sugar, whisking all the time, until all the sugar is added and stiff peaks form. Spoon the meringue over the top of the orange curd, and swirl it into peaks.

5 Bake in the oven for about 1 hour or until the meringue is crisp on the outside and 'marshmallowy' underneath. Serve warm or at room temperature.

LEMON AND PASSION FRUIT TART

SERVES 6

1 x quantity sweet
   shortcrust pastry
   (see page 254)
2 passion fruit
3 eggs and 1 egg yolk
Finely grated zest
   of 1 lemon
125g (4¹/₂oz) caster
   sugar
150ml (¹/₄ pint) double
   cream
Juice of 3 lemons and
   1 orange
Icing sugar, for dusting

23cm (9in) tart tin

Passion fruit works so well with the lemon, intensifying
the tangy flavour.

1 Make the pastry as described on page 254, leaving to chill
for 30 minutes before using.

2 Preheat the oven to 180°C (350°F), Gas mark 4. Line the
tart tin and bake 'blind' (see page 255).

3 For the filling, cut the passion fruit in half and, using
a teaspoon, scoop out the pulp from the centre and push
through a sieve, reserving the seeds in the sieve for later.
Place the eggs, egg yolk, lemon zest and sugar in a bowl and
whisk for a couple of minutes until the egg is all broken up.
Add the cream, lemon and orange juice and the strained juice
from the two passion fruit. Mix well, skimming off any froth
from the top of the mixture.

4 Carefully pour the filling into the cooked pastry case so it
does not spill (sometimes I pour in the filling when it is sitting
on a rack in the oven to avoid spilling it).

5 Clean about ten of the passion fruit seeds by removing them
from the membrane that surrounds them and put to one side.

6 Reduce the oven temperature to 160°C (325°F), Gas mark 3
and bake for 20 minutes, then place the passion fruit seeds on
top. Bake for another 5–15 minutes or until the filling has just
set in the centre – it should only wobble very slightly when
you take it out of the oven.

7 Remove from the oven and allow to cool for about 15 minutes
before removing the tart from the tin and transferring to a
plate or cake stand. When it is cool, dredge a little icing sugar
over the top and cut into slices to serve.

WALNUT AND HONEY TART

1 x quantity sweet
   shortcrust pastry
   (see page 254)
100g (3¹/₂oz) butter
100g (3¹/₂oz) honey
125g (4¹/₂oz) soft light
   brown sugar
75ml (2¹/₂fl oz) double
   cream
200g (7oz) walnuts
   (shelled weight),
   roughly chopped into
   pieces about 5mm
   (¹/₄in) in size

23cm (9in) diameter
   spring-form/loose-
   bottomed tin

This tart is rich and decadent. Make sure you use good, fresh walnuts – not some that have been lurking for ages in the back of the cupboard and may have gone rancid. Serve the tart on its own with lightly whipped cream, or soften some vanilla ice cream, stir in a bit of runny honey, then put back in the freezer to harden before serving.

1 Make the pastry as described on page 254, leaving to chill for 30 minutes before using.

2 Preheat the oven to 190°C (375°F), Gas mark 5. Line the tart tin and bake 'blind' (see page 255).

3 To make the filling, melt the butter in a saucepan, add the honey, sugar and cream, then bring to the boil and boil for 2 minutes. Remove the pan from the heat and stir in the chopped walnuts.

4 Pour the mixture into the cooked pastry case and bake in the oven for 15 minutes until bubbling and golden.

5 Allow to stand on wire rack for about 10 minutes, then remove the tart from the tin. Leave to cool, then cut into slices to serve.

BREAKFAST AND PATISSERIE

BREAKFAST (ENGLISH) MUFFINS

MAKES 10 MUFFINS

**500g (1lb 2oz) strong
white flour
1 tsp salt
350ml (12fl oz) milk
2 tsp caster sugar
1¹/₂ tsp dried yeast or
15g (¹/₂oz) fresh yeast
or 1 x 7g sachet fast-
acting yeast
Ground rice, for
dusting**

In Britain these are of course simply known as 'muffins', but to the rest of the world they are 'English muffins'. This is thanks to an English baker who emigrated to New York around 1880, taking the recipe with him and introducing them to America. They're a great, squishy alternative to toasted bread and are the classic base for eggs Benedict. It's a sin not to eat them dripping with butter; the only other accompaniment you need is a big cup of milky coffee. The picture opposite shows bagels and brioche as well (see pages 166–9)

1 Sift the flour and salt into a large bowl.
2 Heat the milk in a saucepan until it is warm, then stir in the sugar and the yeast. Allow to stand for 5 minutes until the mixture is frothy. If using fast-acting yeast, there is no need to let the mixture stand.
3 Pour most of the liquid into the dry ingredients and mix to a soft but not wet dough. Knead for about 6–8 minutes by hand or in an electric food mixer with the dough hook attached until the dough is smooth and slightly springy. Place the dough in an oiled bowl, cover and leave in a warm place for approximately 1 hour or until it has doubled in size.
4 Knock back the risen dough and knead again for 2–3 minutes, then cover again (I usually leave it on the work surface dusted with ground rice and covered with an upturned bowl or a tea towel) and leave for a further 30 minutes. Meanwhile, dust a baking tray with ground rice.
5 Without knocking back the dough, roll it on a work surface dusted with ground rice into a log about 20cm (8in) long. Cut the log into 10 slices, each approximately 2cm (³/₄in) thick and place on the prepared baking tray, cut side down. Dust the top with ground rice then, using the palm of your

hand, flatten them slightly so they are just about 1.5cm (⁵/8in) high. Cover again and leave to rise for about 30 minutes.

6 Meanwhile, place a heavy cast-iron (if possible) grill pan or frying pan over a medium heat to heat up. When the pan is moderately hot, reduce the heat to very low and cook the muffins (using no oil or butter) about four at a time for approximately 10 minutes on each side. When they are cooked, they will be golden brown on both sides and will sound hollow when tapped on the base.

7 Once they are cooked, remove from the pan and wrap in a clean tea towel while cooking the remaining muffins – this way they will not get too crusty.

30-DAY MUFFIN RECIPE
MAKES 30 MUFFINS

3 eggs
125g (4¹/₂oz) soft dark brown sugar
100g (3¹/₂oz) caster sugar
500ml (18fl oz) milk
125ml (4fl oz) sunflower oil
1 tsp vanilla extract
300g (11oz) plain flour
¹/₂ tsp salt
2 rounded tsp bicarbonate of soda
160g (5³/₄oz) wholemeal plain flour
25g (1oz) bran

These are called 30-day muffins because the batter keeps in the fridge for a whole 30 days, so you can try a different variation every day!

1 Preheat the oven to 180°C (350°F), Gas mark 4. Place muffin cases in a muffin tin (you may need several tins or else bake in batches).

2 Whisk the eggs and sugars together in a large bowl. Add the milk, oil and vanilla extract and mix well.

3 Sift the plain flour, salt and bicarbonate of soda into another bowl, then add the wholemeal flour and bran and stir these into the wet ingredients. This is your basic batter to which various ingredients may be added (see opposite).

4 Fill the muffin cases three-quarters full and bake in the oven for 15–20 minutes or until set and spongy to the touch. Cool on a wire rack.

Banana and maple syrup muffins: Take 400ml (14fl oz) of the basic batter and add 150g (5oz) peeled and mashed banana, 75ml (2^1/$_2$fl oz) maple syrup and stir to combine. Fills 8 muffin cases three-quarters full.

Rhubarb and strawberry muffins: Take 400ml (14fl oz) of the basic batter and add 150g (5oz) finely sliced rhubarb, 100g (3^1/$_2$oz) strawberries, hulled and quartered, 2 extra tablespoons of caster sugar and the finely grated zest of ^{1}/$_2$ orange and stir to combine. Fills 10–11 muffin the cases three-quarters full.

Cherry and almond muffins: Take 400ml (14fl oz) of the basic batter and add 200g (7oz) cherries (fresh or bottled), quartered, 50g (2oz) toasted flaked almonds and the finely grated zest of ^{1}/$_2$ lemon and stir to combine. Fill 8 muffin cases three-quarters full and sprinkle with a few extra flaked almonds and a pinch of caster sugar.

Chunky apple and raisin muffins: Take 400ml (14fl oz) of the basic batter and add 300g (11oz) sharp eating apple, such as Cox's Orange Pippins or Granny Smith, peeled, cored and chopped, 1 teaspoon of ground cinnamon, 100g (3^1/$_2$oz) raisins and 50g (2oz) chopped walnuts (optional) and stir to combine. Fills 9 muffin cases three-quarters full.

Blueberry muffins: Take 400ml (14fl oz) of the basic batter and add 75g (3oz) fresh blueberries. Fills about 10 muffin cases three-quarters full.

BAGELS

450g (1lb) strong
    white flour
1 x 7g sachet fast-
    acting yeast
2 level tsp salt
250ml (9fl oz) warm
    water (use half kettle
    and half cold tap
    water to achieve
    slightly warmer than
    blood temperature)
2 tbsp runny honey
1 tbsp vegetable oil
3 tbsp treacle or
    molasses
Maize or cornmeal,
    for sprinkling
1 egg, beaten
Sesame seeds, sea salt,
    poppy seeds or a
    savoury topping of
    your choice (optional)

If you've never made bagels before, you may be rather surprised to find that they get their dense chewiness from being poached first and then baked. I make these in an electric food mixer using the dough hook, but you can make them perfectly well by hand, too.

1 Sift the flour and salt into the bowl you are making the bread in, add the yeast and mix well.

2 Measure the water in a measuring jug then stir in the honey and oil. With an electric food mixer on the lowest setting, slowly add all the liquid to the dry ingredients. Knead on the lowest setting for 10 minutes, checking to make sure the dough is not too wet and adding more flour if it does look too sticky. It is stiffer than a normal bread dough, but will still have elasticity.

3 If making by hand, make a well in the centre of the flour and pour the liquid in gradually, bringing the dough together with your hands.

4 Turn the dough onto a clean, dry and floured work surface. Using more flour if necessary, start kneading the dough, stretching it away with the palm of one hand and folding it back again with the other, keeping this up for 10 minutes (great muscle builder!). You may need to use more flour as you go, to avoid a sticky dough, which you don't want.

5 Next, place the dough in a lightly oiled large bowl and turn it in the oil to coat. Cover with cling film or a plastic bag to create a draught-free environment and put in a warm (not hot) place for 1–3 hours or until doubled in size.

6 When the dough is nearly ready – doubled in volume – bring a large saucepan of water to the boil (about 4 litres/7 pints) and add the treacle or molasses. Cover and turn off the heat while you shape the bagels. Lightly oil two baking trays and

sprinkle with maize or cornmeal. Remove the dough from the bowl, then punch it down and knead it briefly. Roll it into a rough sausage shape and divide into 7 chunks. As you work with one, keep the others covered with a clean tea towel.

7 There are two ways to shape the bagels. One is to firmly roll out each chunk into a long 'snake-like' shape, then looping the 'snake' and sealing the ends together with a tiny splash of water and squeezing it. The other method is to roll each chunk into a ball. Piercing a hole in the centre with your finger, pull the dough open until you can fit your hand inside stretching it wide, turning it around and squeezing it to keep it even – like a steering wheel. Place on the prepared baking trays and repeat with the rest of the dough.

8 Cover and allow to stand for a further 10–20 minutes to allow the dough to bounce back again.

9 Preheat the oven to 220°C (425°F), Gas mark 7 and heat the saucepan to a gentle simmer. Gently lift each bagel into the water and poach no more than three at a time, turning gently with a couple of slotted spoons, poaching for about 1¹/₂ minutes on each side. Remove the bagels from the water, allowing them to drain first, and place on the prepared trays, spacing them about 3–4cm (1¹/₄–1¹/₂in) apart. Brush with the beaten egg and sprinkle with sesame seeds, sea salt, poppy seeds or a savoury topping of your choice, or just leave them plain, and bake in the oven for 15 minutes, then turn them upside down for a further 10 minutes to cook the bases. Cool on a wire rack.

RACHEL'S BAKING TIPS

✳ When cold, slice the bagels in half and freeze (for up to 3 months) so they can be popped into the toaster straight from the freezer without defrosting.

✳ Bagels are great toasted with butter or spread with cream cheese, thinly sliced smoked salmon and black pepper.

BRIOCHE

MAKES 15-20 INDIVIDUAL BRIOCHES OR 2 LARGE ONES

50g (2oz) caster sugar
60ml (2fl oz) warm
   water
2 x 7g sachet fast-
   acting yeast or 15g
   (1/2oz) dried yeast or
   25g (1oz) fresh yeast
4 eggs, beaten
450g (1 lb) strong
   white flour, sifted
Good pinch of salt
225g (8oz) butter,
   softened and cubed
1–2 eggs, beaten

15–20 individual
   moulds or two large
   brioche moulds (or
   two 13 x 23cm/5 x 9in
   loaf tins)

Brioche is the richest of all yeast doughs as it contains several eggs and lots of butter. If you have an electric food mixer to do all the kneading for you, it is very straightforward to make. In fact, it's much easier than using your hands; because the butter makes it very sticky. We make it like this at the cookery school so the dough can rise overnight in the fridge and be shaped and baked the following morning. Serve brioche warm from the oven with butter and good-quality strawberry jam (make it yourself, see page 276). Leftover brioche lasts for a few days – try slicing and toasting. It also freezes well.

1 In a large bowl, mix the sugar with the warm water and yeast and let stand for 5 minutes until frothy. If using fast-acting yeast, there is no need to let the mixture stand.
2 Add the beaten eggs, flour and salt and mix to a stiff dough with the dough hook.
3 When the mixture is smooth, beat in the cubes of butter one at a time, making sure that each piece is completely absorbed before adding the next one. This kneading stage should take about 30 minutes and the finished dough should have a silky appearance, damp but not sticky to the touch, and coming away easily from the sides of the bowl.
4 Cover the bowl with cling film or a plastic bag and place in the fridge to rest for 8–24 hours.
5 The following day, prepare the brioche moulds by brushing them with melted butter and dusting with flour and set on a baking tray. Remove the dough from the fridge and knock back in the bowl by folding it in on itself. It is crucial to work quickly at this stage, otherwise the butter will begin to melt and the dough will be too sticky to handle.
6 For the larger brioches, divide the dough in two and place

in two lightly oiled loaf tins. For the smaller brioches, weigh the dough into 50g (2oz) pieces and roll into balls. With the side of your hand, roll each ball of dough into a pear shape. Put the balls of dough, heavy end first, into the brioche moulds. Push the top of the dough towards the centre, leaving it just protruding above the body of the dough. Dip the thick end of a chopstick in a little flour and push it down through the dough almost to the bottom (to keep the 'little hat' in place), then remove. Brush the top of each brioche with the beaten egg.

7 Allow the brioches to prove in a warm place for 45 minutes–1 hour until they have doubled in size. Meanwhile, preheat the oven to 180°C (350°F), Gas mark 4.

8 Gently brush the brioches with wash once again. Cook in the oven for 20–25 minutes, until puffed up and risen and a rich golden brown. The loaves of brioche will take longer to cook, about 50 minutes; when fully cooked, they should sound almost hollow when tapped on the base after being removed from the tins. Place on a wire rack to cool.

WAFFLES

MAKES 16-20 WAFFLES

400g (14oz) plain flour
2 tsp baking powder
2 tsp salt
100g (3¹/₂oz) caster sugar
4 eggs
200g (7oz) butter, melted and cooled
600ml (1 pint) milk
Icing sugar, for dusting

Waffles are such a fun breakfast treat, and what a joy to make your own. Most people use an electric machine, but you can still find beautiful antique or new cast-iron waffle irons that can be used on the hob (you will need to use vegetable oil on the cooking surface so the waffles don't stick). Many toasted sandwich makers come with removable plates with a waffle-plate option, so you don't have to invest in a gadget that only makes waffles.

1 Sift the flour, baking powder and salt into a large bowl. Add the sugar and mix well.

2 Whisk the eggs in another bowl, then mix in the melted butter and milk. Pour the wet ingredients into the centre of the dry ingredients, whisking all the time until you have a smooth batter.

3 Heat the waffle machine. Using a ladle, pour some batter into the machine. Do not fill it up too much. Close the lid and cook for about 4–5 minutes or until the waffles are golden brown and cooked through.

4 Remove the waffles and add your own choice of topping.

WAFFLE TOPPINGS

Here are some of my favourites toppings – the quantities are for 1 waffle.

Maple and Blueberry Syrup (see page 275): Dust with icing sugar and drizzle over both syrups.

Banana and yogurt: Add $^1/_2$ sliced banana, top with 2 tablespoons of Greek yoghurt and drizzle with 1 tablespoon of honey. Scatter over chopped pecans or hazelnuts.

Chocolate ice cream and marshmallow waffle sandwich: On top of 1 hot cooked waffle place a scoop of chocolate ice cream and 1 tablespoon of chopped marshmallows. Sandwich with another hot cooked waffle and eat straight away!

RACHEL'S BAKING TIP

If you're feeling particularly decadent, you can serve waffles as the Belgians do, with powdered sugar, whipped cream and berries or even ice cream and chocolate spread, and then head straight for the gym! If you can't face that much for breakfast, you can serve them as a pudding.

BAKED BREAKFAST OMELETTE

SERVES 1

2 eggs, beaten
50ml (1³/4fl oz) milk
Salt and freshly ground
black pepper
35g (1oz) Cheddar
cheese, grated
1 dsp chopped chives
or parsley
30g (1oz) mushrooms,
sliced and cooked
2 streaky bacon
rashers, grilled and
cut into 1cm (¹/2in)
pieces
A knob of butter,
for frying

This is just another method of making an omelette, rather like a frittata. The benefit of baking is that it sets perfectly and doesn't burn on the bottom, as can happen on the hob.

1 Preheat the oven to 230°C (450°F), Gas mark 8.
2 In a large bowl, beat the eggs and milk together very well. Season with salt and pepper.
3 Add the cheese, herbs, mushrooms and bacon and stir gently.
4 Melt the butter in a 20cm (8in) ovenproof, heavy-based frying pan, and when the butter is foaming, add the egg mixture. Turn down the heat and cook for 3–5 minutes until the omelette is light golden on the bottom and set.
5 Place the pan in the oven and cook for 10 minutes or until it has set in the middle.

RACHEL'S BAKING TIP
This mixture can be multiplied and cooked in a larger pan if necessary.

CROISSANTS

MAKES ABOUT 18 CROISSANTS

275ml (9fl oz) milk
25g (1oz) sugar
1½ tsp dried yeast
    or 15g (½oz) fresh
    yeast or 1 x 7g sachet
    fast-acting yeast
450g (1lb) strong
    white flour
275g (10oz) salted
    butter, softened
1 egg, whisked with
    1 tsp milk

There is nothing quite like freshly baked croissants with really good jam and a cup of milky coffee. The yeast in croissants gives them a light crumbly texture, and the layers of butter make them simply irresistible. Apart from butter and jam, they can be filled with all manner of things – almond paste, slices of apple with cinnamon, chocolate, chopped nuts with spices, even cheese and ham for a savoury version. Feel free to experiment!

1 In a small saucepan, heat the milk until warm, remove from the heat and stir in the sugar and the yeast. Allow to sit for 5 minutes to get slightly frothy. If using fast-acting yeast, there is no need to let the mixture stand.

2 Sift the flour into a large bowl and rub in 50g (2oz) of the butter. Add the milk and yeast liquid and mix to a dough. Knead until smooth – for 8–10 minutes by hand or 5 minutes in an electric food mixer with a dough hook. Cover with cling film or a clean tea towel and leave in the fridge for 2 hours.

3 Beat the remaining butter with a rolling pin into a thin slab, about 8mm (3/8in) thick, between sheets of greaseproof paper or cling film. Take the dough out of the fridge and, dusting the work surface and the top of the dough with flour to prevent it sticking, roll into a rectangle about 20 x 40cm (8 x 16in). Using a pastry brush, brush off any excess flour from the pastry.

4 Place the remaining butter on one half of the rectangle, about 2.5cm (1in) from the edges, and fold the other half over it. Roll out the dough into another rectangle of roughly the same size as before and fold in three, as for puff pastry (see page 257), keeping all the sides aligned. Cover with either a plastic bag, cling film or greaseproof paper and place in the fridge for 30 minutes to rest. **Continued overleaf**

5 With the open ends facing towards and away from you, like a closed book, roll out the pastry again, and fold in three as before. Cover with a clean tea towel on the work surface and leave for 15 minutes to allow to rise. (If you wish, you can leave it in the fridge for 8–24 hours. This chills the pastry and butter, making them easier to work with.)

6 Roll into a rectangle once more and fold in three again.

7 Roll out the pastry to approximately ½ cm (1in) thick, 35cm (14in) wide and as long as possible – usually about 55cm (22in). Trim the edges and cut in half lengthways. From each long thin rectangle cut out approximately 9 triangles: the base of each should be about 15cm (6in) wide, but you will have 2 smaller triangles at either end.

8 Starting at the base of each triangle, roll towards the tip and curve the edges of each croissant inwards slightly. Place the croissants on a baking tray with the tip of each triangle tucked underneath and spaced slightly apart to allow room to rise. Brush gently with some of the egg wash and put in a warm place to prove for 30–45 minutes. When they have doubled in size, gently brush them again with egg wash.

9 Meanwhile, preheat the oven to 220°C (425°F), Gas mark 7. Place the croissants in the oven and bake for 10 minutes, then reduce the temperature to 180°C (350°F), Gas mark 4 and bake for 10 more minutes until the croissants are crisp and golden and brown on the bottom. Transfer to a wire rack to allow to cool briefly.

VARIATION

Pains au chocolat: Roll the croissant dough as above and trim the edges. Cut into three long strips instead of two, then cut the strips into small rectangles about 8cm (3¼in) wide. Arrange about 1 tablespoon of chopped good-quality dark chocolate on the centre of each and roll up fully. Transfer to a baking tray, brush with egg wash and allow to rise, as for the croissants. Brush with egg wash again and bake as for croissants. Allow to slightly cool on a wire rack, then serve.

CRUMPETS

MAKES ABOUT 10 CRUMPETS

225g (8oz) plain flour
1/2 tsp salt
150ml (1/4 pint) milk
125ml (4fl oz) water
1 tbsp caster sugar
1/2 x 7g sachet fast-
   acting yeast or 1 tsp
   dried yeast or 7g
   (1/4oz) fresh yeast
2 tbsp sunflower oil,
   for frying

3–4 metal rings or
   pastry cutters

These are gorgeous little yeast-risen teatime treats. Whenever I make them, my children eat them immediately, straight off the pan. Split them in half and the butter and jam or apple jelly melts deliciously into all the little holes.

1 Sift the flour and salt into a large bowl and make a well in the centre. Heat the milk and water together in a small saucepan over a low heat until warm, stir in the sugar and the yeast and leave in a warm place for about 5 minutes until frothy. If using fast-acting yeast, there is no need to let the mixture stand.

2 Pour the warmed milk and yeast mixture onto the flour and beat together with a whisk for about 2 minutes to create a thick but smooth batter.

3 Cover with cling film or a clean tea towel and leave in a warm place for about 1 hour until the mixture has risen and is light and bubbly in texture.

4 Beat the dough again briefly to knock out any air. Place a heavy cast-iron or non-stick frying pan over a very low heat, adding a drop of sunflower oil. Wipe the pan with paper towels to remove the excess oil. Brush the insides of the crumpet rings with oil, then place them in the pan and leave to heat up for 1–2 minutes.

5 Pour in enough mixture to fill the rings halfway up the sides. Cook on the lowest heat possible for about 10 minutes, until bubbles start bursting on the surface and the batter looks slightly drier.

6 Carefully turn over the crumpets, with the rings still attached, remove the rings and cook the crumpets for 10 minutes on the other side, still on a very low heat. Place the first batch of crumpets in a warm oven while cooking the remaining mixture.

BAKLAVA

300g (11oz) shelled
pistachio nuts
or almonds (or a
mixture of both)
1¹/₂ tsp ground
cinnamon
1¹/₂ packs of filo
pastry (1 pack =
around 400g)
125–150g (4¹/₂–5oz)
butter, melted

For the syrup
300ml (¹/₂ pint) water
350g (12oz) caster sugar
125ml (4fl oz) runny
honey
1 stick cinnamon or
1 tsp ground
cinnamon
Zest of ¹/₂ orange
1 tsp whole cloves
1–2 tsp orange-flower
water (optional)

24 x 19cm (9¹/₂ x 7¹/₂in)
ovenproof dish

Ever since I first went to Greece, I have loved these tooth-achingly sweet and nutty diamonds of filo pastry. They are divine to serve after dinner with cups of strong coffee or fresh mint tea.

1 Preheat the oven to 180°C (350°F), Gas mark 4.
2 Grind the nuts in a food processor until they are coarsely but not fully ground. Mix them with the cinnamon. Using a soft pastry brush, lightly butter the ovenproof dish. Gently unfold the filo pastry, covering it immediately with a clean tea towel to stop it drying out and cracking.
3 Start layering the sheets of filo pastry into the dish, brushing each sheet with melted butter before placing the next layer on top. After six layers, spread over one-third of the nuts.
4 Repeat step 3 twice and then add six more layers of filo pastry. Butter the top of the last layer and trim off any overlapping pastry with a sharp knife to create a neat edge. Cut into small diamonds (each 4–5cm/1¹/₂–2in square), making sure the knife goes all the way to the bottom of each.
5 Bake in the middle shelf of the preheated oven for 40–45 minutes until golden brown and crisp, reducing the temperature to 170°C (325°F), Gas mark 3 during cooking if the baklava looks as though it is browning too quickly.
6 Meanwhile, prepare the syrup. In a saucepan set over a medium heat, simmer all the ingredients for about 15 minutes, allowing the liquid to reduce by about one-third. It should be slightly viscous in consistency. Stir occasionally and then leave to cool while the baklava is baking.
7 Remove the baklava from the oven and spoon half the cooked syrup all over the top. Leave for 5 minutes and then spoon over the remaining syrup. Let the baklava go cold before removing the individual pieces from the dish with a palette knife.

ECLAIRS

MAKES ABOUT 25 ÉCLAIRS

1 x quantity choux
   pastry (see page 256)
1 egg, beaten

**For the chocolate
glacé icing**
200g (7oz) icing sugar
25g (1oz) cocoa powder
1–2 tbsp boiling water

**For the crème
chantilly filling**
50g (2oz) icing sugar
   (1 generous tbsp),
   sifted
1 tsp vanilla extract
400ml (14fl oz) whipped
   cream (measure
   when whipped)

2 piping bags
Plain 5–8mm (1/4–3/sin)
   nozzle
Plain 3mm (1/sin)
   nozzle (optional)

Eclairs are typically filled with a sweet vanilla cream known as crème chantilly and topped with chocolate or coffee icing. If you wish, you can make them extra rich and fill them with a combination of crème chantilly and pastry cream (crème patissière), as for Croque en Bouche (see page 228). Eclairs can be prepared in advance: once the unfilled pastries are cooked and cooled, they can be kept in an airtight box for a few days or frozen, although it is best to make the chantilly cream on the day that you are planning on eating the éclairs.

1 Preheat the oven to 220°C (425°F), Gas mark 7. Line a baking tray with parchment paper (not greaseproof paper, as the éclairs may stick when cooked).

2 Make the choux pastry as described on page 256. Place the dough into a piping bag fitted with the plain nozzle and pipe into lengths approximately 10cm (4in) long onto the prepared baking tray, spaced about 4cm (1½in) apart to allow for expansion. Use a small wet knife to stop the dough coming out when you have finished piping each éclair.

3 Brush the éclairs gently with the beaten egg and bake in the oven for 10 minutes. Reduce the oven temperature to 200°C (400°F), Gas mark 6 and continue to cook for a further 15–20 minutes or until the éclairs are puffed up, golden and crisp.

4 Remove the éclairs from the oven and, using a skewer or the tip of a small sharp knife, make a hole in the side or the base of each éclair. Return to the oven and bake for a further 5 minutes to allow the steam to escape. Transfer the éclairs to a wire rack to cool.

5 Meanwhile, make the icing. Sift the icing sugar and cocoa powder into a bowl. Add the boiling water and stir to mix, adding a little more boiling water if necessary until the icing is spreadable but not too watery. ***Continued overleaf***

6 To make the crème chantilly filling, fold the sifted icing sugar and vanilla extract into the whipped cream. Chill until you are ready to use it.

7 When the éclairs are cool, spoon the crème chantilly into a clean piping bag fitted with the small, plain nozzle (or use the same nozzle used for piping the éclairs) and pipe the cream into the éclairs through the hole made by the skewer or knife until they are well filled.

8 Using a small palette knife or table knife that has been standing in a jug of hot water (to make spreading the icing easier), spread the icing over the top of each éclair, dipping the knife into the hot water between each éclair. Serve and watch them being devoured!

VARIATION

Coffee glacé icing: Use coffee glacé icing (see page 269) instead of chocolate.

BAKED MEALS

EASY EMPANADILLAS WITH BLUE CHEESE AND BACON

MAKES 15 EMPANADILLAS

100g (3½oz) bacon rashers, cut into 5mm–1cm (¼–½in) dice, sautéed until cooked and slightly golden

50g (2oz) blue cheese, such as Cashel Blue, Gorgonzola or Stilton, cut into 5mm–1cm (¼–½in) dice

150g (5oz) good-quality bought or homemade puff pastry (see page 257)

1 egg, beaten

Empanadillas, tasty little pastries with different types of fillings, are found in tapas bars all over Spain. I've made them here with puff pastry, but you can make them with hot water crust pastry (see page 257) if you wish.

1 Preheat the oven to 220°C (425°F), Gas mark 7.

2 Place the sautéed bacon and blue cheese in a bowl and mix together.

3 Roll the puff pastry out on a floured work surface until it is about 3mm (⅛in) thick and, using an 8cm (3¼in) plain cutter, cut into rounds. Gently bring together the trimmings of the puff pastry, roll out again and cut into additional rounds to produce about 15 in total.

4 Lay the pastry rounds on the work surface and place a teaspoonful of the filling on one half of the disc, leaving a 1cm (½in) border uncovered. Brush the edges with a little beaten egg, then fold one half over the other half to completely cover the filling. Pinch the sides together to seal and brush with more beaten egg. Bake in the oven for 10 minutes or until golden brown and puffed. Allow to cool slightly before eating.

VARIATIONS

Empanadillas with chorizo: Mix together 25g (1oz) chorizo, cut into 5mm–1cm (¼–½in) dice, and 25g (1oz) Gruyère cheese, cut into small dice. Use for filling as above but sprinkle the empanadillas with a little paprika before baking.

Empanadillas with goat's cheese: Mix together 25g (1oz) chopped black or green olives, 50g (2oz) soft goat's cheese and 2 teaspoons of chopped parsley. Use for filling as above.

ANCHOVY, GOAT'S CHEESE AND CHORIZO PUFF PASTRY SQUARES

MAKES 16–20 SQUARES

300g (11oz) good-quality bought or homemade puff pastry (see page 257)
1 egg, lightly beaten
30g tin anchovies (about 10 anchovies)
25g (1oz) soft goat's cheese, such as Ardsallagh, cut into small pieces about 1–2cm (½–¾in)
40g (1½oz) chorizo, very thinly sliced
50g (2oz) Parmesan cheese, finely grated

These are like a little tapa – super-easy to make and ideal as a canapé with drinks. They can also be prepared in advance. There are so many variations you can try: sun-dried tomatoes with basil and grainy mustard, marinated olives with chopped roasted red peppers, or asparagus tips with creamy fontina cheese or Manchego.

1 Preheat the oven to 230°C (450°F), Gas mark 8.
2 Roll the pastry out on a lightly floured work surface into a rectangle approximately 50cm (20in) long and 18cm (7in) wide and brush a little beaten egg all around the edges.
3 On the centre third (the pastry is to be folded in three), arrange the anchovies interspersed with dots of goat's cheese. Fold one of the short ends over to cover the anchovies and goat's cheese, aligning the edges and pinching them together to seal.
4 On top of the folded-over section, arrange the chorizo and the grated Parmesan. Fold over the other short end, aligning and pinching the edges to seal. Brush the top with a little more beaten egg (it can be frozen or chilled at this stage if you wish).
5 Place on a baking tray and bake in the oven for 10 minutes or until golden on top and at the sides.
6 Allow to stand for 2 minutes, then cut into small squares and serve with drinks.

BAKED CHEESE FONDUE IN A SQUASH

SERVES 2 · VEGETARIAN

1kg (2lb 4oz) round squash (approx-imately 20cm/8in in diameter)

100g (3¹/₂oz) Gouda or Gruyère cheese, grated

25g (1oz) Parmesan cheese, finely grated

75ml (2¹/₂fl oz) double cream

1 small clove of garlic, peeled and finely grated or crushed

Pinch of freshly grated nutmeg

1 tbsp kirsch (optional)

Sea salt

Pinch of freshly ground black pepper

2cm (³/₄in) chunks of crusty bread, such as White Yeast Bread (see page 119), to serve

This fondue was inspired by a recipe of Hugh Fearnley-Whittingstall's. It is one of the most delicious and heart-warming dishes I have ever tasted! The recipe can be halved or multiplied accordingly, depending on what size squash or pumpkin you are using.

1 Preheat the oven to 200°C (400°F), Gas mark 6.

2 Cut the top off the squash approximately 2cm (³/₄in) from the top and set aside as this will be the lid. Scoop out and discard the seeds (or lay them out on a baking tray with a drizzle of olive oil and sea salt and toast in the oven until golden – then peel and eat!). Place the grated cheese inside the squash.

3 In a bowl, mix the cream with the garlic, nutmeg, kirsch (if using) and salt and pepper, then pour onto the cheese and mix together. Put the lid on top and place in an ovenproof dish or roasting tray. Bake in the oven for 50 minutes or until the cheese is melted and bubbling and the flesh inside is soft.

4 Serve with chunks of crusty white bread to dip into the rich creamy cheesy mixture and spoons to scoop out the soft flesh.

BAKED POTATO GALETTE WITH SMOKED SALMON, RED ONIONS AND CREME FRAICHE

SERVES 6-8

625g (1lb 6oz) peeled
   potatoes (weight
   when peeled)
Few good pinches
   of salt
4 tbsp olive oil

To serve
About 8–10 long, thin
   slices smoked salmon
1/2 red onion, peeled,
   very thinly sliced and
   washed (see Rachel's
   baking tip, below)
1/2 lemon
Freshly ground black
   pepper
4 tbsp crème fraîche

23cm (9in) diameter
   frying pan

This is a blissfully simple one-dish meal for a summer lunch or winter brunch. It looks beautiful, serves a large number of people and is easy to prepare. It also works well with Parma ham and roasted peppers with pesto drizzled over the top.

1 Preheat the oven to 220°C (425°F), Gas mark 7.

2 Cut each potato into long, thin lengths approximately 5mm (1/4in) or so thick. Do not rinse them.

3 Toss the matchstick potatoes in a bowl with a few good pinches of salt. Heat the frying pan over a high heat and add the olive oil. Once the olive oil is hot, add the potatoes, pressing them down to make sure they are evenly spread out. Reduce the heat to low and cook for approximately 10 minutes or until the base of the galette is golden.

4 Place the pan in the oven and cook for about 15–20 minutes or until the potatoes are cooked, then flip out onto a warmed serving plate (they can be made ahead to this point and reheated in the pan in a moderate oven for 10 minutes before flipping out).

5 Arrange slices of smoked salmon over the top, then scatter with slices of onion, squeeze over some lemon juice and sprinkle with black pepper. Cut into wedges to serve with a little crème fraîche.

RACHEL'S BAKING TIP

Rinsing the red onion under cold water removes the slightly harsh flavour, which occurs especially if it is sliced in advance.

BAKED RED LENTIL DHAL

SERVES 4-6 ✳ VEGETARIAN

3 tbsp sunflower oil
1 onion, peeled and
   finely chopped
3 cloves of garlic,
   peeled and crushed
   or finely grated
2 tsp coriander seeds,
   ground
2 tsp cumin seeds,
   ground
1 tsp black mustard
   seeds
2 tsp grated root ginger
1/2–1 red chilli,
   deseeded and finely
   chopped
Pinch of ground
   cinnamon
4 green cardamom
   pods, seeds extracted
   and crushed
1 tsp turmeric
1 tbsp tomato purée
250g (9oz) red lentils
700ml (1¼ pints) light
   chicken or vegetable
   stock
Salt and freshly ground
   black pepper
2–3 tbsp chopped
   coriander
Squeeze of lemon or
   lime juice (optional)

This version of the classic Indian dhal is baked in the oven to make it rich and aromatic; serve as a main course with a rice dish such as pilaf (see page 197).

1 Preheat the oven to 180° (350°F), Gas mark 4.

2 Heat the sunflower oil in an ovenproof saucepan or casserole over a low–medium heat, add the onion and garlic, cover and cook for 8–10 minutes until soft.

3 Increase the heat to medium–high, add the spices and cook for 1 minute to toast them.

4 Add the tomato purée and red lentils and stir for 1 minute before adding the stock. Bring to the boil, season with salt and pepper, cover and bake in the oven for 8–10 minutes or until the lentils are cooked and have soaked up all the liquid.

5 Add chopped coriander and season to taste, adding a little lemon or lime juice if necessary.

BAKED POTATO, ONION AND ROSEMARY GRATIN

SERVES 8 ✳ VEGETARIAN

50g (2oz) butter
700g (1lb 8oz) peeled
 onions (weight
 when peeled), sliced
1 tsp sea salt
½ tsp freshly ground
 black pepper
900g (2lb) peeled
 potatoes (weight
 when peeled) thinly
 sliced, about 5mm
 (¼in) thick
100g (3½oz) cheese,
 such as Gruyère,
 smoked Gouda,
 Desmond or
 Gabriel, grated
1 tbsp chopped
 rosemary, thyme
 or sage
225ml (8fl oz) single
 cream

Medium gratin dish
 or 23cm (9in)
 diameter cake tin

I love the wintery flavours of this recipe. It can be made in a gratin dish or a round cake tin and then cut into wedges to serve. It is delicious on its own or served with roast lamb.

1 Melt the butter in a wide sauté pan or frying pan set over a medium heat, add the onions and cook, uncovered, for about 30 minutes, stirring every now and then, until they are golden and caramelised.
2 Mix the salt and pepper in a little bowl and sprinkle some over the onions while they are cooking.
3 Meanwhile, preheat the oven to 180°C (350°F), Gas mark 4. Butter the gratin dish or cake tin.
4 Season the sliced potatoes with the remaining salt and pepper and toss well. Lay half the potatoes in the base of the prepared dish or tin, followed by half of the grated cheese, half of the onions and half of the rosemary. Lay the remaining potatoes over the top, followed by the remaining cheese, onions and rosemary.
5 Pour the cream over the top, cover with foil and bake for 1 hour. Remove the foil and bake, uncovered, for a further 15 minutes. Serve immediately.

BAKED AUBERGINES WITH TOMATOES, BASIL AND PINE NUTS

SERVES 4 · VEGETARIAN

2 large aubergines
Salt and freshly ground
    black pepper
4 tbsp olive oil, plus
    extra for drizzling
1 onion, peeled and
    finely sliced
3 cloves of garlic,
    peeled and crushed
    or finely grated
650g (1lb 6oz) good red
    ripe tomatoes, peeled
    and chopped
Pinch of chilli flakes
1 tsp caster sugar
4 tbsp chopped or torn
    basil leaves
1 ball of mozzarella,
    torn into pieces, or
    25g (1oz) grated
    Parmesan (optional)
4 tbsp pine nuts, lightly
    toasted

Best made in the summer with fresh basil and really ripe tomatoes, this is a lovely dish served on its own or as an accompaniment to roast lamb or chicken. Try adding a few chopped anchovies or olives into the sauce.

1 Preheat the oven to 180°C (350°F), Gas mark 4.
2 Slice the aubergines in half lengthways and, using a teaspoon, scoop out the flesh, leaving a 5mm (1/4in) border around the edge intact. Chop the flesh, then place in a sieve sitting over a bowl adding a good pinch of salt to draw out any bitter juices. Place the aubergine halves on an oiled baking tray, drizzle with a little olive oil and cook for 15 minutes.
3 Meanwhile, heat the olive oil in a saucepan, add the onion and garlic, cover and cook over a low heat for 10 minutes, stirring every now and then, until the onion is soft. Add the drained aubergine flesh, the tomatoes, chilli flakes and sugar, and season with salt and pepper. Cook over a low heat for about 20–30 minutes or until the sauce is reduced. Add the chopped basil and season to taste.
4 Spoon the tomato sauce into the par-cooked aubergines, then add the torn mozzarella or grated Parmesan (if using). Bake in the oven for about 30 minutes or until the aubergine is cooked at the sides and the mixture is hot and bubbling. Sprinkle with the toasted pine nuts and serve.

RACHEL'S BAKING TIP

To toast the pine nuts, put them in the oven for just a few minutes or toast in a saucepan over a medium heat, stirring regularly.

BAKED BUTTERNUT SQUASH RISOTTO WITH SAGE AND TOASTED PUMPKIN SEEDS

SERVES 4-6 * VEGETARIAN

3 tbsp olive oil
1 small onion, peeled and chopped
2 cloves of garlic, peeled and finely grated or crushed
375g (13oz) peeled butternut squash (weight when peeled), cut into 5mm–1cm (1/4–1/2in) cubes
325g (11 1/2oz) risotto rice, such as Arborio or Carnaroli
125ml (4fl oz) white wine
900ml (1 1/2 pints) vegetable or chicken stock
Salt and freshly ground black pepper
100g (3 1/2oz) Parmesan cheese, finely grated
1 tsp finely chopped sage

To serve
Some extra shavings of Parmesan cheese
25g (1oz) pumpkin seeds, toasted (in the oven for a few minutes, or in a pan over a medium heat)

This is a wonderfully comforting winter dish. Baking risotto in the oven rather than cooking it on the hob is so much easier, and means you don't have to stand around stirring!

1 Preheat the oven to 180°C (350°F), Gas mark 4.
2 Heat the olive oil in an ovenproof saucepan or deep ovenproof frying pan set over a low–medium heat, add the onion and garlic, cover and cook for 8–10 minutes until soft.
3 Add the cubed butternut squash and the rice and stir for 1 minute before adding the white wine. Allow the wine to bubble, uncovered, for 1–2 minutes until it has evaporated, then add the stock and bring to the boil.
4 Season with salt and pepper, cover and cook in the oven for 12–15 minutes or until the rice is just cooked, with the tiniest bit of bite (it should not soft and mushy), and has absorbed the stock. Add the grated cheese and chopped sage and season to taste.
5 Serve on warmed plates or in warmed bowls sprinkled with shavings of cheese and toasted pumpkin seeds.

SIMPLE SAUSAGE AND BEAN BAKE

SERVES 4–6

3 tbsp olive oil
1 onion, peeled and sliced
3 cloves of garlic, peeled and crushed or finely grated
Salt and freshly ground black pepper
400g tin tomatoes, chopped
410g tin haricot beans, drained
Few pinches of sugar
225g (8oz) sausages (any type works well), cut into 2cm (3/4in) thick slices

Medium ovenproof pie dish

This is the ultimate baked bean recipe – quick and easy for a family supper. The white haricot beans and the sausages look lovely together, too. You can use any kind of sausage you like for a different result each time. Try Toulouse or plain breakfast sausages, Italian garlic and herb, Polish sausages or indeed any variety that takes your fancy. This dish is equally good reheated the next day; in fact it can taste even better!

1 Preheat the oven to 200°C (400°F), Gas mark 6.
2 Heat the olive oil in a saucepan set over a medium heat, add the onion and garlic, season with salt and pepper, cover and cook, stirring every now and then, for 5–8 minutes until the onions are soft.
3 Add the tomatoes and beans and bring to the boil. Season to taste with a few good pinches of sugar and more salt if necessary.
4 Add the sausages to the tomatoes and beans, then tip everything into the pie dish and bake in the oven for 40 minutes or until the sausages are cooked and the mixture is bubbling. Serve with baked potatoes or pasta or lots of crusty white bread.

RACHEL'S BAKING TIP

I sometimes sprinkle 100g (3½oz) of grated Gruyère or Cheddar over the top halfway through cooking.

PORK EN CROUTE WITH SPICED CABBAGE STUFFING

SERVES 4

50g (2oz) butter
200g (7oz) cabbage,
    quartered cored
    and finely shredded
2 tbsp water
Salt and freshly
    ground black pepper
125ml (4fl oz) double
    cream
1 tsp ground cumin
1 tsp ground coriander
1 tsp English mustard
1 large fillet of pork
    (approximately
    600g/1¹/₃lb), trimmed
150g (5oz) good-quality
    bought or homemade
    puff or flaky pastry
    (see pages 257–8)
1 egg, beaten
Apple sauce (see page
    275), to serve

En croûte means 'in a crust'. Wrapping food in pastry is a traditional French method for cooking meat and even certain types of cheese or pâté. For this dish, pork and cabbage take centre stage. The spices in the stuffing really lift the meat.

1 Preheat the oven to 230°C (450°F), Gas mark 8.
2 Melt the butter in a large saucepan, add the cabbage and water, season with salt and pepper and cook for 5–7 minutes.
3 Add the cream, spices and mustard and simmer slowly for a further 10 minutes. Allow to cool.
4 Split the pork steak down one side and open out flat, taking care not to cut the whole way through. Season with salt and pepper. Add the stuffing along the length of the pork and fold the meat over, bringing the sides together and tucking the ends in.
5 Roll out the pastry on a lightly floured work surface and lay the pork on top. Bring up the ends of the pastry and overlap them on top of the meat. Trim to neaten. Turn the parcel over so that the smooth side of the pastry is on top.
6 If you wish to decorate the pastry, re-roll the trimmings, cut out little leaves and stick to the top with some of the beaten egg. Brush the beaten egg over the exposed pastry and bake in the oven for 10 minutes, reducing the oven temperature to 200°C (400°F), Gas mark 6 for the final 30 minutes. Serve with the apple sauce.

RACHEL'S BAKING TIP
The uncooked pork en croûte can stay in the fridge for up to 24 hours or in the freezer for up to 3 months.

BAKED CHICKEN WITH LEMON AND GARLIC AND PILAF RICE

SERVES 4-6

2 tbsp olive oil
1 chicken
(approximately
2.25kg/5lb), cut
into pieces: breasts,
thighs, drumsticks,
etc.
Salt and freshly ground
black pepper
125ml (4fl oz) white
wine
20 garlic cloves,
unpeeled
Finely grated zest
of 2 lemons and the
juice of 1 lemon
1 large sprig of thyme
1 bay leaf
300ml (1/2 pint) chicken
stock

For the pilaf rice
25g (1oz) butter
1 small onion (about
125g/41/2oz), peeled
and chopped
300g (11oz) basmati rice
750ml (11/4 pints)
chicken or vegetable
stock

To serve
1 baguette, cut into 1cm
(1/2in) thick slices
2 tbsp chopped parsley

This classic French recipe is one of my favourite ways of cooking chicken. It calls for a lot of garlic, but once it is cooked it loses it's pungency and turns deliciously sweet, perfectly complementing the fresh citrusy flavours. As for the pilaf, I strongly recommend this oven-baked method of cooking rice; it is practically foolproof and the rice wonderfully moist and tasty.

1 Preheat the oven to 170°C (325°F), Gas mark 3.
2 Heat a large casserole or saucepan over a medium heat. Add the olive oil and chicken pieces, skin side down, and cook on both sides until golden brown. Season with salt and pepper. Pour off and discard any excess fat.
3 Add the wine and garlic cloves and boil for 2 minutes. Next, add the lemon zest and juice, the herbs and the stock. Bring to the boil, cover and bake in the oven for about 30–40 minutes or until the chicken is cooked.
4 While the chicken is cooking, toast the slices of baguette.
5 To cook the rice, melt the butter in a casserole or saucepan that is large enough to accommodate all the rice, add the onion and season. Cover and cook over a low heat for approximately 10 minutes or until the onion is soft. Add the rice and stir for about 2 minutes until it crackles, then add the stock and some salt and pepper. Bring to the boil then transfer to the oven and cook for about 10 minutes or until the rice is just cooked so that it is slightly al dente and all the liquid absorbed. Cover and keep warm until ready to serve.
6 Serve the chicken with the rice in shallow bowls and sprinkled with chopped parsley. Let each person squeeze the soft garlic out of its skin and spread onto slices of toasted baguette, which can mop up the delicious chicken juices.

BAKED MEDITERRANEAN PASTA

SERVES 6

100g (3¹/₂oz) chorizo,
  finely sliced
1–2 tbsp olive oil
500g (1lb 2oz) penne
  pasta
2 x 400g tinned
  tomatoes, chopped
175ml (6fl oz) boiling
  water
175ml (6fl oz) double
  cream
50g (2oz) chopped
  spring onion
2 tbsp chopped basil
50g (2oz) capers
100g (3¹/₂oz) olives,
  pitted and chopped
6 cloves of garlic,
  peeled and chopped
Salt, freshly ground
  black pepper
1 tsp caster sugar
75g (3oz) soft goat's
  cheese, crumbled
150g (5oz) Gruyère
  cheese, grated
75g (3oz) Cheddar
  cheese, grated

30 x 23cm (12 x 9in)
  ovenproof dish

My husband Isaac made this late one night when we were all starving, and it worked so well that we now regularly make variations of it in the evening – perfect for when you are in a rush.

1 Preheat the oven to 200°C (400°F), Gas mark 6.
2 In a frying pan set over a high heat, cook the chorizo with the olive oil for 2 minutes and drain.
3 In a large bowl, mix together the dried pasta with the tomatoes, the boiling water and cream. Add the chorizo and then the spring onion, basil, capers, olives and garlic. Season with salt, pepper and the sugar.
4 Place the mixture in the ovenproof dish and scatter over the three cheeses, making sure the pasta is completely covered, then bake in the oven for 40–50 minutes or until the pasta is cooked and the sauce golden and bubbling. Cover with foil after 30 minutes if it begins to dry out.

PORK, SPINACH AND MUSHROOM LASAGNE

SERVES 6

375g (13oz) no-need-to-soak lasagne sheets
50g (2oz) Parmesan cheese, finely grated

For the ragu
2 tbsp olive oil
1 large onion, peeled and sliced
900g (2lb) minced pork
6 cloves of garlic, peeled and chopped
2 tbsp chopped sage
Good pinch of freshly grated nutmeg
2 x 400g tins tomatoes, chopped
Salt and freshly ground black pepper

For the sauce
110g (4oz) butter
600g (1¹/₃lb) button mushrooms, sliced
200ml (7fl oz) double cream
10 spring onions, trimmed and sliced

1 x quantity béchamel sauce (see page 273)
100g (3¹/₂oz) Cheddar cheese, grated
100g (3¹/₂oz) Gruyère cheese, grated
3 tsp English mustard
200g (7oz) baby spinach leaves, destalked and shredded

20 x 35 cm (8 x 14in) lasagne dish

This delicious wintery lasagne is made with pork and lots of delicious spinach in a cheesy sauce. It's perfect for a casual dinner as it can be prepared in advance.

1 To prepare the ragu, heat the olive oil in a medium-sized saucepan, add the onion and allow to sweat for 10 minutes. Add the minced pork, garlic, sage, nutmeg and tomatoes and season with salt and pepper. Allow to simmer, stirring regularly, for 30–40 minutes.

2 To prepare the mushroom sauce, melt the butter in a frying pan, add the mushrooms, season with salt and pepper and cook over a high heat for 5 minutes. Add the cream and continue to simmer for a further 5–7 minutes. Remove from the heat and add the spring onions.

3 Meanwhile, make the béchamel sauce (see page 273). Remove the sauce from the heat, add the grated cheeses and stir to mix. Add the mustard and spinach and simmer for a further 3–5 minutes or until the spinach has wilted. Set aside.

4 Taste each sauce as they should be well seasoned (remember to reserve enough of each to cover the top layer of the lasagne). Butter the lasagne dish, then spread a little spinach cheese sauce on the base and cover with a layer of barely overlapping sheets of pasta. Spread a layer of the ragu over the pasta layer, then a layer of spinach sauce, then a layer of the mushroom sauce. Continue with another layer of pasta and so on up to within 2.5cm (1in) of the top of the dish. (Don't make more than five layers.) Spread a mix of the three sauces over the final layer of pasta sheets and sprinkle with the grated Parmesan. Wipe the edges clean and bake in the oven for 30–40 minutes or until is golden and bubbling.

5 Allow to cool for 10 minutes before serving.

BAKED CLAMS

SERVES 4

1.35kg (3 lb) clams
(weight in their
shells)
25g (1oz) butter
25g (1oz) plain flour
1 tbsp finely chopped
shallots
1 tbsp finely chopped
parsley
125 ml (4 fl oz) dry
white wine
125ml (4 fl oz) water
225ml (8 fl oz) double
cream
Salt and freshly ground
black pepper
50g (2oz) butter, melted
50g (2oz) Cheddar or
Gruyère cheese,
grated
25g (1oz) white
breadcrumbs

This is the ultimate New England-style summer meal.
It's light and flavoursome, and really should be served
with crusty white bread and a crisp, dry white wine.
For best results, consume outdoors!

1 Wash the clams under cold running water, discarding
any that will not shut when tapped on the work surface
(these may be dead and therefore not good to eat).
2 Place the butter in a medium-sized saucepan and heat
gently until melted. Add the flour to make a roux and cook,
stirring, for 1–2 minutes, so the flour does not burn. Remove
the pan from the heat.
3 Place the clams, shallots, parsley, wine and water in a
wide saucepan and cook over a medium–high heat. The liquid
should boil for 3–5 minutes or until all the clams have opened.
Remove each clam as it opens, transferring to a separate dish.
4 Once the clams are all cooked, pour the remaining liquid
through a muslin-lined (or use kitchen paper) sieve to remove
any grit. Return the drained liquid to the saucepan and bring
to the boil for 2 minutes. Add the cream and allow the mixture
to come back to the boil. Gradually whisk in the roux to the
boiling mixture to thicken it, and taste for seasoning, adding
salt and pepper if necessary.
5 In a bowl, mix the melted butter with the cheese and the
breadcrumbs. Preheat the grill to hot.
6 Arrange the clams in four ovenproof plates and spoon a little
of the sauce over each. Divide the crumb and cheese mixture
in four and sprinkle over each dish. Just before serving, place
under the hot grill for 1–2 minutes or until golden and
crunchy on top.

COTTAGE PIE

1.5kg (3lb 5oz) large
  potatoes for mashing,
  unpeeled
Salt and freshly ground
  black pepper
150ml (1/4 pint) milk
50g (2oz) butter

For the filling
2 tbsp olive oil
1 onion, peeled and
  chopped
4 large cloves of garlic,
  peeled and grated
1kg (2lb 4oz) minced
  beef
3 carrots, peeled and
  diced into 5mm–1cm
  (1/4–1/2in) cubes
1 tbsp Worcestershire
  sauce
2 tbsp soy sauce
2 tbsp tomato purée
2 tbsp chopped parsley
2 tsp tomato chutney
  (I use Ballymaloe
  Country Relish)
1–2 good pinches of
  caster sugar

For the garlic butter
100g (3 1/2oz) butter,
  softened
3–4 cloves of garlic,
  peeled and crushed
  or finely grated
1 tbsp chopped parsley

Medium pie dish
Piping bag and nozzle
  (optional)

This very simple pie is a firm family favourite. The garlic butter is optional but makes a very delicious accompaniment as it melts into the top of the mashed potato.

1 Preheat the oven to 200°C (400°F), Gas mark 6.

2 To make the mash, place the potatoes in a large saucepan of cold water with a good pinch of salt. Bring to the boil and cook for 10 minutes, then pour out all but approximately 4cm (1 1/2in) of the water and continue to cook the potatoes over a very low heat.

3 In a small saucepan, bring the milk up to boiling point and then remove from the heat. Peel the potatoes while they are still hot, holding them in a tea towel so as not to scald your hands. Mash them immediately. Add the butter, but don't add any milk until they are free of lumps. When the potatoes are fully mashed, add the hot milk – you may not need it all, or you may need some more, depending on the texture of the potatoes. Add some salt and pepper to taste.

4 To make the filling, heat the olive oil in a large saucepan, add the onion and garlic and cook, uncovered, over a low heat until soft and a little golden. Increase the heat, add the minced beef and stir until it changes colour, then add the carrots and remaining ingredients. Reduce the heat to low, cover and cook for a further 15 minutes or until the carrots are tender. Season to taste.

5 Meanwhile, make the garlic butter by mixing all the ingredients together in a bowl. Set aside in the fridge.

6 Place the filling in a large pie dish and top it with the mashed potato, either piping it on using a piping bag or spreading it on and scoring it with a fork. Cook in the oven for 30–45 minutes until it is slightly golden on top and hot and bubbling. Serve with slices of garlic butter melting on top.

PIZZAS

MAKES ABOUT 6 PIZZAS ⁜ VEGETARIAN

For the roasted tomato sauce
450g (1lb) tomatoes, halved
3 cloves of garlic, peeled and kept whole
5 tbsp olive oil
3 tbsp balsamic vinegar
Salt, freshly ground black pepper and 1 tsp caster sugar

For the pizza dough
350g (12oz) strong white flour, sifted
1 level tsp salt
2 tsp caster sugar
50g (2oz) butter
1 x 7g sachet fast-acting yeast
2 tbsp olive oil, plus extra for brushing
175–200ml (6–7fl oz) warm water

My husband Isaac makes great pizzas and the recipes here are all his. He normally uses fast-acting yeast for his pizza dough, but you can of course use fresh or plain dried yeast instead, mixing it with the water and sugar first, as with White Yeast Bread (see page 119). The beauty of pizzas is that one can be as simple or as inventive as one likes with the toppings. I've listed a few of my favourites below. If you have any tomato sauce left over, freeze it.

1 Preheat the oven to 220°C (425°F), Gas mark 7.
2 To make the roasted tomato sauce, lay the halved tomatoes on a baking tray in a single layer, cut side up. Add the whole cloves of garlic randomly on the tray, drizzle with the oil and vinegar and season with salt, pepper and sugar to taste. Cook in the preheated oven for about 20 minutes until very soft and blistered in appearance.
3 Liquidise in a liquidiser or food processor and push through a sieve. Season again to taste. The sauce needs to be thick enough to coat the back of a spoon: if it needs thickening, place in a saucepan, bring to the boil and reduce to thicken, which could take up to 10 minutes.
4 To make the pizza dough, place the flour, salt and sugar in a large bowl and mix. Rub in the butter, add the yeast and mix together. Make a well in the centre of the dry ingredients, add the oil and most, but not all, of the warm water and mix to a loose dough. Add more water or flour, if needed.
5 Take the dough out of the bowl and place on a lightly floured work surface, covered with a clean tea towel, for 5 minutes. Then knead the dough for 10 minutes or until smooth and slightly springy to the touch. Alternatively, knead the dough for 5 minutes in an electric food mixer using the dough hook. Let the dough relax for another 5 minutes. ***Continued overleaf***

6 Divide into 6 balls of dough, each weighing 100–125g (3^1/$_2$–4^1/$_2$oz), and lightly brush with olive oil. If you have time, cover the oiled dough with cling film and place in the fridge for 30 minutes to make it easier to handle.

7 Turn the oven up to 240°C (475°F), Gas mark 9. Place an upside-down baking tray in the centre of the oven, allowing at least 15 minutes to heat up fully.

8 Lightly dust the dough balls and work surface with flour, then roll out each ball into a disc roughly 30cm (12in) in diameter.

9 Place a pizza base on a cool, floured baking tray (upside down if your baking tray has an edge) and spread with 4 tablespoons of the roasted tomato sauce, leaving a 2.5cm (1in) border around the edge. Add your chosen topping (see below).

10 Slide the pizza off the cool tray onto the hot tray in the oven and cook for 5–10 minutes, depending on the heat of the oven and the thickness of the pizza, until the pizza is golden underneath and bubbling on top. I find it better to cook just one or two pizzas at a time. Serve immediately.

TOPPINGS

Take 100–125g (3^1/$_2$–4^1/$_2$oz) pizza dough, rolled into a 30cm (12in) disc and spread with the roasted tomato sauce as above, and add one of the following toppings (in each case enough for 1 pizza), then cook as above.

Pizza with Gruyère, thyme, roasted red onions, spicy sausage and goat's cheese: Sprinkle over 125g (4^1/$_2$oz) grated Gruyère cheese and 1 dessertspoon chopped thyme. Top with 6 onion wedges (which have been drizzled with olive oil, seasoned with salt, pepper and a sprinkling of caster sugar and roasted in a hot oven for 15–20 minutes) and 5 slices of spicy sausage such as Italian or Spanish chorizo. Dot with 3 teaspoons of goat's cheese (such as Ardsallagh) and cook as above.

Basic pizza margarita: Sprinkle over 125g (4^1/$_2$oz) grated Gruyère cheese and cook as above.

Pizza with smoked salmon, cream cheese, capers and chives: Sprinkle over 75g (3oz) grated mozzarella and 50g (2oz) grated Gruyère cheese. Arrange 3 thick slices good-quality smoked salmon on top and cook as above. When the pizza is cooked, sprinkle with 10 capers and 1 tablespoon of chopped chives and drizzle with 3 teaspoons of cream cheese.

RACHEL'S BAKING TIPS

✵ I place my baking tray in upside-down because of the lip. It is easier to slide a pizza on and off a hot tray with no edge. If you have a pizza stone, then this will work even better than the hot upside-down tray. Just place in the hot oven and allow to get really good and hot before cooking pizzas (about 15 minutes before the pizzas go in).

✵ Use semolina or fine polenta flour to dust your work surface before rolling out the pizzas, and for dusting the cool baking tray before transferring the pizzas to the oven, so that the pizzas stick less.

✵ In the winter, cherry tomatoes generally have a better flavour than the larger fruit, so opt for these when making the roasted tomato sauce. The sauce will freeze, or keep in the fridge for four or five days.

YORKSHIRE PUDDING

MAKES 12 · VEGETARIAN

100g (3¹/₂) plain flour
Salt and freshly ground
   black pepper
2 eggs
275ml (9fl oz) milk
15g (¹/₂oz) butter,
   melted and cooled
1 tbsp beef dripping,
   melted, or olive oil

12-hole bun or muffin
   tin or 20 x 30cm (8 x
   10in) roasting tray

A classic served with roast meat and lots of gravy, these can be made in individual portions or made in a roasting tin in one big portion. They are great just as they are, but 1 tablespoon of Dijon mustard added to the batter makes a delicious variation. For light-as-air puddings, place the batter in the fridge for 30–60 minutes before cooking them. (The batter can sit happily in the fridge for up to 24 hours.)

1 Sift the flour into a large bowl, season and make a well in the centre of the flour and add the eggs. Using a whisk, gradually bring in the flour from the sides of the bowl, adding the milk in a steady stream at the same time. When all the flour has been mixed in, whisk in the butter.

2 Preheat the oven to 220°C (425°F), Gas mark 7. Place the bun or muffin tin (or roasting tray, if using) to warm in the preheated oven for 5 minutes, then take it out and pour the beef dripping or olive oil into the holes of the tin. Return to the oven for 1 minute until it is all very hot.

3 Carefully remove the tin from the hot oven and, as quickly as possible, pour the batter into the holes of the tin, filling each one about three-quarters full. Bake in the oven for 15–20 minutes or until puffed up and golden. Remove from the oven, take the individual puddings out of the tin and serve immediately.

VARIATIONS

Popovers: Cook as for Yorkshire puddings (the recipe makes 12 popovers), but use melted butter to grease the tins, instead of the oil or dripping. When cooked, remove from the tins, cool and fill with a blob of marmalade or jam and whipped cream. Dust with icing sugar and serve immediately.

HOLIDAY AND CELEBRATION

EASTER CHOCOLATE TART

SERVES 12

1 x quantity sweet
  shortcrust pastry
  (see page 254)
175ml (6fl oz) double
  cream
125ml (4fl oz) milk
125g (4½oz) milk
  chocolate, chopped
175g (6oz) good-quality
  dark chocolate,
  chopped
2 eggs, well beaten
250g (9oz) sugar-coated
  chocolate eggs,
  to decorate

23cm (9in) diameter
  tart tin

This divine tart is a 'must have' for any self-respecting chocoholic. It looks adorable decorated with little eggs on top.

1 Make the pastry as described on page 254, leaving to chill for 30 minutes before using.

2 Preheat the oven to 180°C (350°F), Gas mark 4. Line the tart tin and bake 'blind' (see page 255).

3 Heat the cream and milk in a saucepan to boiling point, then immediately take off the heat and stir in the chocolate to melt. Allow to cool slightly for a few minutes, then stir in the beaten eggs.

4 Pour the chocolate mixture into the baked pastry case and bake in the oven for 15–20 minutes or until just softly set.

5 Allow the tart to cool for 20 minutes before removing it from the tin. Decorate with the sugar-coated chocolate eggs.

RACHEL'S BAKING TIP

Instead of the chocolate eggs, add a handful of toasted hazelnuts to the chocolate mixture and bake as step 4.

HOT CROSS BUNS

MAKES 20 BUNS

100g (3¹/2) caster sugar
225–300ml (8–10fl oz)
  warm milk
15g (¹/2oz) dried yeast
  or 25g (1oz) fresh
  yeast or 2 x 7g sachets
  fast-acting yeast
450g (1lb) strong
  white flour
75g (3oz) chilled
  butter, cubed
¹/2 tsp cinnamon
¹/4 tsp freshly grated
  nutmeg
2 tsp mixed spice
Pinch of salt
2 eggs, beaten
75g (3oz) currants
50g (2oz) sultanas
25g (1oz) chopped
  mixed peel

For the egg wash
2 tbsp milk, 1 tsp
  caster sugar and
  1 egg yolk mixed
  together, to glaze

For the shortcrust
pastry cross
110g (4oz) shortcrust
  pastry (see page 254),
  rolled out about 3mm
  (¹/8in) thick and cut
  into strips about 5mm
  (¹/4in) wide

Homemade hot cross buns are a special Easter treat, but are really wonderful at any time of year. They go down extremely well (in all senses!) at the cookery school. Eat fresh from the oven, split in half and spread with butter, or toasted and buttered a day or so later. They will also freeze very well.

1 In a measuring jug, mix 1 tablespoon of the sugar with 60ml (2fl oz) of the warm milk and the yeast and let stand in a warm place for 5 minutes until frothy. If using fast-acting yeast, there is no need to let the mixture stand.

2 Sift the flour into a large bowl and rub in the butter. Add the cinnamon, nutmeg, mixed spice, salt and the remainder of the sugar, and mix well together. Add the beaten eggs to the remaining milk, pour in the yeast mixture and mix together. Make a well in the centre of the dry ingredients, add most of the egg and milk and mix to a soft dough, adding more egg and milk if necessary.

3 Knead for 1 minute until smooth. Add the currants, sultanas and mixed peel and continue to knead until the dough is shiny. Alternatively, knead in an electric food mixer using the dough hook.

4 Cover the bowl with cling film and leave in a warm place for 1¹/2–2 hours until it doubles in size. Knock back by kneading for 2 minutes, then leave in the bowl (or covered with a clean tea towel on the work surface) to rest for 5 minutes.

5 Pinch off sections of dough approximately 40g (1¹/2oz) in weight and shape into buns. Place on an oiled baking tray, gently brush with egg wash and, with a sharp knife, mark the top of each bun with a cross. Place a cross of shortcrust pastry onto each bun, tucking the pastry loosely underneath.

6 Allow to rise for 30–45 minutes to double in size and egg wash again carefully.

7 Preheat the oven to 220°C (425°F), Gas mark 7. Bake the buns in the oven for 5 minutes, then reduce the heat to 200°C (400°F), Gas mark 6 and bake for a further 10 minutes or until golden. Remove from the oven and place on a wire rack to cool.

VALENTINE'S DAY HONEY BUNS
MAKES 12 BUNS

75g (3oz) butter
125g (4¹/₂oz) honey
200g (7oz) plain flour
1 tsp baking powder
25g (1oz) caster sugar
Pinch of salt
75ml (2¹/₂fl oz) milk
2 eggs

For the topping
75g (3oz) icing sugar
1 tbsp runny honey
¹/₂ tbsp boiling water

12-hole bun tray or muffin tin and 12 paper cases

Make these little cupcakes on Valentine's Day for your own 'honey bun'. Guaranteed to win you a kiss.

1 Preheat the oven to 180°C (350°F), Gas mark 4. Line the bun tray or muffin tin with the paper cases.
2 Melt the butter and honey together in a saucepan, then set aside to cool slightly.
3 Sift the flour and baking powder into a large bowl, then add the caster sugar and salt.
4 Whisk the eggs in another bowl, add the milk and the melted butter and honey and pour this mixture into the dry ingredients. Stir together until a soft dough forms, then divide among the 12 paper cases (they can be filled almost to the top of the paper cases). Bake in the oven for 15 minutes or until golden and well risen. Allow to cool.
5 Next, make the topping. Sift the icing sugar in a bowl. In a separate bowl, mix the honey and boiling water together, then pour into the sifted icing sugar. Stir to mix, adding a little more water if it is not a spreadable consistency.
6 Once the buns have cooled, use a table knife to spread the icing over the top of them.

FLORENCE'S ORANGE CAKE

SERVES 8–10

225g (8oz) butter,
    softened
225g (8oz) caster sugar
Finely grated zest
    of 1 orange
4 eggs
225g (8oz) plain flour
1 tsp baking powder
Freshly squeezed juice
    of 2 oranges (for use
    in the cake, filling
    and icing)

For the orange filling
125g (4¹/₂oz) butter,
    softened
225g (8oz) icing
    sugar, sifted
Finely grated zest
    of 1 orange

For the orange
glacé icing
300g (11oz) icing
    sugar, sifted
Crystallised flowers
    (optional; to make
    your own, see page
    271), to decorate

Two 20cm (8in)
    diameter sandwich
    tins or 28cm (11in)
    diameter spring-
    form/loose-bottomed
    tin

Florence is my mother-in-law Darina's aunt, and this cake is legendary at Ballymaloe. It keeps very well for a couple of weeks.

1 Preheat the oven to 180°C (350°F), Gas mark 4. Brush the sides of the sandwich tins (or cake tin) with melted butter and dust with flour. Line the base of each with greaseproof or parchment paper.

2 Cream the butter in a large bowl or in an electric food mixer until soft. Gradually add the sugar and orange zest and continue to beat until the mixture is light and fluffy. Add the eggs one at a time, beating well between each addition. Sift the flour and baking powder into the mixture and stir in gently, then stir in 1 tablespoon of the orange juice.

3 Divide the mixture evenly between the two tins (or pour into the single tin), making a slight hollow in the centre of each cake so that it will rise evenly without forming a peak. Bake in the oven for 25–30 minutes or until a skewer comes out clean when inserted into the centre of the cakes. Allow to sit for 5 minutes then turn out onto a wire rack and allow to cool.

4 Meanwhile, make the orange filling. Cream the butter until very soft, then add the icing sugar and orange zest. Gradually beat in 1 tablespoon of the orange juice to create a smooth, soft mixture.

5 To make the glacé icing, add enough orange juice to the icing sugar for a spreadable icing. (If it is too soft, it will run off the cake, but if it is too stiff, it will be difficult to spread.)

6 When the cakes are cool, carefully slice each in half horizontally (or the single cake into two or three, depending on its thickness), spread with a little of the orange filling and sandwich the pieces together. Spread icing over the top and sides and decorate with the crystallised flowers (if using).

VANILLEKIPFERL

MAKES ABOUT 60 BISCUITS

350g (12oz) plain
  flour, sifted
2 tsp baking powder
250g (9oz) butter,
  softened
2 tsp vanilla extract
1 egg, beaten
100g (3½oz) caster
  sugar
50g (2oz) ground
  hazelnuts
Pinch of salt
100g (3½oz) icing
  sugar

These extremely pretty little biscuits make an impressive Valentine's Day treat. Vanillekipferl translates as 'vanilla mountain tops' because of all the delicate icing sugar snow. In addition, the word 'kipferl' relates to the German word '*kipfel*', or 'crescent', because the biscuits are traditionally crescent-shaped.

1 Preheat the oven to 180°C (350°F), Gas mark 4.
2 Mix the flour, baking powder, butter, vanilla extract, egg, caster sugar, ground hazelnuts and salt together in a large bowl or an electric food mixer, until a dough forms.
3 Flatten into a round 2cm (³/₄in) thick with the palm of your hand, cover with cling film and chill in the fridge for 30 minutes.
4 Using your hands, roll the dough into walnut-sized balls, then flatten them slightly. They do not spread very much so can be placed close to each other on two or more baking trays.
5 Bake in the oven for approximately 10–15 minutes until pale golden (they will be overcooked if too golden) and begin to feel slightly firm. Allow to stand on the baking trays for a few minutes to cool.
6 Sift the icing sugar into a wide shallow bowl. Once the biscuits have almost cooled (they should not cool completely) and firmed up, toss them in the sugar, coating completely.

DARINA'S SIMNEL CAKE

SERVES 16–20

110g (4oz) cherries,
stoned and cut into
two or four,
depending on size
350g (12oz) sultanas
350g (12oz) currants
350g (12oz) raisins
110g (4oz) homemade
candied peel (see
page 272), chopped
50g (2oz) nibbed
(chopped) almonds
50g (2oz) ground
almonds
Finely grated zest
of 1 lemon
Finely grated zest
of 1 orange
60ml (2fl oz) Irish
whiskey

For the almond paste
680g (1½lb) caster
sugar
680g (1½lb) ground
almonds
2 egg yolks, beaten
50ml (1¾fl oz) Irish
whiskey
A few drops of almond
essence
Icing sugar, for
dusting

For the cake
225g (8oz) butter,
softened
225g (8oz) soft light
brown sugar
6 eggs, beaten
275g (10oz) plain flour
1 tsp mixed spice

This is my mother-in-law Darina's recipe for simnel cake, which we make at the cookery school. Traditionally eaten at Easter, it is similar to Christmas Cake (see page 236–7) in that it contains lots of dried fruit and has a thick layer of almond icing covering the top and sides. Unlike Christmas cake, it also has a layer of delicious almond paste baked into the centre. The 11 balls on top of the cake represent 11 of the 12 Apostles – Judas is missing because he betrayed Jesus.

1 Line the base and sides of the cake tin with greaseproof paper and wrap a collar of brown paper around the outside, which will help prevent the cake from drying out (see page 264).

2 Add the cherries to a large bowl and mix in the dried fruit, chopped almonds, ground almonds and grated lemon and orange zest. Add about half of the whiskey and leave for 1 hour to macerate.

3 To make the almond paste, place the caster sugar in another bowl and mix with the almonds. In a separate bowl, mix the beaten egg yolks, whiskey and almond essence, then add to the sugar and almonds and mix to a stiff paste, adding more egg if necessary. Sprinkle the work surface with icing sugar, turn out the almond paste and gently knead until smooth.

4 Preheat the oven to 180ºC (350ºF), Gas mark 4.

5 To make the cake, cream the butter in a large bowl or in an electric food mixer until soft. Add the sugar and beat the mixture until it is light and fluffy. Gradually pour in the beaten eggs, beating well between each addition so that the mixture doesn't curdle. Sift in the flour with the mixed spice and stir in gently. Add the grated apple to the dried fruit and stir, gently but thoroughly, into the mixture, being careful not to beat the mixture again or the cake will be heavy.

1 large or 2 small
   cooking apples, such
   as Bramley, grated
   as far as the core
1 egg, for glazing

23cm (9in) diameter,
   8cm (3¼in) deep
   cake tin, or 20 x 20cm
   (8 x 8in) square
   cake tin

6 Pour half of the cake mixture into the prepared tin. Roll about one-third of the almond paste into a 22cm (8½in) round or square, depending on the shape of the cake tin. Place this on top of the cake mixture in the tin and cover with the remaining mixture. Make a slight hollow in the centre, dip one hand in a bowl of water and pat it over the surface of the cake to ensure that the top is smooth when cooked. Cover the top with a single sheet of brown paper cut to size.

7 Cook for 1 hour in the oven. Reduce the heat to 170°C (325°F), Gas mark 3 and bake for another 2–2½ hours or until a skewer inserted into the centre comes out clean. Pour the rest of the whiskey over the cake and leave to cool in the tin.

8 The following day, carefully remove the cake from the tin. Do not remove the lining paper but wrap in some extra greaseproof paper and foil until required.

9 When you wish to ice the cake, roll some of the remaining almond paste into a 23cm (9in) round or square, approximately 8mm–1cm (³⁄₈–½in) thick. Roll 11 little balls, each the size of a walnut in its shell, and set aside. Meanwhile, preheat the oven to 220°C (425°F), Gas mark 7.

10 Separate the egg into two bowls. Mix 1 teaspoon of water with the yolk and lightly beat the egg white.

11 Brush the cake all over with the egg white and top with the round/square of almond paste, then roll the remaining almond paste to cover the sides as neatly and as evenly as possible. Press down the top and the sides with your hands to bind them together, and neaten with a sharp knife. Lightly score the top of the cake into 4cm (1½ in) squares or diamonds. Brush with the egg yolk, stick the 'Apostles' around the outer edge of the top and carefully brush with more beaten egg yolk.

12 Place on a lower shelf of the oven and toast for 15–20 minutes or until slightly golden, taking care as it can burn if it is too close to the top of the oven. Carefully remove from the baking tray and allow to cool on a wire rack. Cut while warm or store for several weeks when cold.

PINK MERINGUES WITH RASPBERRY CREAM OR BLUE MERINGUES WITH BLUEBERRY CREAM

MAKES 8 LARGE OR 16 SMALL HALF MERINGUES (4 GENEROUS PAIRS, 8 SMALLER PAIRS)

4 egg whites
Pinch of salt
300g (11oz) caster sugar
1/2 tsp vanilla extract
Pink or blue food
    colouring

For the raspberry cream
75g (3oz) fresh or
    frozen raspberries
2 tbsp icing sugar
Squeeze of lemon juice
400ml (14fl oz) stiffly
    whipped cream,
    (measured when
    whipped)

For the blueberry cream
75g (3oz) fresh or
    frozen blueberries
2 tbsp icing sugar
400ml (14fl oz) stiffly
    whipped cream,
    (measured when
    whipped)

Piping bag and
    1.5cm (5/8in) nozzle
    (optional)

These pretty meringues make a memorable christening gift, particularly when presented in a pretty basket. They're also perfect for children's birthday parties. For a girl use pink food colouring and raspberry cream; for a boy, use blue colouring and blueberries.

1 Preheat the oven to 140°C (275°F), Gas mark 1. Line two baking trays with parchment paper.
2 Place the egg whites and a pinch of salt into a large spotlessly clean bowl and whisk until soft peaks form. Gradually add the caster sugar one tablespoon at a time, whisking between each addition, until it has all been added and the meringue is satiny and forms stiff peaks when the whisk is lifted from the mixture.
3 Using a large metal spoon, fold in the vanilla extract. Using a piping bag fitted with a 1.5cm (5/8in) nozzle or a spoon, pipe or scoop the mixture into individual meringues approximately 7cm (2 3/4in) wide onto the prepared baking trays.
4 To achieve the ripple colour effect, dip a wooden or metal skewer into your chosen food colouring and swirl it through each meringue.
5 Bake in the oven for 30 minutes. Test one by lifting and gently pressing on the base of a meringue – it should be crisp but give way with a bit of pressure – they will crisp more when cooling. Turn off the oven, and allow to cool in the oven with the oven door slightly ajar for best results. If possible, allow them to cool completely in the oven.
6 When ready to serve, make the cream. Place the raspberries

or blueberries and sugar in a food processor and whiz until smooth. Push the mixture through a sieve into a bowl to remove the pips. Fold as much purée as you wish through the whipped cream, leaving it rippled if you like. Place a generous tablespoon of the raspberry or blueberry cream on one half of the meringue and sandwich together with another meringue. Serve any remaining purée on the side.

RACHEL'S BAKING TIP

The meringues will keep for two or three days in an airtight container unfilled, but need to be eaten within half an hour once they have been filled.

PARTY DOUGHNUTS
MAKES ABOUT 24 DOUGHNUTS

450g (1lb) strong
  white flour
3/4 tsp salt
40g (1¹/₂oz) chilled
  butter, cubed
225ml (8fl oz) milk
75g (3oz) caster sugar
1¹/₂ tsp dried yeast
  or 15g (¹/₂oz) fresh
  yeast or 1 x 7g sachet
  fast-acting yeast
2 egg yolks
Vegetable oil, for frying
225g (8oz) caster sugar
  mixed with 2 tsp
  ground cinnamon,
  to serve

A guaranteed hit with kids and very simple to make. The doughnuts can be prepared in advance and stored in the fridge right up to the point when they need to be cooked – ideal for a children's birthday party! I cook these in a wide pan on the hob.

1 Sift the flour and salt into a large bowl. Add the butter and, using your fingertips, rub it in until the mixture resembles breadcrumbs.
2 Heat the milk until warm in a saucepan, then stir in the sugar and yeast. Remove from the heat and allow to stand for 5 minutes until the yeast goes frothy. If using fast-acting yeast, there is no need to let the mixture stand. Using a whisk, mix in the egg yolks.
3 Pour most of this liquid into the flour and mix to a soft but not wet dough (you may need all the liquid). Knead the dough (by hand or in an electric food mixer using the dough hook)

for approximately 5 minutes or until the mixture is smooth and slightly springy. Place the dough in an oiled bowl and coat it in the oil. Cover with oiled cling film or a clean tea towel and leave in a warm place for about 1 hour or until it has doubled in size.

4 Knock back the risen dough and knead for 2–3 minutes. Roll out on a floured work surface to 1cm (1/2in) thick then, using a 5cm (2in) plain cutter, cut out about 24 rounds. Into the centre of each round insert your forefinger to go all the way down through the dough. With your forefinger, lift up the doughnut and swing it around in the air! This will make the hole in the doughnut wider.

5 Place the doughnuts on an oiled baking tray and tidy up into a round, cover again with oiled cling film or a tea towel and leave in a warm place for approximately 30–45 minutes until nearly doubled in size.

6 Meanwhile, heat the oil in a deep fryer to a temperature of 180–190°C (350–375°F) (I normally use a wide saucepan filled with about 5–6cm/2–21/2in of oil), or until a breadcrumb dropped into the oil sizzles. Carefully place the doughnuts in the oil with a slotted spoon and cook for 2–3 minutes on each side until golden brown. Remove from the oil with the slotted spoon and toss immediately in the sugar or cinnamon sugar and serve.

RICH HAZELNUT BROWNIES WITH VANILLA ICE CREAM AND SHERRY

MAKES 16 BROWNIES

175g (6oz) very dark, good-quality chocolate (70–80% cocoa solids)
175g (6oz) butter, cubed
25g (1oz) good-quality cocoa powder, sifted
3 eggs
225g (8oz) caster or soft light brown sugar
1 tsp vanilla extract
100g (3½oz) plain flour
75g (3oz) hazelnuts, toasted, skinned and roughly chopped
Icing sugar and cocoa powder, for dusting (optional)
Pedro Ximenez sherry (or similar), for serving

20 x 20cm (8 x 8in) square cake tin

What mother wouldn't love these amazing, sticky brownies served with ice cream soaked in indulgent Pedro Ximenez sherry on Mothering Sunday? Pedro Ximenez is a thick, dark and sticky variety of sherry made from pressed raisins and I use it here because of its toffee-like flavour, but you could also use a Moscatel in its place. The toffee sauce (see page 274) would also be a perfect accompaniment.

1 Preheat the oven to 180°C (350°F), Gas mark 4. Line the base and sides of the tin with parchment paper.
2 Melt the chocolate, butter and cocoa powder together in a heatproof bowl set over a saucepan of simmering water. Do not let the base of the bowl touch the water. Remove from the heat.
3 In a separate large bowl, whisk the eggs, sugar and vanilla extract for 2 minutes. Continuing to whisk, add the chocolate mixture until well combined. Sift in the flour and fold through with the hazelnuts with a spatula or metal spoon.
4 Spoon the mixture into the prepared tin and bake in the oven for 19–25 minutes. When cooked it should be dry on top but still slightly 'gooey' and 'fudgy' inside. Don't be tempted to leave it in the oven any longer than this or you will have cake and not brownies. Allow to cool in the tin, then cut into squares.
5 Serve the brownies stacked up on their own or in individual bowls with a scoop of vanilla ice cream and a shot of sherry poured over the ice cream for the grown-ups! You could dust with half icing sugar and half cocoa powder for a final touch.

LIME YOGHURT CAKE WITH ROSEWATER AND PISTACHIOS

SERVES 8

225g (8oz) self-raising
    flour
1 tsp baking powder
Pinch of salt
75g (3oz) ground
    almonds
100g (3½oz) caster
    sugar
2 medium eggs
1 generous tbsp or 50g
    (2oz) runny honey
250ml (9fl oz) natural
    yoghurt, unsweetened
150ml (¼ pint)
    sunflower oil
Finely grated zest
    of 1 lime

For the syrup
150ml (¼ pint) water
100g (3½ oz) caster
    sugar
Juice of 1 lime
1–2 tbsp rosewater

For decorating
Rose petals (optional)
50g (2oz) unsalted
    pistachios, roughly
    chopped (optional)

22cm (8½in) diameter
    spring-form/loose-
    bottomed tin

This extraordinary cake can be scattered with rose petals to make it even more special. It's extremely feminine and is therefore perfect for Mothering Sunday or for sharing with girlfriends for a birthday or hen night. It's very moist so keeps extremely well in the fridge for a few days.

1 Preheat the oven to 180°C (350°F), Gas mark 4. Line the base and sides of the cake tin with greaseproof paper.
2 Sift the flour, baking powder and salt into a large bowl. Add the ground almonds and caster sugar and mix.
3 Mix the eggs, honey, yoghurt, sunflower oil and lime zest together well in a medium-sized bowl. Make a well in the centre of the dry ingredients and slowly pour in the wet ingredients, bringing them together with a whisk until they are just combined. (Add some chopped pistachios to the mixture if you wish, or retain for decorating.) Pour this mixture into the prepared tin and bake in the oven for 50 minutes or until a skewer inserted into the middle comes out clean. Allow to cool in the tin for about 20 minutes.
4 While the cake is cooling, make the syrup. In a small saucepan, boil the water and sugar for about 5 minutes until it is reduced by half. Add the lime juice and boil for a further 2 minutes, then cool and add the rosewater according to your taste.
5 With a fine skewer, make holes on top of the warm cake and, with a tablespoon, spoon the syrup all over the top. Scatter the pistachios over, if you wish, and leave to settle for 1 hour. Decorate with rose petals, if using. Serve with cream, natural yoghurt, sliced mangos or berries.

WHITE-FROSTED COCONUT CELEBRATION CAKE

SERVES 8–10

175g (6oz) butter,
   softened or at room
   temperature
350g (12oz) caster sugar
6 eggs, separated
1 tsp vanilla extract
250g (9oz) plain flour
50g (2oz) cornflour
2 level tsp baking
   powder
1/2 tsp bicarbonate
   of soda
50g (2oz) desiccated
   coconut, plus extra
   for sprinkling
320ml (10 1/2fl oz)
   buttermilk
100ml (3 1/2fl oz) canned
   coconut milk (you can
   buy 160ml tin now)
Pinch of salt
1/2 tsp cream of tartar
1 x quantity coconut
   butter icing for the
   filling (see page 267)

For the white frosting
2 large egg whites
200g (7oz) caster sugar
100g (3 1/2oz) golden
   syrup
Pinch of salt
1/4 tsp cream of tartar
1 tsp vanilla extract

Two 23cm (9in)
   spring-form/loose-
   bottomed tins

This is a special cake and requires more work than others, so set the time aside because it's well worth the effort. It is a delicious light and crumbly recipe, which came from my friend Dervilla when another friend wanted a coconut cake for her wedding. The frosting is a variation of the classic American recipe and the golden syrup gives it a beautiful ivory colour. Scattering coconut over the top adds a delicately pretty touch.

1 Preheat the oven to 160°C (325°F), Gas mark 3. Lightly butter and flour the cake tins and line the bases with parchment paper.

2 Cream the butter in a large bowl or in an electric food mixer until soft. Add 300g (11oz) caster sugar and beat until the mixture is light and fluffy.

3 Beat the egg yolks into the butter and sugar mixture, one by one, beating well between each addition. Add the vanilla extract and beat again.

4 Sift the flour, cornflour, baking powder and bicarbonate of soda into a bowl. Stir in the desiccated coconut. Measure the buttermilk and coconut milk into a measuring jug and whisk together. Slowly add the flour mix and the buttermilk mix to the butter mixture, alternating between each one (beginning and ending with the flour) and beating between each addition.

5 Place the egg whites in a large, spotlessly clean bowl, add the salt and whisk until foamy. Add the cream of tartar and whisk until soft peaks form. Add the remaining 50g (2oz) caster sugar and whisk again until stiff peaks form. Gradually fold this into the cake batter with a large metal spoon until all the egg white is just mixed through. Do not

overmix or it will deflate the cake.

6 Pour the mixture into the prepared cake tins and smooth the tops. Bake for 35–40 minutes or until a skewer inserted into the middle comes out clean.

7 Allow the cakes to cool for 15 minutes in the tins, then, if you can, cool them right side up by inverting them onto a flat plate and sliding them back onto the wire rack to cool.

8 Make the coconut butter icing for the filling as described on page 267.

9 To make the frosting, place the egg whites, sugar, golden syrup, salt and cream of tartar in a stainless steel or heatproof bowl set over a saucepan of simmering water. The base of the bowl should not touch the water. Bring the water to a steady simmer. With a hand mixer or a balloon whisk (to build up your muscles!), whisk the mixture until you have shiny, satiny soft peaks. Remove the bowl from the simmering water and continue to whisk for a further 2 minutes – it will get a bit stiffer. Whisk in the vanilla extract.

10 Immediately ice the middle, top and sides of the cake with a palette knife, fluffing the frosting up to form little peaks all over the cake. You need to work fast to ice the cake, as the icing sets very quickly. Sprinkle some desiccated coconut over the top, leaving the sides free of coconut to show off your ivory-coloured frosting. Well done – it's finished!

VARIATION

Lemon curd filling: Instead of using the coconut butter icing as the filling, use lemon curd (or make your own – see page 278) instead, which is equally delicious.

CROQUE EN BOUCHE

MAKES 40 PROFITEROLES

1 x quantity choux
   pastry (see page 256)
1 egg, beaten
1 x quantity crème
   patissière (see
   page 270)
Pale pink and blue
   sugared almonds,
   crystallised flowers
   or rose petals (see
   page 271), optional

For the crème chantilly
1 tbsp icing sugar,
   sifted
1/2 tsp vanilla extract
200ml (7fl oz) whipped
   cream (measure
   when whipped)

For the caramel
375g (13oz) caster
   sugar
Pinch of cream
   of tartar
150ml (1/4 pint) water

Two piping bags
Plain 5–8mm (1/4–3/8in)
   nozzle
Plain 3mm (1/8in)
   nozzle (optional)

Croque en bouche – translated as 'crunch in the mouth' –
is a spectacular French wedding cake made from profiteroles
dipped in caramel and then arranged in a pyramid. Though
I use golden unrefined sugar for nearly everything else,
I recommend white caster sugar for making caramel as it is
far easier to tell when it is changing colour and caramelising.
A croque en bouche can be quite small, for just a few people,
or it can be six feet high! It only keeps for an hour or two
before serving, so plenty of extra hands would be needed
for making a huge one. Of course, you can also serve them
as profiteroles, using chocolate sauce instead of caramel
(see the variation on page 230).

1 Preheat the oven to 220°C (425°F), Gas mark 7.
2 Make the choux pastry as described on page 256. Line
a baking tray with parchment paper. Put the choux pastry
into the piping bag fitted with the large nozzle and pipe
the dough into 40 walnut-sized rounds, spaced about 4cm
(1¹/₂in) apart on the tray to allow for expansion. Use a
small wet knife to stop the dough coming out when you
have finished piping each profiterole.
3 Brush the profiteroles gently with the beaten egg and
bake in the oven for approximately 20–25 minutes or until
they are puffed up, golden and crisp. Remove the profiteroles
from the oven and, using a skewer or the tip of a small sharp
knife, make a hole in the side or the base of each profiterole.
Return to the oven and bake for a further 5 minutes to allow
the steam to escape. Allow the profiteroles to cool on a
wire rack.
4 While the profiteroles are cooling, make the crème chantilly
by folding the sifted icing sugar and vanilla extract into the
whipped cream. Fold the pastry cream (crème patissière) and

the crème chantilly together in one bowl and chill in the fridge until you are ready to use it.

5 When the profiteroles are cool, place the pastry cream mixture in a piping bag fitted with the small, plain 3mm (1/8in) nozzle (or the same one used for piping the profiteroles) and pipe the pastry cream into the profiteroles through the hole made by the skewer until they are filled. Chill in the fridge until you are ready to serve them, about 1–2 hours.

6 To make the caramel, place the sugar, cream of tartar and the water in a small saucepan and stir over a low heat until the sugar is dissolved. Do not stir after this point. Increase the heat to high and allow the sugar syrup to cook for a further 5–10 minutes until it has caramelised; gently swirl the pan to even out the caramel – it should be the colour of whiskey. Remove from the heat and set over another pan filled with boiling water, to keep the caramel from cooling down too quickly and hardening.

7 Using tongs, dip each profiterole, on the unpierced side, into the caramel and place caramel side down in a circle, on a large serving plate. This will be the base of the pyramid. Arrange another round of profiteroles, caramel side down, on top of the first round and then continue, making the rounds slightly smaller all the time, until it forms a cone.

8 Drizzle any remaining caramel over the top when you have finished piling the profiteroles up. Be very careful when assembling this as the caramel will be extremely hot. Decorate, with sugared almonds, crystallised flowers or rose petals, if you wish. To serve, break each profiterole off with a knife.

VARIATION

Chocolate profiteroles: Follow steps 1–5 and then make the hot chocolate sauce described on page 274. When you are ready to serve, pile the profiteroles on a large plate with a lip, or on individual plates. Dust very generously with icing sugar, then pour over the hot chocolate sauce and serve immediately.

CHRISTMAS PUDDING WITH BOOZY TOFFEE SAUCE

MAKES 2 X 1 LITRE (1.75 PINT) PUDDINGS (EACH SERVES 8-12)

100g (3¹/₂oz) raisins
100g (3¹/₂oz) sultanas
100g (3¹/₂oz) dried
  cranberries
100g (3¹/₂oz) candied
  peel (see page 272),
  chopped
100g (3¹/₂oz) currants
100g (3¹/₂oz) dates
  (stoned weight),
  halved
100ml (3¹/₂fl oz) Irish
  whiskey, plus extra
  for serving
100g (3¹/₂oz) ground
  almonds and 10
  whole, skinned ones
2 cooking apples,
  unpeeled and grated
Finely grated zest and
  juice of 1 lemon
6 tbsp golden syrup
200g (7oz) butter,
  chilled and grated
180g (6¹/₂oz) soft dark
  brown sugar
4 eggs, beaten
230g (8¹/₂oz) gluten-free
  flour or 250g (9oz)
  self-raising flour,
  sifted
¹/₂ tsp baking powder
¹/₄ or whole nutmeg,
  finely grated
¹/₂ tsp ground
  cinnamon
1 x quantity boozy
  toffee sauce (see page
  274), to serve

Two 1 litre (1³/₄ pint)
  pudding basins

I love the cranberries in this recipe, which give the pudding a delightfully zingy flavour. The toffee sauce also makes a nice change from brandy butter.

1 In a saucepan, gently simmer the dried fruit in the whiskey for 3 minutes. Remove from the heat, cover and leave for at least 1 hour.

2 Mix the ground almonds, apples and lemon zest and juice together in a bowl.

3 Pour 3 tablespoons of golden syrup into each of the pudding basins and arrange 5 almonds and a few pieces of soaked fruit decoratively in the golden syrup.

4 Using a wooden or metal spoon, mix the grated butter, sugar and eggs together well in a large bowl. Next, add all the remaining ingredients and mix thoroughly together. Spoon into the pudding basins and flatten out. Gently bang the bowls on the work surface to release any air bubbles.

5 Cut two rounds of parchment paper to fit neatly over the top of the mixture, then cut out two more rounds 5mm (¹/₄in) wider than the rim of the basin. Place them over the basin and tie with a long piece of string under the lip of the bowl and over the top again. Tie at the other side to make a handle.

6 Place the basins in a large saucepan each and carefully pour hot water around the puddings to come three-quarters of the way up the sides. Cover and steam for 3 hours, keeping the water in the saucepan topped up all the time.

7 Remove the basins from the water and allow to cool. Remove the top paper lid and cover with a new one. Store in a cool place. Reheat by steaming for 1 hour in the same way as above, then turn out and pour a little whiskey over and ignite. Serve with the boozy toffee sauce.

WALNUT CAKE WITH AMERICAN FROSTING

SERVES 8

200g (7oz) plain flour
Pinch of salt
1 generous tsp baking
  powder
100g (3¹/₂oz) butter,
  softened
225g (8oz) caster sugar
1 tsp vanilla extract
2 eggs, separated
100g (3¹/₂oz) shelled
  walnuts, roughly
  chopped
100ml (3¹/₂fl oz) milk

For the vanilla
buttercream filling
75g (3oz) butter,
  softened
125g (4¹/₂oz) icing
  sugar, sifted
¹/₂ tsp vanilla extract

1 x quantity American
  frosting (see page
  268)
Rose petals or 8 walnut
  halves, to decorate

Two 20cm (8in)
  diameter or three
  18cm (7in) diameter
  sandwich tins

This cake makes a perfect autumnal wedding cake – in fact, we had it for our own wedding, baked by our dear friend Dervilla. We decorated it with sparklers and dark red rose petals, which made for a rather dramatic and beautiful effect. It keeps well, so you could send a slice to anyone who was unable to come to the reception. You don't need a wedding to enjoy this cake, however, as it's great for any special occasion.

1 Preheat the oven to 180°C (350°F), Gas mark 4. Brush the cake tins with melted butter and dust with flour. Line the base of each with greaseproof or parchment paper.
2 Sift the flour with the salt and baking powder. Cream the butter in a large bowl or in an electric food mixer until soft. Add the sugar and vanilla extract and beat until the mixture is light and fluffy. Beat in the egg yolks and then stir in the chopped walnuts. Fold in a quarter of the flour and milk into the mixture, alternating each, until they are incorporated.
3 In a separate bowl, whisk the egg whites until they are stiff. Stir a quarter into the cake mixture and then gently fold in the rest. Divide between the tins, making a slight hollow in the centre of each so that the cake rises evenly rather than forming a peak.
4 Bake in the oven for about 16–20 minutes until firm to the touch or until a skewer inserted into the centre of each cake comes out clean. Remove from the oven and allow to sit for 5 minutes before turning out onto a wire rack to cool.
5 Meanwhile, make the buttercream filling. Cream the butter until very soft, then beat in the icing sugar and the vanilla extract. When the cake is cold, sandwich the layers together with the filling. *Continued overleaf*

6 Make the American frosting as described on page 268.

7 Spread quickly over the cake with a palette knife, regularly dipping the knife into a jug of boiling water to help spread the icing. It sets very quickly at this stage, so speed is essential.

8 Scatter with rose petals, if using, or arrange the walnut halves around the top of the cake, and allow the icing to set until it feels dry on the surface.

RACHEL'S BAKING TIP

Make sure that the walnuts you use for this cake are fresh. Any leftover walnuts will keep best in the freezer. Like many cakes with nuts in, this cake keeps very well if properly stored for a couple of weeks.

ST STEPHEN'S DAY MUFFINS

MAKES 6 LARGE MUFFINS OR 12 BUNS OR 24 MINI MUFFINS

1 egg
75ml (3fl oz) milk
25g (1oz) butter, melted
2 tbsp sherry, Irish
   whiskey or brandy
125g (4$\frac{1}{2}$oz) leftover
   Christmas pudding,
   broken into lumps
125g (41$\frac{2}{2}$oz) plain flour
1 tsp baking powder
$\frac{1}{2}$ tsp mixed spice
75g (3oz) caster sugar
Icing sugar, for dusting

12-hole or 24-hole
   muffin tin and paper
   cases

St Stephen's Day, as it is known in Ireland, is the day after Christmas (aka Boxing Day). And what better way to use up any bits of leftover Christmas Pudding than with these festive and delicious muffins. They are divine with a cup of coffee or tea and can be frozen.

1 Preheat the oven to 180°C (350°F), Gas mark 4. Line your chosen muffin tin with paper cases.

2 Whisk the egg in a bowl, then add the milk, melted butter, sherry, whiskey or brandy and the pieces of Christmas pudding.

3 Sift the flour, baking powder and mixed spice into another bowl. Add the caster sugar and mix well. Make a well in the centre, add the wet ingredients and mix together until a soft lumpy batter forms.

4 Spoon the mixture into the paper cases and bake in the oven for 20–25 minutes for large muffins, 15–20 minutes for the buns and about 10–15 minutes for the mini muffins.

5 Allow to cool on a wire rack then dust with icing sugar to serve.

CHRISTMAS CAKE

SERVES 12–20

225g (8oz) sultanas

225g (8oz) raisins

110g (4oz) homemade candied peel, chopped (see page 272)

75g (3oz) stoned dates, chopped

75g (3oz) dried apricots, chopped

50g (2oz) currants

25g (1oz) crystallised ginger, finely chopped

125ml (4fl oz) brandy or Irish whiskey

275g (10oz) butter, softened

275g (10oz) soft light brown sugar

5 eggs

1 tsp finely grated orange zest

50g (2oz) ground almonds

275g (10oz) plain flour

1 tsp mixed spice

1/4 tsp ground cinnamon

1/4 tsp freshly grated nutmeg

For Darina Allen's almond paste

450g (1lb) ground almonds

450g (1lb) caster sugar

1 egg

2 tbsp brandy or Irish whiskey

Ingredients continued opposite

This delicious Christmas cake came about by accident when I started experimenting with dried fruits and flavourings. I use dates, apricots and a little crystallised ginger as well as the usual sultanas, raisins and currants. As with all traditional Christmas cakes, if this is made a few weeks in advance you will get a lovely moist texture. But this cake can also be made (much to the busy person's relief) just a few days in advance, or even the day before! My mother-in-law, Darina, covers her Christmas cake with almond paste and then toasts it in the oven for extra flavour, so this is what I do with this cake. However, feel free to ice it if you cannot bear to have your Christmas cake without the traditional white icing! Use the American Frosting recipe given on page 268.

1 Place the dried fruit and the crystallised ginger in a bowl. Pour on the brandy or whiskey and allow to soak for at least 2 hours.

2 Preheat the oven to 150°C (300°F), Gas mark 2. Line the cake tin with greaseproof paper and wrap a collar of brown paper around the outside, which will help prevent the cake from drying out (see page 264).

3 Cream the butter in a large bowl or in an electric food mixer until soft. Add the sugar and beat until the mixture is light and fluffy. Add the eggs, one at a time, beating well between each addition. Stir in the orange zest and ground almonds, then sift in the flour and spices and fold in gently. Fold in the dried fruit and any brandy or whiskey left in the bowl. Transfer the mixture to the prepared cake tin. Bake in the oven for $2^{1}/_{2}$–$3^{1}/_{4}$ hours (a round tin will take longer) until a skewer inserted into the middle of the cake comes out clean. Cover the cake, still in the tin, with foil and allow to cool. Once the cake has cooled, remove it from the tin and

A couple of drops of almond essence
Icing sugar, for dusting

To brush on the cake
1 small egg white, lightly beaten
2 egg yolks

23cm (9in) diameter cake tin or 20 x 20cm (8 x 8in) square cake tin

Festive cutters

cover again in foil until you are ready to cover it with almond paste.

4 Preheat the oven to 220°C (425°F), Gas mark 7. To make the almond paste, mix the ground almonds and sugar together in a bowl. In another bowl, beat the egg, add the brandy or whiskey and the almond essence, then add to the dry ingredients and mix to a stiff paste; you may not need all the egg. Sprinkle the work surface with icing sugar, turn the almond paste out onto the surface and gently knead until smooth.

5 Remove the foil and greaseproof paper from the cake. Take about half of the almond paste and place it on a work surface that has been dusted with icing sugar. Roll out until it is about 1cm (^{1}/$_2$in) thick. Brush the top of the cake with the lightly beaten egg white and turn the cake upside down onto the almond paste. Cut around the edge of the cake, then carefully turn the cake the right side up with the lid of almond paste attached to the top.

6 Next, measure the circumference of the cake with a piece of string. Roll out two long strips of almond paste and trim both edges to the height of the cake with a palette knife. Brush the cake and the almond paste lightly with egg white and press the strip against the sides of the cake. Do not overlap or there will be a bulge. Use a straight-sided water glass to even the edges and smooth the join, and rub the cake well with your hand to ensure a nice flat surface.

7 At this stage, carefully place the cake on a large, oiled baking tray. Roll out the remainder of the almond paste approximately 5mm (^{1}/$_4$in) thick and, using festive cutters, cut out star, heart, holly or Santa shapes. Brush the whole surface of the cake with the beaten egg yolks and stick the shapes on top and around the sides, if you wish. Brush these with egg yolk as well.

8 Bake the cake in the oven for 10–20 minutes (not too near the top of the oven) until it is golden and toasted. Remove from the oven, allow to cool, then transfer to a serving plate.

FESTIVE JAM COOKIE SANDWICHES

MAKES ABOUT 35 SANDWICHES

425g (15oz) plain flour
75g (3oz) caster sugar
2 tsp vanilla extract
2 tsp finely grated lemon zest (from 1 large lemon)
4 egg yolks
325g (11½oz) butter, softened
Raspberry or strawberry jam (or make your own see pages 276–7)
Icing sugar, for dusting

6cm (2½in) plain cutter
3cm (1¼in) plain or flower-shaped cutter

These gorgeous little vanilla and lemon-scented cookies sandwiched together with the jam of your choice make a great Christmas cookie – the icing sugar looks like snow!

1 Preheat the oven to 180°C (350°F), Gas mark 4.

2 Sift the flour into a large bowl or electric food mixer and add the sugar, vanilla extract, finely grated lemon zest, egg yolks and butter. Mix until it all comes together to a dough. Remove from the bowl and flatten to a round with the palm of your hand or with a rolling pin to about 2cm (3/4in) thick and chill in fridge for about 30 minutes.

3 Roll the dough out on a lightly floured work surface until it is about 5mm (1/4in) thick, then, using the 6cm (2½in) plain cutter, cut the dough into discs.

4 Take half the discs and, using either the plain or flower-shaped 3cm (1¼in) cutter, cut holes out of the centre of each, like little round windows. Bring the discarded scraps together and make more discs and cut holes in the centre of these. You want to end up with about 35 whole discs and about 35 discs with the centres cut out (equal amounts).

5 Place the discs on several baking trays and bake in the oven for 8–10 minutes until pale golden and ever so slightly firm.

6 Allow to stand for a couple of minutes, then remove from the trays and transfer to wire racks to cool.

7 When the discs are cool, spread 1/2–1 teaspoon of jam on the whole discs and top with the discs with the hole in them so that you can see the jam through the little windows. Dust with icing sugar and serve.

MINCE PIES

MAKES 24 MINI OR 16 MEDIUM-SIZED MINCE PIES

1 x quantity sweet
   shortcrust pastry
   (see page 254)
250g (9oz) mincemeat
   (just over half a jar)
   (or make your own,
   see page 278)
1 egg, beaten
Icing sugar, for dusting

Shallow 24-hole fairy
   cake tin or 16-hole
   muffin tin
6cm (2^1/$_2$in) plain
   or fluted cutter
4cm (1^1/$_2$in) plain or
   fluted cutter or 3cm
   (1^1/$_4$in) star cutter

Mince pies freeze very well, taking some of the headache out of all that Christmas preparation. If I make lots of these before Christmas, I freeze them raw and then cook them on the day. Cooked mince pies can be stored in a biscuit tin or airtight box and warmed through gently before serving. They are perfect with a glass of spicy mulled wine or a cup of coffee for a festive snack.

1 Preheat the oven to 200°C (400°F), Gas mark 6. Brush the tin with melted butter.

2 On a floured work surface, roll out the pastry to 3mm (1/8in) thick and, using the 6cm (2½in) cutter, cut out 24 circles for the bases. Then use the smaller plain/fluted cutter or star cutter to cut out 24 circles/stars for the lids. Re-roll the trimmings if necessary.

3 Line the holes of the cake tin with the larger pastry rounds. Fill each base with a teaspoon of mincemeat and top with one of the smaller rounds or stars. Brush the tops of the mince pies with the beaten egg.

4 Bake in the oven for 10–13 minutes until pale golden. Cool for 5 minutes before removing from the tin and transfer to a wire rack to cool. Dust with icing sugar to serve.

FINNISH CAKE WITH CARAMELISED GINGER

SERVES 8

75g (3oz) butter
55ml (4 tbsp) milk
125ml (4fl oz) soured
   cream
1 egg
175g (6oz) soft light
   brown sugar
50g (2oz) crystallised
   ginger, chopped
175g (6oz) plain flour
1 tsp baking powder
2 tsp ground cinnamon
1 tsp mixed spice

23cm (9in) diameter
   spring-form/loose-
   bottomed tin or 20 x
   20cm (8 x 8in) square
   cake tin

This is a powerhouse of flavours in a soft, moist cake.

1 Preheat the oven to 180°C (350°F), Gas mark 4. Butter and flour the sides and line the base of the tin with greaseproof paper.

2 Melt the butter and milk together in a small saucepan. Remove from the heat and allow to cool to room temperature.

3 In a medium-sized bowl, whisk together the soured cream, egg and brown sugar until smooth, then whisk in the chopped ginger. Add the melted butter and milk and mix together.

4 Sift the dry ingredients into a separate large bowl. Make a well in the centre, pour in the liquid mixture and whisk together until smooth. Pour the mixture into the prepared tin and smooth the top. Bake in the oven for approximately 45 minutes until golden brown and a skewer inserted into the middle of the cake comes out clean.

5 Leave in the tin for 5 minutes, then carefully transfer to a wire rack to cool.

VARIATION

This cake can also be iced with a simple lemon icing made with 175g (6oz) sifted icing sugar and the finely grated zest of 1 lemon. Mix together and then soften with 3–5 tablespoons of lemon juice to make a soft paste. Spread gently on the cooled cake with a palette knife.

GINGERBREAD HOUSE AND PEOPLE

MAKES APPROXIMATELY 40 GINGERBREAD BOYS AND GIRLS
OR 1 GINGERBREAD HOUSE AND ALL THE TRIMMINGS

300g (11oz) butter
125g (4½oz) caster sugar
125g (4½oz) soft dark brown sugar
225g (8oz) golden syrup or treacle
725g (1lb 9oz) plain flour
2 tsp bicarbonate of soda
3 tsp ground ginger
1 tsp ground cinnamon

For the icing for the gingerbread boys and girls
175g (6oz) icing sugar
1–2 tbsp boiling water

For decorating the gingerbread boys and girls
Smarties
Chocolate buttons (milk or white chocolate)
Gold and silver balls
Or anything else that takes your fancy

For the 'glue' and icing for the house
2 egg whites
500g (1lb 2oz) icing sugar, plus extra for dusting

Ingredients continued overleaf

Our boys love it when it is time to make a gingerbread house at Christmas; they normally start asking for it at the end of November! You need to put aside a couple of hours, but it is great fun for the whole family – you can get very creative and as tasteful or as tacky as you wish. This recipe can also be used for making gingerbread people.

1 Preheat the oven to 180°C (350°F), Gas mark 4. Line 2 baking trays with parchment paper.

2 In a large saucepan, melt the butter together with the sugars and golden syrup or treacle. Sift the flour, bicarbonate of soda and ground ginger and cinnamon into a large bowl. Add the melted butter and sugar and mix together.

3 Knead the mixture for a few seconds until it comes together, adding a teaspoon or so of water if necessary, but without allowing it to get too wet. Flatten the dough slightly into a round about 2cm (³/₄in) thick, wrap with cling film and place in the fridge for 30 minutes.

4 To make the gingerbread boys and girls, remove the dough from the fridge, dust the work surface with flour and roll all of the dough out to about 5mm (¹/₄in thick). Cut out the girl and boy shapes using boy/girl cutters, transfer onto the baking trays and cook in the oven for 12 minutes, until they are slightly firm, a little darker at the edges and slightly drier on top. Allow the shapes to firm up for a few minutes, then place them on a wire rack to cool. When they have cooled, they can be iced, if you wish.

5 To make the icing, sift the icing sugar into a bowl and add the water. Beat until the icing comes together, adding a little more water if necessary. (Be careful not to add too much or the icing will be too runny.) *Continued overleaf*

For decorating
the house
**Hundreds and
thousands
Chocolate buttons
(milk and sugared
chocolate)
Jelly Tots
Dolly Mixtures
Sugar strands, for
sprinkling
Flake bar for the
chimney
Or any other sweets
you wish**

Piping bag and nozzles

6 Using a small palette knife or the back of a spoon dipped into boiling water (to make the icing easier to spread), spread the icing over the gingerbread boys and girls. If you wish to pipe on details, such as faces and hair, spoon the icing into a small piping bag with just the smallest corner cut off. While the icing is still slightly 'unset' on the biscuits, arrange the silver balls or whatever decorations you are using, then set aside for the icing to set.

7 To make the gingerbread house, first make templates in paper to the measurements overleaf. These are handy not just for now, but for when the dough is cooked and you need to trim the walls and roof, to ensure all the edges are straight.

8 Place a sheet of parchment paper on the work surface, dust with flour and roll out about one-quarter of the dough to 5mm (1/4in) thick. Place one of the paper templates on the dough and cut round with a sharp knife, then slide the dough, still on its parchment paper, onto a baking tray. Repeat with remaining dough, re-rolling the trimmings, until you have a front and back wall, two side walls and two roof panels. Re-roll any leftover dough to make into Christmas trees or boys and girls – there should be enough for 6–8. Carefully trim excess paper from around each piece on the baking trays.

9 Bake all the sections in the oven for 12–15 minutes or until slightly firmed and just a little darker at the edges. Remove from the oven and allow to sit for a few minutes on the baking trays to firm up. One by one, lift the pieces, still on the paper, and trim around the template to give clean, sharp edges. To make an open door for the house, cut one out of the front wall and cut out windows, if you wish. Place on a wire rack for a few minutes, then turn over and peel off the trimmed paper. Leave all the pieces to cool completely.

10 Meanwhile, prepare a board for the house to sit on. I like to use a large wooden chopping board, which can be covered with tin foil, if you choose.

11 To make the icing 'glue' for the house, place the egg whites in a large bowl, sift in the icing sugar, then stir to make a

thick, smooth icing. Spoon into a piping bag with a small, star-shaped nozzle.

12 To assemble the house, pipe generous lengths of icing along the vertical wall edges, one by one, to join the walls together. Using a bowl or some other object or objects to support the walls from the inside, hold the walls gently in place with your hands until the icing is dry. Leave the roofless house to dry for at least 30 minutes until the icing is firmly set.

13 Once dry, remove the supports and pipe a thick line of icing along one long side of a roof piece and along the top edge of all the walls. Stick the two roof sections together at an angle and set the two pieces on top of the house. You can arrange the roof so that there is a slight overhang on either side of the house. Hold the roof gently in place for a few minutes until it dries, then leave it to dry for a further 30 minutes.

14 While the roof is drying, attach the door to the doorway – so that it looks slightly ajar – by running a line of icing glue down one side and along the base. Stick a small piece of a Flake bar onto the roof as a chimney.

15 Using the icing, pipe around the windows, and stick sweets around the door and on the front of the house. To make snow on the roof and icicles hanging from it, start with the nozzle at a 90-degree angle to the roof and squeeze out a pea-sized blob of icing. Keeping the pressure on, pull the nozzle down and then pull away, leaving a pointy trail of icing. Repeat all around the edge of the roof.

16 Using the icing, stick milk chocolate and sugared buttons onto the roof for tiles. Glue the gingerbread trees or boys and girls around the house, then scatter the board with sugar strands.

RACHEL'S BAKING TIP

The gingerbread house will stay fresh for a week, although, after all the work putting it together and icing it, the temptation is to keep it for the few weeks over Christmas, by which time it will be quite stale and not so good to eat!

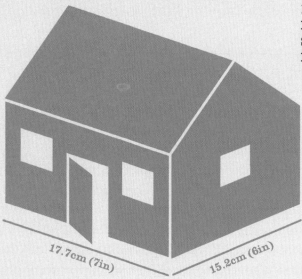

Dimensions
Front & back: 12.7 x 17.7cm (5 x 7in)
Sides: 12.7 x 15.2cm (5 x 6in)
Roof: 7.6 x 17.7cm (3 x 7in)

17.7cm (7in)

15.2cm (6in)

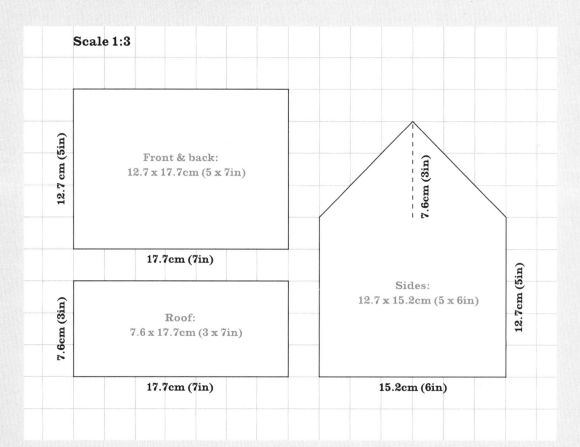

Scale 1:3

12.7 cm (5in)

Front & back:
12.7 x 17.7cm (5 x 7in)

17.7cm (7in)

7.6cm (3in)

Roof:
7.6 x 17.7cm (3 x 7in)

17.7cm (7in)

7.6cm (3in)

Sides:
12.7 x 15.2cm (5 x 6in)

12.7cm (5in)

15.2cm (6in)

DODO'S STOLLEN

MAKES 2 LOAVES

100g (3¹/₂oz) raisins
100g (3¹/₂oz) sultanas
100g (3¹/₂oz) currants
100g (3¹/₂oz) candied peel, chopped (see page 272)
50ml (1³/₄fl oz) Jamaican rum
100g (3¹/₂oz) ground almonds
1 tsp vanilla extract
15g (¹/₂oz) dried yeast or 25g (1oz) fresh yeast or 2 x 7g sachets fast-acting yeast
225ml (8fl oz) warm milk
500g (1lb 2oz) strong white flour, sifted
Pinch of salt
Pinch of freshly ground black pepper
1 tsp ground coriander seeds
¹/₂ tsp ground cardamom
¹/₄ tsp freshly grated nutmeg
Finely grated zest of 2 lemons
150g (5oz) butter, cubed
100g (3¹/₂oz) caster sugar
225g (8oz) marzipan (see page 272)
Icing sugar, for dusting

This slightly modified recipe for traditional German Christmas cake is an old family recipe from my brother-in-law, Dodo. Don't be put off by the number of ingredients; it is not a difficult recipe. Although the cake can be eaten on the day it's made, try keeping it for a week in an airtight container to let the flavours mature. Stollen also freezes very well.

1 Place all the dried fruit in a large bowl together with the rum, ground almonds and vanilla extract. Cover and allow to soak while you make the dough.

2 Place the yeast and warm milk in a separate bowl and allow to stand in a warm place for 5 minutes until frothy. If using fast-acting yeast, there is no need to let the mixture stand.

3 Place the flour, salt and pepper, spices and lemon zest in another bowl and mix together. Make a well in the centre and pour in the yeast mixture.

4 Using one hand with your fingers outstretched like a claw (or a wooden spoon), bring as much flour as is necessary from the sides of the bowl into the liquid to form a soft dough. Cover with oiled cling film or a clean tea towel and allow to stand for 10 minutes.

5 Knead in the cubed butter and sugar using the dough hook of an electric food mixer (you can use your hand, but it's a bit messy). Turn out on a lightly floured work surface and knead for 10 minutes until smooth and slightly springy. (This can also be done in an electric food mixer with a dough hook.) When the dough is smooth and elastic, place it in an oiled bowl and allow to stand for approximately 2 hours until the dough has doubled in size.

6 Knock back the risen dough, turn out onto a lightly floured work surface and allow to stand for a further 10 minutes.

Continued overleaf

7 Roll out the dough into a square about 2.5cm (1in) thick. Place the soaked fruit evenly over the surface, then knead the dough again, being careful to incorporate all the fruit evenly.

8 Cut the dough into two equal pieces and roll the first piece out to approximately 15 x 20cm (6 x 8in) and about 2.5cm (1in) high. Divide the marzipan into two equal pieces of 110g (4oz) each, then roll each piece of marzipan to form a sausage shape just less than the length of the dough.

9 Taking one piece of dough, place the marzipan lengthways across the centre of the dough, leaving a little space at each end. Carefully fold the dough over the marzipan and place it seam-side down onto a large, greased baking tray. Repeat with the other piece of dough.

10 Cover and allow to rest for 1 hour or until it has doubled in size. Preheat the oven to 200°C (400°F), Gas mark 6.

11 Bake the stollen in the oven for 40–45 minutes. Allow to cool, then dust with icing sugar and serve.

BASIC RECIPES AND TECHNIQUES

EQUIPMENT

Chances are that you already have a lot of the following baking equipment in your cupboard or kitchen drawer. Any missing items can be bought from cook shops, by mail order or from larger supermarkets and need not be bought all at once but built up gradually as and when required. As with anything, the better the quality of your equipment, the better your results will be and the longer they will last. This applies to measuring scales, food mixers and cake tins as well.

BAKEWARE

Baking tray: Choose rigid flat trays that won't bend or warp during cooking, preferably with only one lip so they can be easily gripped as you take them out of the oven and cooked biscuits can be easily removed.

Brioche tin: Available in individual or larger round tins with sloping, wide, fluted edges and a small-diameter flat base. They can also be used for jellies and mousses.

Cake or sandwich tins: Ideally, choose one with a loose base so that the baked cake can be easily removed. They are available in a range of sizes, either round or square, deep-sided (7.5cm/3in), and with or without a non-stick coating. Look out for shallower rectangular or square traybake tins.

Fairy cake tin: This is a shallow metal tin with 12 holes.

Loaf tin: A deep rectangular tin used to bake bread or a tea loaf, such as Cornish Saffron Bread (see page 122). They are available in a range of sizes, but a 900g (2lb) tin measuring 13 x 23cm (5 x 9in) is the most useful.

Muffin tin: A deep metal tin or flexible heatproof silicone mould either with 6 or 12 holes.

Swiss roll tin: A rectangular baking tin with shallow straight sides and available in different sizes.

Springform tin: A round loose-based tin with a spring clip to open the sides for easy removal of a baked cake. It is traditionally used when making cheesecakes or chocolate mousse cakes.

Tart tin: This is available in a range of sizes from tiny individual ones right up to a large 25cm (10in) diameter ones with fluted edges.

EVERYDAY ESSENTIALS

Balloon whisk/hand-held electric beater: The type will depend on how energetic you feel. For quick jobs a hand-held balloon whisk will make light work of whipping cream, while a hand-held electric beater will save time and muscle power when whisking meringue.

Biscuit/cookie/scone cutters: You can buy a variety of fun shapes now, but to begin with choose two sets: one plain and one with fluted edges, ideally in a storage tin to keep the different sizes together.

Measuring jug: As with scales, this is essential for measuring liquids correctly.

Mixing bowls: You will need at least three different sizes. A large stainless steel bowl is useful for whisking egg whites and making bread.

Parchment paper: Sometimes called non-stick baking paper, this paper does not need greasing, unlike greaseproof paper, making it ideal to line the base and sides of deep cake tins or baking trays.

Pastry brush: Essential for lightly greasing a baking tray or for glazing bread or pastries with egg before baking.

Rolling pin: Choose a long wooden rolling pin; the wider the diameter, the fewer revolutions needed when rolling.

Scales: These are essential when baking as measurements need to be exact.

Sieve: Choose a fine-mesh metal sieve and use to sift out any lumps in cocoa powder or flour before adding in to the recipe.

Skewer: Choose a small, fine metal skewer and use to test if a large cake is cooked. Insert into the centre of the cake and if the skewer comes out with uncooked cake sticking to it then the cake isn't quite cooked. If clean, it is ready.

Spatula: Flexible plastic spatulas make light work of scraping out the last remains from the bowl or when scooping icing into a piping bag.

Wire rack: This is essential for turning a baked cake or loaf out onto so that the steam can escape and prevent the base from becoming soft and soggy.

ADDED EXTRAS

Baking beans: These ceramic 'beans' are poured into an uncooked pastry case lined with greaseproof paper and used to hold the sides of the tart up during 'blind baking' (see page 255). Once the shape is set the beans are removed and the tart baked for a few more minutes until golden. Uncooked rice, dried pulses or pasta can also be used in the same way. Keep them in a jar and use over and over.

Bundt or kugelhopf tin: This has a patterned edge and hollow centre.

Dredger: A small plastic, china or metal container with a lid with small perforations either to sprinkle flour over a work surface when kneading bread or rolling out pastry or to dust a cake or biscuits with icing sugar.

Food mixer: A free-standing electric mixer saves time and effort when making large cakes or bread, leaving hands free to spoon in additional ingredients or to quickly line a tin while the mixer is in action. Choose one that comes with different hooks – a whisk, a pastry or cake beater and a dough hook.

Icing bags and piping nozzles: Available in two sizes: ones for fine icing and decoration, and larger ones for piping whipped cream. The nozzles are either metal or plastic with nylon piping bags. Disposable plastic bags may also be bought from specialist cake decorating or cook shops. (See pages 269–70 for making your own.)

Palette knife: This is not a knife in the true sense as it is not used for cutting. Its flexible blade has a curved end that makes it an invaluable tool for spreading icing or cream over cakes or to slide under baked biscuits or tarts to transfer to a wire rack or serving plate. Invest in two different sizes if you can.

Ramekins: Small, straight-sided dishes, usually with a capacity of 150ml (1/4 pint) and great for making individual brûlées, mousses and soufflés.

PASTRY

Many people are nervous of making pastry, but it isn't as tricky as you might think, it is just about following the right steps. Always try to measure the ingredients accurately and go easy on the liquid. Keep everything as cool as you can. Be sure to chill the pastry for about 30 minutes before baking to stop it becoming sticky or shrinking too much during cooking.

SHORTCRUST PASTRY

MAKES 400G (14OZ)

This basic pastry is used in many popular recipes, from mince pies to quiches; it's also one of the easiest pastries to start with. The uncooked dough can be frozen or kept in the fridge for a couple of days.

200g (7oz) plain flour, sifted
Pinch of salt
100g (3¹/₂oz) chilled butter, cubed
¹/₂–1 medium egg, beaten

✳ Place the flour, salt and butter in a food processor and whiz briefly. Add half the beaten egg and continue to whiz. You might add a little more egg, but not too much as the mixture should be just moist enough to come together. If making by hand, rub the butter into the flour (1) until it resembles coarse breadcrumbs (2) then, using your hands, add just enough egg to bring it together (3).
✳ With your hands, flatten out the ball of dough until it is about 2cm (³/₄in) thick (4), then wrap in cling film or place in a plastic bag (5) and leave in the fridge for at least 30 minutes or, if you are pushed for time, in the freezer for 10–15 minutes.

VARIATIONS

Sweet shortcrust pastry: In place of the pinch of salt, use 1 tablespoon of icing sugar.
Soured cream shortcrust pastry: Replace the egg with 2 tablespoons of soured cream (or crème fraîche), adding just enough to bring it together.

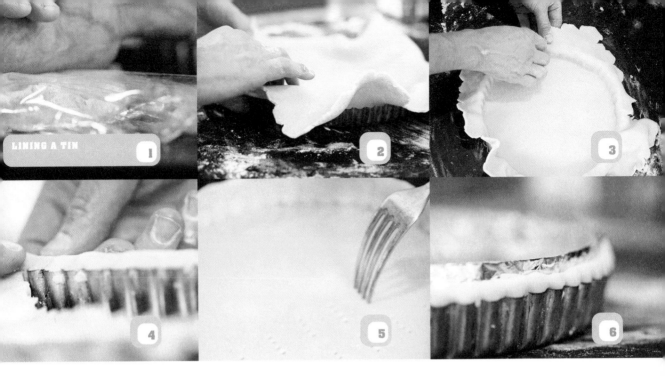

LINING A TIN

1

2

3

4

5

6

Herby shortcrust pastry: Add about 1 teaspoon of finely chopped herbs, such as thyme or marjoram, to the flour before mixing it.

TECHNIQUE: LINING A TIN

✳ Remove the pastry from the fridge and place between two sheets of cling film (larger in size than your tart tin) (1). Using a rolling pin, roll the pastry out to no thicker than 5mm (1/4in), or even thinner for small tartlet tins. If the tin is round, make sure to keep the pastry in a round shape and also large enough to line the base and sides of the tin.
✳ Remove the cling film and place in the tart tin (2). If you wish, retain the top layer of cling film to help you shape the pastry. Press the pastry into the edges (3) and, using your thumb, 'cut' the pastry along the edge of the tin for a neat finish (4). Remove the cling film, if used, prick over the base with a fork (5) and chill the pastry in the fridge for 30 minutes or the freezer for 10 minutes (it can keep for weeks like this in the freezer).

TECHNIQUE: BLIND BAKING

✳ To pre-bake a pastry case before adding filling, first chill the pastry, then line your tin. Line the pastry with foil, greaseproof or parchment paper, leaving plenty to come up the sides (6). Fill with baking beans or dried pulses. (Alternatively, for a really smooth finish use clingfilm to line the pastry: place 2 sheets over the pastry, add the beans and bring the edges into the centre.) Whichever method you choose, bake 'blind' in a 180°C (350°F), Gas mark 4 oven for 15–20 minutes or until the pastry feels dry.
✳ Remove the paper and beans, brush with a little leftover beaten egg and return to the oven for 2 minutes. If there are any little holes or cracks in the pastry, just patch it up with any leftover raw pastry before you return it to the oven. Remove from the oven and set aside in the tin while you make the filling. The pastry can be baked a day in advance and kept covered until you need it.

CHOUX PASTRY

MAKES ABOUT 850G (1LB 12OZ))

Choux pastry is spooned or piped into shapes
and then baked for chocolate profiteroles or
éclairs (see pages 228–230 and 179) and is
deceptively easy to make.

100g (3¹/₂oz) strong white or plain flour
Pinch of salt
150ml (¹/₄ pint) water
75g (3oz) butter
3 eggs, beaten

✴ Sift the flour and salt into a large bowl
and set aside.

✴ Place the water and butter in a medium-
sized saucepan with high sides (not a low

sauté pan) set over a medium–high heat,
stirring, until the butter melts (1). Allow
the mixture to come to a rolling boil then
immediately remove the pan from the heat.
Add the flour and salt (2) and beat very
well with a wooden spoon until the mixture
comes together.

✴ Reduce the heat to medium and replace
the saucepan, stirring for 1 minute until
the mixture starts to 'fur' (slightly stick
to the base of the pan) (3). Remove from
the heat and allow to cool for 1 minute.

✴ Pour about one-quarter of the beaten egg
into the pan (4) and, using the wooden spoon,
beat very well. Add a little more egg and beat
well again until the mixture comes back
together. Continue to add the egg, beating

vigorously all the time, until the mixture has softened, is nice and shiny and has a dropping consistency (5). You may not need to add all the egg or you may need a little extra. If the mixture is too stiff (not enough egg) then the choux pastries will be too heavy, but if the mixture is too wet (too much egg) they will not hold their shape when spooned onto greaseproof paper (6).

✳ Although the pastry is best used right away, it can be placed in a bowl, covered and chilled for up to 12 hours, until ready to use.

HOT WATER CRUST PASTRY

MAKES 250G (9OZ)

This is a simple pastry often used for meat pies.

75g (3oz) butter, cubed
100ml (4fl oz) water
225g (8oz) plain flour
Pinch of salt
1 egg, beaten

✳ Place the butter and water in a medium-sized saucepan and heat gently, stirring occasionally, until the butter melts, then allow the mixture to come to a rolling boil.

✳ Meanwhile, sift the flour and salt into a large bowl. Make a well in the middle and add the egg.

✳ Pour the hot liquid into the flour and stir with a wooden spoon to mix.

✳ Spread the mixture out on a large plate with the wooden spoon and allow to cool (about 15 minutes), then wrap in cling film and place in the fridge for 30 minutes until firm. Use according to the recipe you are making.

PUFF PASTRY

MAKES APPROXIMATELY 1.25KG (2LB 12OZ)

Puff pastry takes a little more time and effort to perfect, but it's worth having a go and the results are delicious. If you're pressed for time, you can buy good-quality puff pastry from supermarkets – look for one that contains butter. This recipe makes generous quantities, so you can store any leftover pastry in the fridge for 48 hours or in the freezer for up to three months.

450g (1lb) flour (strong or baker's
  flour, if possible),
Pinch of salt
1 tbsp freshly squeezed lemon juice
200–275ml (7–9fl oz) cold water
  (the amount of water will depend
  on the absorbency of the flour)
450g (1lb) chilled butter, still in
  its wrapper

✳ Sift the flour and salt into a large bowl. Mix the lemon juice with 200ml (7fl oz) water, pour into the flour and, using your hands, mix to a firm dough, adding more water if necessary. This dough is called *détrempe* (a mixture of flour and water). Flatten it slightly and cover with a plastic bag, cling film or greaseproof paper and allow to rest in the fridge on a baking tray (which aids the chilling process) for 30 minutes.

✳ Roll the *détrempe* into a rectangle about 1cm (1/2in) thick. Remove the butter from the fridge, still in its wrapper and, using a rolling pin, 'beat' it until it forms a slab about 1.5–2cm (5/8–3/4in) thick. Remove the wrapper, place in the centre of the dough rectangle and fold the dough over the edges of the butter to make a neat parcel.

Turn the dough over and, dusting the work surface with flour to stop the dough sticking, roll it gently out into a rectangle approximately 40cm (16in) long and 20cm (8in) wide, positioned so that one narrow end is facing you. Brush off the excess flour with a pastry brush, then fold neatly into three by lifting the end furthest away from you and placing it on the rectangle, so that only one-third of the pastry is left uncovered, and aligning the sides as accurately as possible. Fold the other end on top. Seal the edges with your hands or a rolling pin.

Give the dough a one-quarter turn (90 degrees), so the folds are running vertically in front of you. Roll out away from you, again into a rectangle (to roughly the same measurements as before), brush off any excess flour and fold in three again. Seal the edges, cover with cling film or greaseproof paper and allow to rest in the fridge for another 30 minutes.

Repeat steps 3 and 4 twice more (always ensuring you start the process with the folds in the pastry running vertically), so that in the end the dough has been rolled out six times and has rested in the fridge three times for 30 minutes each time. Chill for at least 1 hour before using.

FLAKY PASTRY

MAKES APPROXIMATELY 1.25KG (2LB 12OZ)

This pastry contains less butter than puff pastry and gives the same lovely flaky result. It is suitable for any dish where you might use puff pastry, except perhaps vol au vents. Flaky pastry may be kept wrapped in the fridge for 48 hours or it may be frozen.

500g (1lb 2oz) strong or plain flour (if using plain flour, more water may be needed)
Pinch of salt
325g (11½oz) butter, chilled
175ml (6fl oz) cold water (add a few ice cubes on a warm day)

Sift the flour and salt into a bowl and divide the butter into four equal parts. Keeping the rest of the butter in the fridge, rub one part of it into the flour, then slowly mix in the cold water until a soft, but not sticky dough forms. (Depending on the absorbency of the flour, you may need slightly less water, or you may need slightly more.) Cover with a plastic bag or cling film and allow to rest in the fridge on a baking tray (which aids the chilling process) for 30 minutes.

Take a second portion of butter out of the fridge and cut it into small pieces. Sprinkle the work surface with flour to stop the dough sticking and roll out the pastry into a strip approximately 40cm (16in) long and 20cm (8in) wide, positioned so one narrow end is facing you. Brush off the excess flour with a pastry brush, then dot the butter over the nearest two-thirds of the pastry. Lift the end furthest away from you (the pastry that has no butter on it) and fold it over one-third of the pastry dotted with the butter, aligning the sides as accurately as possible. Fold the other end on top.

Give the pastry a one-quarter turn (90 degrees), so the folds are running vertically in front of you. Roll out the pastry away from you, again into a rectangle (to roughly the same measurements as before), brush off any excess flour, and fold in three again. Cover and leave to rest once more in the fridge for another 30 minutes.

Using the third portion of butter, repeat steps 2 and 3.

✳ Using the last portion of butter, repeat steps 2 and 3 one more time. If the pastry then appears streaky, roll and fold it once again. Cover and allow to rest in the fridge on the baking tray for at least 30 minutes before using it to cover a pie.

TECHNIQUE: TOPPING A PIE WITH PASTRY

✳ Roll out the pastry on a lightly floured surface until a little larger than the top of the pie dish. To double-check, hold the pie dish over the pastry.

✳ Pour the filling into the pie dish. Cut strips of pastry the width of the dish rim and long enough to go all the way around the dish. Brush the top edge of the pie dish with water or beaten egg, then press the strips in place.

✳ Brush the top of the pastry rim with a little more water or egg, then lift the remaining pastry over the rolling pin and drape over the top of the dish. Press together the edges of the pastry to seal, then trim off the excess.

✳ If using puff or flaky pastry, make light horizontal cuts around the pastry edge to encourage the pastry to rise and separate into layers (this is called 'knocking up').

✳ Crimp the edge by pressing the index finger and thumb of one hand into the top edge of the pastry, leaving a small gap between each imprint, then press the point of a small knife into each gap. Continue around the edge of the pie for a scalloped effect.

✳ Re-roll any pastry trimmings and cut diamond-shaped leaves with a small knife, or cut hearts, flowers or stars with small biscuit cutters. Stick onto the pie top with a little beaten egg and then glaze the top with more egg before baking.

BREADS

Making bread is immensely satisfying and doesn't take as long as you might imagine. Although you need to be around while the dough rises, this actually requires no effort on your part except a quick peek every now and then to check how it's getting on, enabling you to do other things in the meantime. Mixing and kneading can even be done in an electric food mixer if you have one with a dough hook. Bread is fun to make with children (I love doing this with my boys), and, unlike pastry, it won't turn that rather gruesome grey from overhandling, but actually benefits from quite rough kneading.

If you don't have time to wait for the bread to rise, there are also yeast-free alternatives, such as my speedy white or brown soda bread, corn bread or scones (see pages 117–18, 124–5 and 128). They are all equally delicious and need only 15 minutes to make and shape before baking.

WHICH FLOUR TO USE?

When making yeast breads, it is important to use a flour that has a high gluten content, such as strong white, wholemeal or granary flour (a mix of wholemeal, white and rye flours with added malted wheat grains). Those with a lower gluten content such as rye, buckwheat or millet flour can be mixed with other flours to improve their gluten levels while still maintaining their distinctive flavour. Gluten is crucial to bread making as it's what gives bread its chewy, open texture.

Spelt, a nutty stoneground wheat flour, has a lower gluten content than other wheat flours and so can be tolerated by many who find wheat flours difficult to digest. However, do take care not to prove (see glossary) bread

made using spelt flour for too long or you may find that the dough will collapse.

For those following a coeliac diet, gluten must be completely avoided, so make breads with a mix of gram, quinoa, cornmeal, potato or rice flours and xanthum gum, a powder available from health food shops that will mimic the properties of gluten and aid the stretch and rise of a bread.

USING YEAST

Yeast is available in three forms, fresh yeast, dried yeast and fast-acting dried yeast. Both fresh and dried yeast need to be activated in warm water and fed with a little sugar. As the yeast begins to produce carbon dioxide, it will cause the water to bubble and create a frothy, beer-like head on top, which is known as 'sponging', but if this doesn't happen in 5–10 minutes then the chances are the yeast will not work. Make sure that the water is just warm to your little finger; too hot and the yeast will be killed, but too cold and it will not be activated. The easiest way is to measure two-thirds cold tap water into a measuring jug and then top up with one-third boiling water. The water should feel comfortable to the touch.

Fast-acting dried yeast doesn't need to be activated first and can either be stirred straight into the flour or into warm liquid and used immediately. This form of yeast is essential for bread machines. Fresh yeast can be kept well wrapped in the salad drawer of the fridge, while dried yeast and fast-acting dried yeast can be kept in the storecupboard. Check the use-by dates on the back of the packets before using as old yeast will produce a poor rise or no rise at all.

BASIC WHITE BREAD

MAKES 2 LOAVES

2 tsp caster sugar
425ml ($^3/_4$ pint) warm water
$2^1/_2$ tsp dried yeast or 20g ($^2/_3$oz) fresh yeast or $1^1/_2$ x 7g sachets fast-acting yeast
750g (1lb 10oz) strong white flour,
2 tsp salt
40g ($1^1/_2$ oz) chilled butter or 4 tbsp olive oil

✳ In a measuring jug, mix the sugar with 150ml ($^1/_4$ pint) of the warm water and the yeast and let it stand in a warm place for 5 minutes until frothy (1). If using fast-acting dried yeast, there is no need to leave it to stand (check the packet instructions or tin).

✳ Sift the flour and salt into a large bowl. Add the butter and rub it in until it resembles fine breadcrumbs. Alternatively, make a well in the centre and add the oil, if using. Pour in the yeast mixture and most of the remaining warm water and mix, adding the remaining water or a little extra if needed, to a loose, soft but not sticky dough (2).

✳ Knead for 10 minutes by pushing the front half of the dough away with the heel of your hand while holding the back of the dough with your other hand (3). Fold the stretched part of the dough back on itself (4), give it a quarter turn and repeat until the dough is a smooth, springy and elastic ball. This will encourage the yeast to multiply and to help develop the gluten that will, in turn, help the dough to stretch and rise fully. If using an electric food mixer fitted with a dough hook, knead for just 5 minutes.

✳ Put the dough into a large oiled bowl, cover the top with cling film and leave in a warm place – either near the oven, on a chair near a radiator, or in a bowl of hot but not boiling water – for 1–2 hours, depending on the temperature, to rise (or 'prove') until it is doubled in size.

* When the dough has risen, 'knock back' or punch down with a fist to deflate the dough (5). Scoop out the dough (6) onto a lightly floured work surface.

* Knead the dough for 2–3 minutes (7) and then allow to rest for 10 minutes. Preheat the oven to 220°C (425°F) Gas mark 7.

* Cut the dough in half, then shape each into an oval, about 23cm (9in) long (8). Press each piece into a lightly oiled 13 x 23cm (5 x 9in) loaf tin, cover loosely with oiled cling film and leave in a warm place for 20–30 minutes for a second or final rising until the bread is level with the top of the tin.

* Be careful not to over-prove or the bread will begin to deflate. Remove the cling film and check if the dough is ready by pressing on it lightly with a fingertip. It should feel spongy rather than firm and the indentation made with your finger should spring back slowly. Dust with flour or glaze with beaten egg (9), or leave plain and glaze after baking with melted butter or a sugar or salt glaze.

* Bake for 30–35 minutes, turning the oven temperature down to 200°C (400°F) Gas mark 6 after 15 minutes until the bread is well risen, browned and the base sounds hollow when tapped. Turn out of the tin immediately after it is cooked; if left in the tin the base can become soggy. Cool on a wire rack and store in a pottery bread crock, wooden bread bin or wrapped in a tea towel.

TECHNIQUE: PLAITING DOUGH

To make a plait, divide the dough into three equal pieces. Using both hands, roll each piece into a long sausage shape. The thickness of each 'sausage' will depend on how fat you want the plait and how long you want the bread, but I normally roll each strand to about 2–3cm (3/4–11/4in) wide and 30cm (12in) long. Pinch the three ends together at the top, tucking the messy end underneath, and bring each outside strand into the centre (1), alternating strands, to form a plait (2). Pinch the plaited ends together and tuck in neatly underneath. Transfer to a floured baking tray (3), cover with a clean tea towel and place somewhere warm to double in size. Brush with egg, or dredge with flour, and bake.

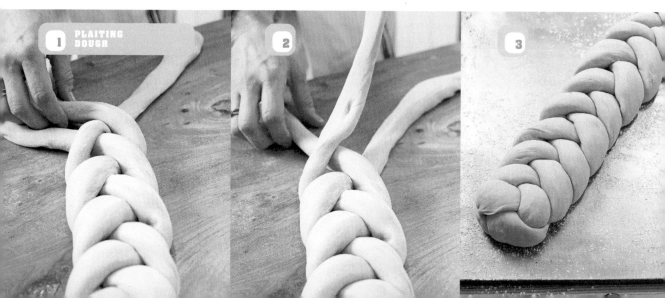

1 PLAITING DOUGH   2   3

CAKES

Whether it's your child's birthday, a special celebration or a Saturday afternoon get-together, nothing beats a homemade cake. Cakes are much easier to make than you may think; the trick is to weigh out ingredients precisely and resist the temptation to open the oven door too early. Even if your first attempts don't look perfect, chances are they will still taste good and you can always hide imperfections by adding fun decorations; but, as with all cooking techniques, practice makes perfect.

To tell if a cake is done, it should look well risen and golden brown and shrinking very slightly from the sides of the tin. Press lightly in the centre of the cake with a fingertip and if the mark springs back it is ready; if a slight dent remains, cook for a few more minutes and then retest; for deeper cakes, test with a skewer (see page 253). Bear in mind that fan ovens cook quicker than conventional ones, so reduce the temperature by 10 per cent and check 5 minutes earlier than the given time.

BASIC SPONGE CAKE
SERVES 6-8

175g (6oz) butter, softened
175g (6oz) caster sugar
3 eggs, beaten
175g (6oz) self-raising flour, sifted
**20cm (8in) diameter spring-form/
loose-bottomed tin or two 18cm (7in)
diameter sandwich tins**

✴ Preheat the oven to 180°C (350°F), Gas mark 4. Grease and line the spring-form tin or sandwich tins (see page 264). Cream the butter in a large bowl (1) or in an electric food mixer until soft. Add the sugar and beat until the mixture is light and fluffy (2).

✳ Beat the eggs into the butter and sugar mixture a little at a time, beating well after each addition (3). If the butter and sugar are not creamed properly, and if you add the eggs too fast, the mixture will curdle, resulting in a cake with a heavier texture. If the mixture does begin to curdle, don't panic; add a spoonful or two of the flour to help stabilize the mixture. Then add alternate spoonfuls of egg and flour until it has all been added. Even if you can't bring the mixture back, cook it anyway and don't let on!

✳ Sift the flour over the mixture (4) and fold in with a spatula or metal spoon to make a dropping consistency (see page 280).

✳ Pour the mixture into the prepared cake tin or divide between the sandwich tins (5 & 6). Smooth the top and bake in the oven for approximately 20 minutes until the cake is risen, golden brown and spongy to the touch.

✳ Allow to cool in the tin for a few minutes, then turn out and peel off the lining paper. Turn the right side up and allow to cool on a wire rack.

TECHNIQUE: LINING A CAKE TIN

✳ Stand the cake tin on a sheet of greaseproof paper and draw around the base (1). Cut out the disc and place on the base of the tin (2).

✳ Use a butter wrapper or some softened butter applied with greaseproof paper to grease the sides of the tin (3). Sprinkle over flour and then shake off the excess.

TECHNIQUE: COLLARING A TIN

✳ Draw around the outside of the tin and cut a square or circle of greaseproof or non-stick parchment paper for the base of the tin. Cut a strip the height of the tin plus 2cm (³⁄₄in) and long enough to go around the sides with a little extra to overlap. Fold up 2cm (³⁄₄in) from one of the long sides then snip at intervals all the way along.

✳ Lightly butter or oil the inside of the tin (if using greaseproof paper) or leave ungreased if using parchment paper. Add the strip of paper with the cut edge at the bottom, carefully pressing into the corners if you are using a square tin. Add the paper for the base so the snipped edges are covered. If using greaseproof, butter or oil it lightly.

1 LINING A CAKE TIN

2

3

MAKING MERINGUE 1

MERINGUE

Although meringue is just a simple combination of egg white and sugar, many people are nervous of making it. The secret to light, fluffy meringue is to use a large, clean, grease-free bowl (glass or steel bowls are best) and a clean whisk, egg whites that are at room temperature, and to whisk for long enough that the white stands upright on your whisk, but no longer.

BASIC MERINGUE
MAKES 1 ROULADE OR 8 LARGE MERINGUES

4 egg whites
225g (8oz) caster sugar

✳ Place the egg whites in the spotlessly clean and dry bowl of an electric food mixer (1) (or use a hand-held electric beater) and whisk using the fastest speed possible until soft peaks form (2).
✳ Add the sugar all in one go and whisk at full speed for approximately 4–5 minutes until stiff peaks form (3).
✳ To cook the meringue, see the method for Coconut Meringue Roulade (page 85) and Baked Alaska (page 89).

TECHNIQUE: EGG WHITE WHIPPING STAGES
Soft peak: The egg whites are bright white and fluffy and just hold their shape when the whisk is lifted out of the mixture. Because they are so soft they fold easily into chocolate or fruit mousses, roulades and soufflés.
Stiff peak: The egg white stands in firm tall peaks when the whisk is lifted, so this is most suited to meringues where the mixture will need to be self-supporting during cooking.

DECORATING AND FILLING CAKES

Once your cake has cooled, you can begin having fun with decoration. Nowadays supermarkets stock a wealth of cake decorations – from colourful sprinkles, sugar flowers and swirls to metallic balls. If you're short on time, you can buy ready-to-roll icing and even icing for writing with. All these simple options mean that even if you are a cake-making beginner, you can still create attractive and delicious cakes. However, do try making your own icing; it's very easy and tastes better than shop-bought. Butter and cream cheese icings (see below) are ideal for starting out.

Of course, if you really want to pull out all the stops, you can split cakes to produce layers. If the cake is delicate and likely to be crumbly, freeze it first for 30 minutes to firm up. You will also need to double the quantity of icing. Split the cakes horizontally using a serrated knife and spread each layer with icing, then re-assemble the cake and spread the remaining icing on the top.

CREAM CHEESE ICING
MAKES 175G (6OZ)

75g (3oz) chilled cream cheese
25g (1oz) butter, softened
1/2 tsp vanilla extract
75g (3oz) icing sugar, sifted

⁕ Beat the cream cheese and butter together with a wooden spoon or in an electric food mixer until combined.

⁕ Add the vanilla extract and sifted icing sugar and mix to combine. The icing should be smooth and quite thick.

⁕ Using a palette knife, spread the icing over the cooled cake, dipping the knife in a bowl of hot water if the icing is hard to spread out. Store in the fridge.

BUTTER ICING
MAKES 325G (11.5OZ)

100g (3¹/₂oz) butter, softened
200g (7oz) icing sugar, sifted
1 tbsp milk or water

⁕ Place the butter in a large bowl and beat thoroughly with a wooden spoon until it is very soft.

⁕ Add the sifted icing sugar and a drop of milk or water and beat until smooth. Spread over the cooled cake as in step 3, above.

VARIATIONS

Coconut butter icing: In a dry pan, toast 25g (1oz) desiccated coconut until lightly golden, then transfer to a cold plate and allow to cool completely. Add 175g (6oz) sifted icing sugar and the finely grated zest of 1 lemon to the softened butter and beat until light and smooth. Add the toasted coconut and 60ml (2fl oz) canned coconut milk and mix well.

Coffee butter icing: Add 3–4 tablespoons of cooled very strong coffee with the icing sugar in step 2 and beat until smooth.

VANILLA BUTTERCREAM ICING

150ml (¼ pint) milk
125g (4½oz) caster sugar
2 egg yolks
175g (6oz) butter, softened
1 tsp vanilla extract

✴ Place the milk and sugar in a small saucepan and bring to a gentle boil, stirring to dissolve the sugar.

✴ Whisk the egg yolks in a small bowl, then pour the milk onto the yolks, whisking continuously. Return the mixture to the pan and cook over a low–medium heat, stirring all the time with a wooden or silicone spatula until it thickens and the mixture just coats the back of a spoon – this may take approximately 10 minutes. Do not allow the mixture to get too hot or it will scramble (if it does, quickly remove the pan from the heat and pour the mixture through a sieve). Pour into a bowl or jug and allow to cool slightly.

✴ Meanwhile, place the butter in a bowl (I usually do this in an electric food mixer with a whisk) and whisk until soft and light.

✴ Gradually add the almost cooled (not cold but room temperature is good) custard to the butter, whisking all the time, until is combined. Add the vanilla extract and mix.

AMERICAN FROSTING

MAKES 600ML (1 PINT)

This delicious soft icing is a little tricky to make, so follow the instructions exactly. Quick and accurate decisions are necessary in judging when the icing is ready and then it must be applied to the cake immediately. If the icing is not cooked enough, it will still taste good, but will not dry out properly on the outside. If cooked too much, it will be difficult to spread over the cake.

2 egg whites
425g (15oz) caster or
   granulated sugar
100ml (3½fl oz) water

✴ Ensure your cake is ready before you start, as this icing begins to set very quickly. Bring to the boil a saucepan of water large enough to hold a heatproof bowl. Place the egg whites in the bowl and whisk with a hand-held electric beater until very stiff.

✴ In a separate saucepan over a medium–high heat, dissolve the sugar in the water and boil for 5–10 minutes until the liquid is thick and syrupy and has reached the 'thread' stage – when the last few drops that fall from a metal spoon dipped into the syrup come off in one long, quite thick and syrupy thread.

✴ Pour the boiling syrup over the stiffly beaten egg whites, whisking all the time with the hand-held beater. Place the bowl in the saucepan of simmering water. Continue to whisk over the water for 10–15 minutes until the icing is snow white, very thick and meringue-like.

✴ Spread quickly over the cake with a palette knife, regularly dipping the knife into a jug of boiling water. The icing sets very quickly at this stage, so speed is essential.

GLACÉ ICING

MAKES 200ML (7FL OZ)

Glacé icing is runny and sets to a hard, shiny coating. Try adding different colourings and use to decorate cookies or fairy cakes.

200g (7oz) icing sugar
About 2 tbsp boiling water

✳ Sift the icing sugar into a bowl. Add some of the boiling water and stir to mix, adding a little more boiling water if necessary, until the icing is spreadable but not too watery.

VARIATIONS

Chocolate glacé icing: Sift 25g (1oz) cocoa powder into the sifted icing sugar.
Coffee glacé icing: Add 1 tablespoon of coffee essence with the boiling water.
Orange glacé icing: Add the freshly squeezed juice of 1 orange with the boiling water.

TECHNIQUE: EASY ICING FINISHES

Chocolate shavings: See the easy chocolate curls on page 271. Use to completely cover a simple cream-covered sandwich cake or to adorn the sides of a birthday cake, then add crystallised flowers to the top (see page 271).
Funny faces: Children are always delighted by cupcakes decorated with piped faces and wild curly hair in a contrasting colour. Use vanilla buttercream icing (see opposite) either left plain or coloured very pale pink, then decorate with piped melted dark chocolate. Or encourage them to make up their own designs either with homemade icings or tubes of ready-made icing, adding sweets for hair bows, earrings or sunglasses.
Smooth and glossy: For a glass-like finish when using chocolate ganache, royal or glacé icing, dip a palette knife into hot water and smoothe over the icing to remove marks.
Soft swirls: Effective on butter or buttercream icings, American frosting or cream-topped cakes. Spread a round-bladed knife back and forth for a soft wave-like effect. If the cake is very crumbly, it can be helpful to either spread with a very thin layer of apricot jam or butter icing to stick the crumbs in place and to then spread more liberally with the rest of the icing.
Swirls and curls: Make up a piping bag (see below) and spoon in melted chocolate or glacé icing, then fold down the top and snip off the tip. Pipe squiggly random lines over the top of an iced sandwich cake, plain loaf cake, muffins or baked custard tarts. You could also pipe chocolate squiggles directly on to parchment paper and leave to harden. Lift off the paper and break into random shards for stylish additions to chocolate mousses, cakes or ice cream desserts.

TECHNIQUE: MAKING A GREASEPROOF PIPING BAG

Don't be put off by piping. It's amazing how effective a simple cake can look with a pretty pastel-coloured fondant (or ready-to-roll icing) dotted with royal icing, with slightly larger dots to 'glue' candles in place. In many cases there is no need to even using a piping nozzle, just snip off the tiniest piece from the end of a paper piping bag and away you go.
✳ Cut a piece of greaseproof or parchment paper, approximately 25cm (10in) square, then fold in half to make a triangle. Fold the triangle in half again along the long folded edge and pinch all the way up the new halfway crease with your fingers.
✳ Open out and then, with your finger and thumb marking the pinch mark, fold the left-

hand point of the triangle into the crease to form a cone.

✳ Bring the right-hand point over and around the cone so the three points meet at the top. Fold the top points over several times to secure the cone shape and to stop it unravelling.

✳ To use, spoon in the icing. Fold the top of the bag over several times to enclose the icing then snip off the tip of the bag and begin piping. If using a piping nozzle, add to the bag and snip off the tip so that the tube sits comfortably, then spoon in the icing and fold the top of the bag down.

CREME PATISSIERE (PASTRY CREAM)
MAKES 450ML (16FL OZ)

The cream can be frozen or may be made a couple of days in advance and stored in the fridge before using.

4 egg yolks
100g (3¹/₂oz) caster sugar
25g (1oz) plain flour, sifted
1 vanilla pod with a line scored down the side, or ¹/₂ tsp vanilla extract
350ml (12fl oz) milk

✳ In a bowl, whisk the egg yolks with the sugar until light and thick, then stir in the flour.

✳ Place the vanilla pod (if using) in a saucepan with the milk and bring it slowly just up to the boil. Remove the vanilla pod and pour the milk onto the egg mixture, whisking all the time. Return the mixture to the pan and stir over a low–medium heat until it comes up to a gentle boil. (It must boil for it to thicken.) Continue to cook,

stirring all the time (or use a whisk if it looks lumpy), for 2 minutes or until it has thickened.

✳ Remove the saucepan from the heat, add the vanilla extract (if using) and pour into a bowl. If the mixture goes a little lumpy while cooking, remove the saucepan from the heat and whisk well. If it is still lumpy when cooked, push it through a sieve.

✳ Cover with cling film and allow to cool. It must be covered, or the surface must be rubbed with a tiny knob of butter to prevent a skin forming.

CREME CHANTILLY
MAKES 225ML (8FL OZ)

1 tbsp icing sugar, sifted
¹/₂ tsp vanilla extract
200ml (7fl oz) whipped cream (measure when whipped)

✳ Fold the sifted icing sugar and vanilla extract into the whipped cream.

✳ Cover and chill in the fridge until you are ready to use it.

RASPBERRY CREAM
MAKES 450ML (16FL OZ)

75g (3oz) fresh or frozen raspberries
2 tbsp icing sugar, sifted
400ml (14fl oz) stiffly whipped cream (measured when whipped)

✳ Place the raspberries and icing sugar in a food processor and whiz until smooth.

✳ Push the mixture through a nylon sieve to remove the pips.

Fold the raspberry purée through the whipped cream. You can leave it slightly marbled if you wish.

VARIATION

Blueberry cream: Replace the raspberries with blueberries and continue as above.

CRYSTALLISED FLOWERS

1 egg white, lightly whisked
75g (3oz) caster sugar
Edible flowers, such as fruit blossom,
   primroses, violets or violas,
   or rose petals

Preheat the oven to 150°C (300°F), Gas mark 2. Spread out the sugar on a baking tray and dry in the oven for about 15 minutes. Remove and allow to cool.

Dip a small paintbrush into the egg white and carefully brush the flowers using just enough egg white to cover the surface (1). Sprinkle the sugar over the flowers, covering all the petals (2).

Gently shake off any excess sugar and arrange carefully on a tray lined with greaseproof or parchment paper and place somewhere dry (and even slightly warm, such as near a radiator or in an airing cupboard) and allow to dry overnight.

Remove from the tray and use to decorate cakes or desserts (3).

EASY CHOCOLATE CURLS

Unwrap a block or half a block of good-quality cooking chocolate (55–75% cocoa solids), depending on how many curls you would like to make, and turn over so the smooth underside is uppermost.

Hold a swivel-bladed vegetable peeler close to the chocolate edge and run along the top of the bar to shave off curls. If the curls are very small or difficult to do, warm the chocolate briefly in the microwave in 10 second bursts on full power, then try again. Any broken chocolate shards can be melted or chopped and added to muffins.

CRYSTALLISED FLOWERS | 1 | 2 | 3

MARZIPAN

MAKES 450G (1LB)

Homemade marzipan is far more delicious that the shop-bought variety. Use for decorating or for Simnel and Christmas cakes (see pages 216 and 236). It will keep in the fridge for three or four weeks.

225g (8oz) caster or granulated sugar
75ml (2½fl oz) water
175g (6oz) ground almonds
1 drop natural almond essence
1 egg white, lightly beaten

✳ Bring the sugar and water to the boil in a heavy-based saucepan and cook to 116°C (240°F) or to the 'soft ball' stage (see glossary), keeping the sides of the saucepan brushed down with water (see glossary).
✳ Remove the pan from the heat and stir until the syrup is cloudy. Add the ground almonds, almond essence and lightly beaten egg white and mix well.
✳ Transfer to a bowl and allow the marzipan to cool and become firm.

TECHNIQUE: USING MARZIPAN

Marzipan is ideal for making petit fours (small sweets that are often served with after-dinner coffee).

Shaped petit fours: Roll out the marzipan thickly and stamp out tiny shapes using petit four cutters, then put onto a wire rack and coat with melted chocolate. When set, transfer to pastel-coloured petit four cases.

Striped petit fours: Make up a batch of hazelnut marzipan or colour half the quantity above. Roll each half out to a rectangle the same size and place one on top of the other, then cut in half and put on top to make four layers. Cut into small squares or slices for eye-catching striped petits fours.

Colouring and shaping: Colour small pieces of marzipan with different paste or liquid food colourings and then form into tiny fruits or vegetables, moulding into shapes with your hands dipped in a little icing sugar. Try making into mini carrots to decorate the top of Carrot Cake (see page 67) or shape into mini sandwiches or cakes for a dolly's tea party, but always remember to check with visiting children that no one has a nut allergy.

CANDIED PEEL

DECORATES 10-15 CAKES

5 oranges
5 lemons
5 grapefruit (or 15 of just one fruit)
1 tsp salt
1.25kg (2lb 12oz) caster sugar

✳ Cut the fruit in half and squeeze out the juice. (Reserve the juice for another use, perhaps home-made lemonade.) Put the peel into a large bowl, add the salt and cover with cold water. Leave to soak for 24 hours.
✳ Next day, throw away the soaking water, put the peel in a large saucepan and cover with fresh cold water. Bring to the boil, cover and simmer very gently for about 3 hours or until the peel is soft. It should mash between the tips of your fingers easily when it is cooked.
✳ Remove the peel from the pan and discard the water. Scrape out any remaining flesh and membrane from inside the cut fruit, using a teaspoon, leaving the white

pith and rind intact.

✴ In a clean large saucepan, dissolve the sugar in 1 litre (1³/₄ pints) of water, then bring to the boil, stirring to dissolve the sugar. Add the peel and simmer gently for 30–60 minutes until it looks translucent (shiny and 'candied') and the syrup forms a thread when the last drop falls off a metal spoon. Remove from the heat and allow to stand for 20–30 minutes to slightly cool.

✴ Put the candied peel into sterilised glass jars (see page 276) and pour the syrup over. Cover and store in a cold place or in the fridge. It should keep, stored like this, for at least three months.

SAUCES

My favourite sauces are quick and easy to put together and packed full of taste.

BECHAMEL SAUCE
MAKES 900ML (1 PINT 8FL OZ)

This flavoured white sauce is the base of many baked savoury dishes.

850ml (1 pint 6fl oz) cold milk
1 carrot, scrubbed and cut in half
1 onion, peeled and cut in half
4 peppercorns
Sprig of thyme
Sprig of parsley
50g (2oz) butter
50g (2oz) plain flour
salt and freshly ground black pepper

✴ Put the milk into a large saucepan with the carrot, onion, peppercorns, thyme and parsley. Bring to the boil, then reduce the heat and simmer for 4–5 minutes. Take the pan off the heat and leave to infuse for approximately 10–15 minutes. Pass the milk through a sieve into a large jug. Discard the vegetables.

✴ Place the butter in a medium-sized saucepan and heat gently until melted. Add the flour and cook, stirring, for 1–2 minutes, so the flour does not burn.

✴ Remove the pan from the heat and gradually pour in the milk, whisking all the time.

✴ Place the pan back on the heat and whisk until the sauce thickens. Season to taste with salt and pepper.

CREME ANGLAISE
MAKES 450ML (16FL OZ)

This light, custardy sauce is perfect for pouring over crumbles or sweet pies. If the mixture goes a little lumpy while cooking, remove the saucepan from the heat and whisk well. If it is still lumpy when cooked then push it through a sieve.

4 egg yolks
100g (3¹/₂oz) caster sugar
1 vanilla pod with a line scored down the side, or ¹/₂ tsp vanilla extract
350ml (12fl oz) milk

✴ In a large bowl, whisk the egg yolks with the sugar until light and thick.

✴ Place the vanilla pod (if using) in a saucepan with the milk and slowly bring just up to the boil. Remove the vanilla pod (scrape out some of the seeds if you want a stronger vanilla flavour) and pour the milk onto the egg yolks and sugar, whisking all the time.

✳ Return the mixture to the saucepan with the vanilla extract (if using) and stir over a low heat until it has thickened sufficiently to coat the back of a spoon. Do not allow it to boil.

✳ Remove the pan from the heat and pour into a bowl. Cover with cling film and allow to cool. It must be covered, or the surface must be rubbed with a tiny knob of butter, to prevent a skin forming.

TOFFEE SAUCE
MAKES ABOUT 650ML (22FL OZ)

110g (4oz) butter
250g (9oz) soft light brown sugar
  (or half brown and half caster sugar)
275g (10oz) golden syrup
225ml (8fl oz) double cream
1/2 tsp vanilla extract

✳ Place all the ingredients in a saucepan set over a high heat and boil for approximately 4–5 minutes, stirring regularly, until it has thickened. Serve warm.

BOOZY TOFFEE SAUCE
MAKES 400ML (14FL OZ)

110g (4oz) butter
225g (8oz) soft light brown sugar
  (or half brown and half caster sugar)
225ml (8fl oz) double cream
60ml (2fl oz) brandy
60ml (2fl oz) sweet sherry

✳ Place the butter, sugar and cream in a saucepan and bring to the boil, stirring all the time. Boil for 4 minutes or until the sauce has thickened.

✳ Remove the pan from the heat, allow to cool for 1 minute, then add the brandy and sherry.

HOT CHOCOLATE SAUCE
MAKES 300ML (10FL OZ)

200ml (7fl oz) double cream
200g (7oz) good-quality dark chocolate
  (70% cocoa solids), chopped
1–2 tbsp Cointreau, Grand Marnier,
  brandy or rum, or 1 tsp finely grated
  orange zest (optional)

✳ Pour the cream into a saucepan and bring to the boil.

✳ Add the chopped chocolate and stir until the chocolate has melted.

✳ Add the liqueur or grated orange zest (if using). Remove from the heat and reheat gently when needed.

COFFEE SAUCE
MAKES 275ML (9FL OZ)

225g (8oz) caster or granulated sugar
75ml (2 1/2fl oz) water
225ml (8fl oz) strong coffee
1–2 tbsp Irish whiskey, Cointreau,
  Grand Marnier or brandy (optional)

✳ Set a small–medium sized saucepan over a medium heat, add the sugar and water and stir with a wooden spoon until the sugar dissolves and the water comes up to the boil. Boil for 7–10 minutes, not stirring, until the syrup turns to caramel. If it starts to caramelise at one side of the saucepan, which it often does, don't stir it, but gently 'swirl' the syrup in the pan to even it out. The syrup should be a rich caramel colour throughout, about the colour of whiskey.

✳ Take the pan off the heat, add the coffee immediately and place it back on the heat for 1–2 minutes to dissolve the caramel into the coffee. Remove from the heat and add the alcohol (if using). If the sauce gets a little thick once cool, add a little more coffee or water to thin it out slightly.

RASPBERRY SAUCE
MAKES ABOUT 225ML (8FL OZ)

This sauce keeps for up to 48 hours in the fridge and freezes well.

250g (9oz) fresh or frozen raspberries
1 tbsp caster sugar
2 tbsp freshly squeezed lemon juice

✳ Put the raspberries in a liquidiser or food processor along with the sugar and lemon juice and whiz to a pulp. Taste and add some more sugar or lemon juice if necessary.
✳ Strain through a sieve and place in the fridge until you are ready to use it. Give it a little mix before serving, as sometimes it separates.

VARIATION

Strawberry sauce: Replace the raspberries with 250g (9oz) fresh or frozen hulled strawberries.

BLUEBERRY SYRUP
MAKES 450ML (16FL OZ)

500g (1lb 2oz) fresh or frozen blueberries
2 tbsp water

Finely grated zest of 1 lemon
225ml (8fl oz) maple syrup

✳ Place the blueberries and the water in a medium-sized saucepan set over a medium heat. Using a potato masher, mash the blueberries until they are juicy. Simmer, uncovered, for 8–10 minutes until the mixture has thickened.
✳ Take off the heat and push the mixture through a sieve using a metal spoon, making sure to press through all of the blueberry juice.
✳ Place the blueberry purée back in the (cleaned) saucepan set over a medium heat and add the maple syrup. Simmer, uncovered, for another 8–10 minutes until the blueberry syrup has thickened.

APPLE SAUCE
MAKES 350ML (12FL OZ)

450g (1lb) cooking apples, such as Bramley or Grenadier
1–2 dsp water
50g (2oz) caster or granulated sugar, amount depending on the tartness of the apples

✳ Peel, quarter and core the apples. Cut the quarters in half and place in a heavy-based saucepan with the sugar and water. Cover and heat gently.
✳ As soon as the apple has broken down, remove the pan from the heat and beat into a purée with a wooden spoon, then stir and taste for sweetness. Serve warm.

JAMS AND PRESERVES

Making your own jam or marmalade is really easy and very satisfying. As well as making great gifts, they are delicious baking accompaniments: spread over breakfast muffins or fresh-out-the-oven bread; sandwich between layers of a classic sponge cake, and even use them as a 'glue' to stick decorations onto a cake.

Jam sticks and burns very easily, so do make sure you stir it while it is cooking. It is better not to make a huge quantity at once as the jam will take longer to cook, thereby losing some of the fresh fruit flavour. Finally, add a label so you can remember what flavour the jam is and when it was made.

STRAWBERRY JAM
MAKES 4 X 375G (13OZ) JARS

1kg (2lb 4oz) granulated sugar
**1kg (2lb 4oz) fresh or frozen
  strawberries, hulled**
Juice of 2 lemons

☀ Preheat the oven to 180°C (350°F), Gas mark 4. Place the sugar in an ovenproof bowl and put in the oven for about 15 minutes to warm through.

☀ Meanwhile, place the strawberries with the lemon juice in a large, wide saucepan set over a medium heat. Using a potato masher, mash the fruit to the desired consistency, either smooth or leaving whole fruit pieces. Turn up the heat, bring to the boil and cook for 2 minutes until juicy.

☀ Add the warm sugar to the strawberries. Stir until the sugar has dissolved, then boil for another 6 minutes, stirring frequently. If there is any scum on top (a pale pink froth, from dust or impurities in the fruit), skim it off with a slotted spoon and discard. Remove the pan from the heat while you test the jam to see if it is set (see below). If the jam hasn't set, boil for a minute or so longer and test again.

☀ Remove the pan from the heat, pot into sterilised jars (see below) and cover with lids or jam covers while still hot.

TECHNIQUE: TESTING WHETHER THE JAM HAS SET

To test whether your jam or marmalade is set, put a teaspoonful on a chilled saucer and place in the fridge. When the jam is cold, run your finger through the 'blob' – if a wrinkle forms in the skin on top, then it is set.

TECHNIQUE: STERILISING JARS

To sterilise jars for jams and preserves, wash them in hot soapy water, then rinse and dry. Place the jars upturned on a baking tray in a warm oven preheated to at least 120°C (250°F), Gas mark $1/2$ for approximately 15 minutes until completely dry. Leave them upturned on a clean tea towel until ready to use. Alternatively, you can put them through a hot cycle in the dishwasher.

TECHNIQUE: COVERING JARS

Covering jars is vital to prevent their contents from going mouldy. You can buy packets of waxed and cellophane discs from good cook shops or larger supermarkets. Place the smaller waxed paper discs, waxed side downwards, onto the still very hot jam, jelly or marmalade. Add a cellophane disc and secure in place with a rubber band. The heat from the preserve will create an airtight seal and kill any bacteria or mould spores from the air trapped between the cellophane and the waxed disc.

A sterilised screw-topped lid may be used if preferred and, if making chutney, this is essential to stop vinegar evaporation. If the jam has to cool to stop the fruit from sinking, do not add the waxed and cellophane lids until completely cold.

VARIATION

Raspberry jam: Instead of strawberries, use the same quantity of raspberries (fresh or frozen) as above, but omitting the lemon juice. Place the raspberries in the pan, bring to the boil and cook for 2 minutes until they are juicy. Add the warm sugar and continue as above.

GRANDPA'S CHUNKY SEVILLE ORANGE MARMALADE
MAKES 8–10 X 375G (13OZ) JARS

2.5kg (5lb 8oz) Seville oranges, washed
6.75 litres (12 pints) water
5.5kg (12lb 2oz) granulated sugar

✴ Place the washed oranges in a heavy-based saucepan with the water. Put a plate on top to prevent them bobbing over the surface of the water. Cover with the lid of the saucepan and simmer for approximately 2 hours or until the oranges are soft. Cool and drain, reserving the water.
✴ Preheat the oven to 180°C (350°F), Gas mark 4. Place the sugar in an ovenproof bowl and put in the oven for about 15 minutes to warm through.
✴ Place a chopping board on a large baking tray to catch any juice from the oranges. Cut the oranges in half and scoop out the soft centres, then slice the zest into slices approximately 3–5mm (1/8–1/4in) thick (or thicker if you prefer).
✴ Place the pulp with the pips into a muslin bag (or a clean 'J' cloth or something similar) and pour any escaped juice into a large, wide, stainless steel saucepan, along with the reserved cooking water and the sliced oranges. Bring to the boil, then add the warm sugar. Stir over a high heat until all the sugar is dissolved. Boil rapidly for about 20 minutes until setting point is reached (see opposite). If the marmalade hasn't set, boil for a minute or so longer and test again.
✴ Remove the pan from the heat, pot into sterilised jars and cover with lids or jam covers while still hot (see page 276).

SWEET ONION JAM
MAKES 2–3 X 375G (13OZ) JARS

25g (1oz) butter
680g (1 1/2lb) onions, peeled and
    thinly sliced
150g (5oz) caster sugar
1 tsp salt
1 tsp freshly ground black pepper
100ml (3 1/2fl oz) sherry vinegar or
    balsamic vinegar
250ml (9fl oz) full-bodied red wine
2 tbsp crème de cassis

✴ Melt the butter in a saucepan and add the onions, sugar, salt and freshly ground black pepper. Stir, then cover the saucepan and cook for 30 minutes over a gentle heat, stirring from time to time to prevent it from sticking to the bottom of the pan.

⁕ Remove the lid and add the vinegar, wine and crème de cassis and cook, uncovered, for another 30 minutes, stirring every now and then. It should be slightly thick by now. Pour into sterilised jars (see page 276) and cover while hot. It thickens as it cools.

LEMON CURD
MAKES 250ML (9FL OZ)

75g (3oz) butter
150g (5oz) caster sugar
Finely grated zest and juice of 3 lemons
2 eggs
1 egg yolk

⁕ Place the butter, sugar, lemon zest and juice in a saucepan and heat very gently until the butter is melted.

⁕ Put the eggs and egg yolk in a bowl and beat thoroughly.

⁕ Pour the beaten eggs into the melted butter mixture and stir carefully over a low heat until the mixture has thickened and will coat the back of a spoon. If the heat is too high the mixture will scramble. If it does, quickly push it through a sieve. Remove the pan from the heat and pour into a bowl or into a sterilised jar (page 276).

VARIATION
Seville orange curd: Heat 150g (5oz) butter, 250g (9oz) caster sugar, the finely grated zest of 1 Seville orange and the juice of 3 Seville oranges very gently until the butter is melted. Beat 4 eggs and 2 egg yolks together thoroughly, then stir into the melted butter mixture. Continue as above.

MINCEMEAT
MAKES 2.7KG (6LB)

This delicious mincemeat will keep happily in a cool dark place for at least a year. If you are making your own suet (the fat that surrounds the beef kidney), make sure that every trace of blood has been removed before you whiz it in the food processor, otherwise it will cause the mincemeat to go off.

2 large cooking apples, peeled, cored and cut into large chunks
Finely grated zest and juice of 2 oranges and 2 lemons
250g (9oz) shredded suet, or butter, chilled and grated
275g (10oz) raisins
275g (10oz) sultanas
275g (10oz) currants
125g (4½oz) candied peel (see page 272), chopped
650g (1lb 7oz) soft dark brown sugar
50g (2oz) nibbed (chopped) almonds, or chopped pecans
2 tsp mixed spice
75ml (2½fl oz) Irish whiskey or brandy

⁕ Place the apple chunks in a small saucepan with 1 teaspoon of water, cover and cook over a low heat for about 8–10 minutes until the apples are cooked down to a pulp. Allow to cool.

⁕ Mix with all the remaining ingredients in a large bowl and put into sterilised jars (see page 276). Leave to mature, if possible for at least two weeks before using.

GLOSSARY

Bain-marie Sometimes called a water bath, this is a roasting tin half filled with hot water. Delicate dishes, such as custard or savoury terrines, are usually cooked in this way as they are protected from the oven's fierce heat so stopping the eggs from curdling or the terrines from drying out.

Bake blind To pre-bake a pastry case before the filling is added. The uncooked case is lined with greaseproof paper, parchment paper or clingfilm and weighted down with baking beans (or uncooked pulses, rice or pasta). The case is then partially baked with the paper to set the shape and then the baking beans and paper are removed and the case is returned to oven until it is cooked. (See also page 255.)

Beat To mix energetically with a wooden spoon or hand-held electric beater until ingredients are smoothly blended and lump-free.

Béchamel sauce A classic sauce made by first infusing hot milk with onion, mace, a bay leaf, some peppercorns and a few parsley stalks. The milk is passed through a sieve, then added to a roux (a mixture of melted butter and plain flour) as if making a basic white sauce. (See also page 273)

Blanching Originally this meant to soak whole almonds, hazelnuts or pistachios in boiling water for a few minutes so that the brown skins may be easily removed. Now, it more commonly means to partially cook vegetables in boiling water for a minute or two.

Body temperature or body heat This term is used in bread-making to describe warm water or milk that is just tepid – 37°C (98.4°F) – the perfect temperature to activate yeast.

Bring together Once liquid is added to a rubbed-in pastry or a dry shortbread-style mix, the crumbs are squeezed together with your hands to make a ball of dough.

Brushing down the sides of the saucepan When boiling sugar for marzipan or boiled sugar petits fours, small splatters of syrup will brown on the sides of the saucepan spoiling the mixture, so remove them by brushing the sides of the pan with a pastry brush dipped in hot water.

Caramelise To heat sugar or a sugar syrup until it is a deep golden-brown colour.

Casserole To slow-cook a meat or vegetable mixture with stock in a deep ovenproof dish, with a lid, in the oven. Choose either china or pottery dishes or ovenproof dishes that can be used on the hob first to seal the meat and vegetables and then transferred to the oven.

Cream To beat softened butter and sugar together in a bowl with a wooden spoon or hand-held electric beater until smooth and pale in colour.

Crystallise To brush edible flower petals, herb flowers or leaves, cherries on stalks, tiny sprigs of grapes or physalis berries with egg white and then to lightly coat with

caster sugar. Allow to stand for several hours or overnight and then when dry use to decorate cakes and summer desserts. (See also page 271.)

Cube (or dice) To cut fruits, vegetables or butter into small even-sized cubes.

Curdle When a cake or sauce splits or separates when beaten eggs are added too quickly.

Détrempe The dough base used when making puff pastry (see page 257) to which butter is then rolled and folded into.

Dropping consistency Usually applying to rubbed-in cakes, the mixture should be soft so that it slides off the spoon reluctantly after a few seconds, but not so soft that it simply pours off.

Dust To sprinkle a light 'dusting' or fine coating of sifted icing sugar or cocoa powder over cakes or a little flour over bread from a sieve or dredger.

Egg wash Can be either 1 egg yolk beaten with 1 tbsp water and an optional pinch of salt brushed over bread or pies before baking for a deep golden crust or 1 egg white with 1 tbsp water for a paler crust with a soft sheen.

Fold in To gently mix sifted flour or fruits into a creamed or whisked mixture with a large, deep-bowled spoon or serving spoon, ideally cutting and swirling through the mixture with the spoon on its side in a figure-of-eight motion.

Glaze or glazing This can be done either before baking, with beaten egg, milk and a sprinkling of sugar, or after baking, with melted butter, olive oil, a milk and sugar syrup or fruit-flavoured sugar syrup, jam or honey for a glossy finish.

Grind Most often done to nuts in baking by very finely chopping in a food processor, liquidiser, electric spice or baby-food mill.

Hard-ball stage When a teaspoon of boiled sugar syrup can be moulded easily into a ball that resists pressure when dropped into a glass of iced water, or when a sugar thermometer reads 121–130°C (250–266°F). (See also 'Soft-ball stage'.)

Knead To work bread, scone or pastry dough using your fist, by pressing from the centre to the edge and then folding the edges back to the centre with the other hand before turning slightly and repeating. Repeat just a few more times to smooth the surface on scone or pastry dough, or 10 minutes for bread to develop the gluten. (See also pages 260–61.)

Knock back (or punch down) This quite literally means to punch a fully risen yeast dough with your fist to force the air out before kneading and shaping.

Lardons A French term for small strips or cubes of bacon, mostly used to describe diced pancetta rather than diced streaky bacon.

Mornay sauce A light cheese sauce made with a roux base and milk.

Nibbed This is a rather old-fashioned term meaning coarsely chopped. It is most often used when describing almonds.

Prove This is a term used in bread-making where the mixed dough is left to rise in a warm place until it has doubled in volume.

Relax (rest) To chill pastry for 15 minutes or so to minimise shrinking during baking. This is done when making pastry or batter for pancakes or crêpes so that the starch can swell, giving a lighter cooked finish, or after bread dough is kneaded for the second time before shaping.

Roux To stir plain flour into melted butter as a thickening base when making a white or béchamel sauce.

Rub in To press diced butter and flour between your fingers and thumbs to mix and break down into fine crumbs. It can also be done in a food processor or using an electric food mixer.

Sift To press or shake icing sugar, cocoa powder or flour through a sieve to remove any lumps and give a light 'dusting'.

Simmer To gently heat a liquid in a saucepan until bubbles just break the surface, or 'shimmer'.

Soft-ball stage When a boiled sugar syrup will form soft sticky balls that can be flattened when a teaspoon of the syrup is dropped into a glass of iced water, or a sugar thermometer reads 112–116°C (234–241°F). (See also 'Hard-ball stage'.)

Sponge or sponging Fresh or dried yeast is mixed with warm liquid and a little sugar to begin fermentation. After 5 minutes the mixture will be frothy and ready to use. If fast-acting yeast is used, the mixture doesn't need to stand but can be added straight to the dry ingredients.

Steam To gently cook over simmering water either by adding to a covered steamer pan set over a saucepan of simmering water or by cooking a cake or pudding in a covered basin on a trivet or inverted saucer in a saucepan half filled with simmering water, so that the ingredients do not come into direct contact with the steam.

Sweating onions To gently fry chopped or sliced onions in oil or a mixture of oil and butter until softened but not browned.

Vanilla sugar Caster sugar flavoured with a vanilla pod. Rinse, dry and recycle a used pod then add to a half-filled jar of caster sugar. Store for a week, shaking the jar from time to time to allow the flavours to develop, before using. Sprinkle over cakes or biscuits.

Whip To beat whipping or double cream using a balloon whisk or hand-held electric beater until the cream is softly thickened and just holding its shape.

Whisk Using a balloon whisk or hand-held electric beater to beat eggs and sugar together into a mousse-like mixture for a fatless sponge cake or to beat egg whites into a fluffy mass for meringues and other dishes.

Zest The thin, coloured rind of a citrus fruit, pared or grated without any of the white pith and added to cakes and biscuits for its flavour.

INDEX

vanilla buttercream icing 268
Irish coffee meringue roulade 86
Italian hazelnut cake 47

J

jams 276–7
  Bakewell bars 22
  coconut and raspberry tart 152
  fairy cakes 39
  festive jam cookie sandwiches
    239
  raspberry jam 277
  raspberry jam steamed
    pudding 97
  strawberry jam 276
  Swiss roll 63
  testing for a set 276
jars, sterilising 276

K

kheema naan 114
Kugelhopf 61–2

L

lamb: kheema naan 114
lasagne: pork, spinach and
    mushroom 199
leeks: calzone di magro
    ('without meat') 145
  chicken and leek pie 140
lemon: baked chicken with lemon
    and garlic and pilaf rice 197
  coconut meringue roulade with
    lemon curd cream 85–6
  cookies 14
  lemon and passion fruit tart 159
  lemon cupcakes 36
  lemon curd 278
lentils: baked red lentil dhal 187
lime yoghurt cake with rosewater
    and pistachios 224
lining tins 255, 264

M

macaroon tart, coconut 152
maize meal: corn bread 124
maple syrup: baked bananas
    with 98
  banana and maple syrup
    muffins 165
marble cake, chocolate and
    vanilla 48
marmalade: chocolate, marmalade
    and hazelnut cake 59

Grandpa's chunky Seville
    orange marmalade 277
marzipan *see* almond paste
mascarpone: baked bananas
    with orange and honey
    mascarpone 98
  Pavlova meringue roulade with
    cherries and rosewater
    mascarpone 86
Mediterranean pasta 198
Meredith's zucchini bread 72
meringue 265
  baked Alaska 89–90
  blue meringues with blueberry
    cream 218–20
  coconut meringue roulade 85–6
  mocha-pecan meringue ice
    cream sandwiches 91
  pink meringues with raspberry
    cream 218–20
  Seville orange meringue pie 158
milk, sour 108
mincemeat 278
  mince pies 240
  mincemeat Eccles cakes 35
mocha cake 55
mocha-pecan meringue ice cream
    sandwiches 91
muffins: breakfast (English)
    163–4
  St Stephen's Day 235
  30-day muffin recipe 164
mushrooms: baked breakfast
    omelette 171
  beef, stout and anchovy pie 151
  pork, spinach and mushroom
    lasagne 199
  roast mushroom and goat's
    cheese tartlet 141
mustard dip, pretzels with 134

N

naan bread 113–14

O

oats: apple and oat crumble 81
  date bars 26
  oat and vanilla shortbread
    cookies 16
  oatcakes 131
  oatmeal and chocolate
    cookies 12
  oatmeal and raisin cookies 12
olives: baked Mediterranean

pasta 198
  calzone puttanesca 143–4
  pissaladière 136
  red onion, olive and rosemary
    focaccia 107–8
  sun-dried tomato, rosemary
    and olive bread 110
omelette, baked breakfast 171
onions: baked potato, onion and
    rosemary gratin 189
  beef, stout and anchovy pie 151
  cheese and onion corn bread 124
  pissaladière 136
  pizza with Gruyère and roasted
    red onions 203
  quiche Lorraine 145
  red onion, olive and rosemary
    focaccia 107–8
  sweet onion jam 278
oranges: almond and orange
    butter fingers 24
  baked bananas with orange
    and honey mascarpone 98
  candied peel 272
  chocolate, marmalade and
    hazelnut cake 59
  date, orange and cardamom
    tart 157
  Florence's orange cake 213
  glacé icing 269
  Grandpa's chunky Seville
    orange marmalade 277
  iced orange cake 43
  orange and almond puffs 35
  orange cookies 14
  orange cream cheese icing 67
  scones 31
  Seville orange meringue pie 158
  white chocolate and orange
    cookies 14

P

pains au chocolat 174
paired biscuits 40
paper-thin crispbread 127
party doughnuts 220–1
pashwari naan 114
passion fruit: lemon and passion
    fruit tart 159
pasta: baked Mediterranean
    pasta 198
  pork, spinach and mushroom
    lasagne 199
pasties, beef 148

ACKNOWLEDGEMENTS

This book would not have happened without the help of many people – I am indebted and immensely grateful to all of you.

A huge thanks to: Jenny Heller and everyone at Collins, especially Lizzy Gray, Emma Callery, Anna Martin, Chris Gurney; Fiona Lindsay, Alison Lindsay, Mary Bekhait and Leonie Drury at Limelight Management; Emma Smith and Katrin Smejkal at Smith & Gilmour; Mark Read, Annie Rigg and Wei Tang; Noel Murphy, Tina Young and Dagmar Vesely; Rita and all the staff at Paul UK; and the Baker and Spice team. Thank you to Dervilla O'Flynn and Susan Mannion – you both gave me so much help and support throughout; and thanks to everyone who was kind enough to share their recipes with me. Finally, special thanks to my husband Isaac and my family, and to Myrtle, Tim and Darina Allan.

Thank you everyone for making this so much fun.